D0214842

CHARACTERS AND AUTHORS IN LUIGI PIRANDELLO

Characters and Authors in Luigi Pirandello

ANN HALLAMORE CAESAR

CLARENDON PRESS · OXFORD
1998

Oxford University Press, Great Clarendon Street, Oxford OX2 6DP

Oxford New York
Athens Auckland Bangkok Bogota Bombay
Buenos Aires Calcutta Cape Town Dar es Salaam
Delhi Florence Hong Kong Istanbul Karachi
Kuala Lumpur Madras Madrid Melbourne
Mexico City Nairobi Paris Singapore
Taipei Tokyo Toronto Warsaw
and associated companies in
Berlin Ibadan

Oxford is a trade mark of Oxford University Press

Published in the United States by
Oxford University Press Inc., New York

British Library Cataloguing in Publication Data
Data available

Library of Congress Cataloging in Publication Data
Caesar, Ann.
Characters and authors in Luigi Pirandello / Ann Hallamore Caesar.
Includes bibliographical references and index.
1. Pirandello, Luigi, 1867–1936—Characters.   I. Title.
PQ4835. I7Z5377   1998
852'.912—dc21   97-35958
ISBN 0-19-815176-4

1 3 5 7 9 10 8 6 4 2

Typeset by Best-set Typesetter Ltd., Hong Kong
Printed in Great Britain
on acid-free paper by
Bookcraft Ltd
Midsomer Norton, Somerset

For Mike, Geoffrey, and Joe

I think therefore I am is the statement of an intellectual who underrates toothache. *I feel therefore I am* is a truth much more universally valid.

(Milan Kundera)

Preface

Luigi Pirandello is known primarily in the English-speaking world for his contribution to modern European drama with plays such as *Sei personaggi in cerca d'autore* and *Enrico IV*. What is less well known is that he was also a prolific writer of essays, poetry, short stories, novels, and even film-scripts: indeed he himself believed that writing for the stage was no more than a temporary aberration which would not long delay his return to narrative.

Studies of Pirandello's work in English have usually given priority to his plays, choosing to read his other writings as an apprenticeship for his vocation as dramatist. In recent years in his native Italy on the other hand, there has been a keen awareness of the innovative nature of his narrative writing as a whole and in particular of his short stories and novels.

I set out in this book with the intention of discussing Pirandello's work across the genres without giving any one practice a special weighting. He was a restless writer who not only experimented with different literary forms, but who also refused to allow himself to be coerced into respecting the limits of any one genre. The concept of the 'well-made' work, be it novel, play, or essay, was abhorrent to him. From his earliest work as a student in Bonn through to his last years as an international celebrity and Nobel prize winner he detested rules, canons, anything that sought to define and by that definition contain the impulse of the creative moment. It soon became evident that the force driving the work forward was the character him- or herself. It also became clear that the relationship as Pirandello presented it between author and character was not a happy one, being neither mutually supportive nor collaborative. More often than not authors and characters—and anybody else involved in the creative process—were shown to be at each other's throats. Frustrations, recriminations, and incomprehension are the hallmark of the relationship, one that concerns not only characters and their authors but extends to characters and their actors, and even directors, and so infiltrates every aspect of the creative process.

But the power of the character as a generating force behind these narratives is only a part of the story. It leads into the question of what makes a literary character, whether they are 'people' in any intelligible sense. Much of the book is taken up with a study of the plethora of life-histories that Pirandello's fictions provide, of how characters make and unmake each other, and themselves. He shows characters, usually men, pinned down by the surfeit of information that the community has about them, and others, usually women, who without a past that is public knowledge struggle without success to know themselves. What his characters have in common is their investment in the spoken word. The word is action, only through language can they realize themselves—*la parola viva* ('the living word'). Whatever the genre, short story, novel, poem, or play, Pirandello's characters seek to tell, often painfully, not always articulately, their life-story, struggling through the spoken word and therefore through their interlocutor to make sense of themselves.

Acknowledgements

Many people have helped me in the writing of this book. My thanks go to members, past and present, of the Department of Italian at Cambridge University. In particular I wish to express my gratitude to Robin Kirkpatrick, Patrick Boyde, and Judy Davies, and to the many students with whom I have read and discussed Pirandello over the years. Among those friends and colleagues who have so generously taken time to read and comment on earlier drafts, I am particularly indebted to Jennifer Lorch for her wonderfully incisive comments and to Laura Lepschy who provided helpful advice at just the right moment. My greatest debt, and pleasure in acknowledging it, goes to Michael Caesar.

I have drawn on material for three of the chapters from essays that have previously appeared in books or journals: 'Pirandello and the Drama of Creativity', in P. Collier and J. Davies (eds.), *Modernism and the European Unconscious* (Polity Press, Cambridge, 1990), 215–28; 'The Branding of Women: Family, Theatre and Female Identity in Pirandello', *Italian Studies*, 45 (1990), 48–63; 'Changing Costume, Changing Identity: Women in the Theatre of Pirandello, Bontempelli and Wedekind', *Romance Studies*, 20 (Summer 1992), 20–9 (repr. *Luigi Pirandello: The Theatre of Paradox* (Lampeter, Edwin Mellen, 1996), 197–209) and 'Telling Tales: Pirandello and the Short Story', *The Yearbook of the Society for Pirandello Studies*, 13 (1993), 1–17.

I should like to thank the Universities of Bologna, Glasgow, Manchester, and Wales, and the Institute of Romance Studies in London, for inviting me to speak on Pirandello. My thanks go also to the Faculty of Modern and Medieval Languages at the University of Cambridge and Corpus Christi College for allowing me to take leave to complete the book.

A. H. C.

Contents

Note on Translations and Sources

All quotations from primary literary sources appear in their original form followed by my own translation unless otherwise attributed. In the case of nineteenth- and twentieth-century criticism I have similarly included the original followed by a translation. Titles of literary and non-literary writings by Pirandello appear for the first time in the original followed by a translation and thereafter in the original only. Dates in the text refer to the original date of publication.

A new and complete Italian critical edition of all Luigi Pirandello's works is in the process of being published. It includes so far the following:

Novelle per un anno (3 vols., Milan, Mondadori, 1985–90).

Tutti i romanzi (2 vols., Milan, Mondadori, 1973).

Maschere nude (2 vols. publ. so far, Milan, Mondadori, 1986–93).

Where I have not been able to use the above, I have quoted from the following editions: *Maschere nude, Opera omnia* (4 vols., Milan, Mondadori, 1948–9); *Saggi, poesie, scritti varii* (Milan, Mondadori, 1977).

Pirandello in Translation

Not all of Pirandello's work has been translated into English and in many cases the English translation is now out of print. What follows is not a full list but those editions that I have drawn on for the purposes of this book.

Plays

The first English translation of the *Collected Plays* of Pirandello began publication in 1987 (3 vols. so far, London and New York, John Calder and Riverrun Press): i. *Henry IV, The Man with the Flower in his Mouth, Right You Are (if You Think You Are), Lazarus* (1987); ii. *Six Characters in Search of an Author, All for the Best, Clothe the Naked, Limes from Sicily* (1988); iii. *The Rules of the Game, Each in His Own Way, Grafted, The Other Son* (1992).

Luigi Pirandello: Three Plays (The Rules of the Game, Six Characters in Search of an Author, Henry IV) (London, Methuen, 1985).

The Mountain Giants: A Myth, tr. Felicity Firth, *The Yearbook of the British Pirandello Society*, 10 (1990).

Novels

The Late Mattia Pascal, tr. Nicoletta Simborowski (London, Dedalus, 1987).

The Notebooks of Serafino Gubbio or *Shoot!*, tr. C. K. Scott Moncrieff (London, Dedalus, 1990).

One, None and a Hundred Thousand, tr. Samuel Putnam (New York, Howard Fertig, 1982).

Short Stories

Luigi Pirandello, *Short Stories, a selection*, tr. Frederick May (London, Oxford University Press, 1965).

Essays

On Humor, introduced, translated, and annotated by A. Illiano and P. F. Testa (Chapel Hill, NC, University of California, 1974).

1

Real and Implied Authors

> Isn't every writer (even the purest lyric poet) always a 'playwright' insofar as he distributes all the discourses among alien voices, including that of the 'image of the author' (as well as the author's other *personae*)?
>
> (Mikhail Bakhtin, *The Aesthetics of Verbal Creation*)

Among the most enduring images of Luigi Pirandello left by his friends, family, and colleagues are those which show him performing or reading aloud from plays or novels. There are early photographs of him as a student in the late 1880s, hamming it with friends in improvised amateur dramatics on the balcony of his uncle's house in Rome and, forty years on, pictures of him as, with a singular intensity, he takes his cast through one of his play-scripts or rehearses his lead actress Marta Abba. Nor is the evidence left to us us only photographic. There are many verbal accounts of Pirandello in performance. In one of them, a close friend and frequent visitor to Pirandello's home in Rome, Arnaldo Frateili, recalls how unsettling he found it to listen to Pirandello read to him the opening chapters of *Uno, nessuno e centomila* (*One, None and a Hundred Thousand*) in which the protagonist describes the start of his journey into madness.[1] Perhaps to reassure his readers that this response was not the product of an unduly nervous sensibility on his part, Frateili goes on to describe another incident that took place at about the same time, where the impromptu audience knew neither Pirandello nor what he was doing. When his family was still young, Pirandello used to teach mornings in a girls' college while after lunch he would withdraw to his study at home to write. On one such afternoon, builders working on a

---

[1] Arnaldo Frateili, 'Pirandello uno e due', *Almanacco Letterario Bompiani*, 16 (1938), repr. in Leonardo Sciascia (ed.), *Omaggio a Pirandello* (Milan, Mondadori, 1967), 83–6.

temporarily erected platform next door looked in through the window to see a man sitting at his desk rolling his eyes and gesticulating wildly, all the while talking to himself. Thinking him insane, or possibly possessed by the devil, they gathered around and watched until, the period of writing over, an embarrassed Pirandello became aware for the first time of the audience so close to hand.

What these vignettes reveal is that Pirandello's propensity for acting is not reserved for his theatre alone, nor is it the case that he only acts out parts that have first been written down. The two episodes described by Arnaldo Frateili refer to different stages in the creative process: in the first Pirandello is reading aloud from his manuscript and so he is acting out a part that is already written. What is interesting here is that he is translating into performance a monologue that is not destined to be a play, but a novel. In the second episode the builders are watching an earlier stage in the creative process, where the author is at work writing, bringing into existence new characters. What such descriptions reveal to us is that Pirandello wrote from within the character, he did not adopt a position outside his creation, and so intense was the relationship between author and character that it brought down the barriers between the written and the spoken word. Once a literary character is embodied, he expresses himself in speech. Speech implies presence. To the onlooker Pirandello appears, consciously or otherwise, to be acting, while the process of creative composition is played out in gestures and in words. Characters speak aloud through his voice, and their presence is registered in the involuntary movements of his face and body. It is, in the words of the builders peering in through the window, as if he were 'possessed', as though the writer has become the medium through which the character can materialize and find expression. The primacy of the fictional character is the touchstone of all Pirandello's creative and theoretical writings—what has its origins in unconscious processes becomes a theoretically sophisticated philosophy of literature. What for Frateili was essentially a psychological trait, part of the singularity of the man, becomes for Pirandello the motivating force behind his fictions and his literary aesthetics.

Born in 1867 in a hamlet called Caos, in a remote corner

of Sicily near Agrigento (then known as Girgenti),[2] Luigi Pirandello's cultural roots belong in the 1880s and 1890s, so his was first and foremost a nineteenth-century formation, and one that coincided with the moment when literary realism began to enjoy popularity and prestige. His school years were spent in Sicily, but he moved to Rome in 1887 to continue his studies. In 1889, after two years as a student at the University of Rome, an altercation with one of his professors led the 22-year-old student to transfer to Bonn University, where he remained until 1891 when he graduated in philology with a thesis on the dialect of his native region in Sicily.[3] During his years in Bonn, Pirandello believed that his artistic future would be in poetry; his collection of poems, *Elegie renane* (*Elegies of the Rhine*), named after Goethe's *Elegie romane* which he was translating at the time, were written while he was living in Germany.[4] But the two years abroad also saw the beginning of a very productive period as essayist. His views on literature first outlined in book reviews and short articles were to reappear, elaborated but often substantially unchanged, in two important volumes that he completed and published in 1908, *L'umorismo* (*On Humour*)[5] and *Arte e scienza* (*Art and Science*).[6] By then he had been living for some fifteen years in Rome. At first, as a yet unknown writer, he had been assisted by a monthly maintenance cheque from his father while he tried to gain entry into the artistic circles of the Umbertine capital. Befriended by an artist from Messina, Ugo Fleres, he was introduced to other Southerners who had settled in the city, amongst whom the most important was to be Luigi Capuana. Until he moved to a university chair in Catania in

---

[2] An autobiographical fragment of 1893 begins: 'Io dunque son figlio del Caos; e non allegoricamente, ma in giusta realtà' ('I am therefore a child of Chaos; and not allegorically but in all reality'), *Saggi, poesie, scritti varii*, ed. Manlio Lo Vecchio-Musti (Milan, Mondadori, 1973), 1281. The text will hereafter be abbreviated to *Spsv*. All translation unless otherwise stated is mine.

[3] Luigi Pirandello, *Laute und Lautentwickelung der Mundart von Girgenti* (Halle a. S., Drück der Buchdrückerei des Waisenhauses, 1891).

[4] Luigi Pirandello, *Elegie renane* (Rome, Unione Coop Editrice, 1895), and *Elegie romane di Goethe* (Livorno, Giusti, 1896). The two edns. have been collected in Luigi Pirandello, *Tutte le poesie*, intr. Francesco Nicolosi (Milan, Mondadori, 1960).

[5] Luigi Pirandello, *L'umorismo* (Lanciano, Carabbo, 1908), rev. and ext. (Florence, Battistelli, 1920). This 2nd edn. is included in *Spsv* 17–160.

[6] Luigi Pirandello, *Arte e scienza* (Rome, Modes-Libraio Editore, 1908). Repr. *Spsv* 161–79. By 1905 Pirandello had published almost three-quarters of his short stories, three novels, and five collections of poetry.

1902, this fellow Sicilian writer was to be both friend and protector. When Pirandello took up residence in Rome, he still felt that he would pursue a literary career in poetry; it was Capuana who actively encouraged him to write narrative and also gave him material help by ensuring that his stories and novels found publishers. This is how Pirandello remembered what was to be a crucial moment in his literary career:

Fino a tutto il 1892 non mi pareva possibile che io potessi scrivere altrimenti che in versi. Devo a Luigi Capuana la spinta a provarmi nell'arte narrativa in prose.[7]

Up until the end of 1892, I did not believe that I could write in anything other than verse. It was Luigi Capuana who gave me the incentive to experiment in the art of prose narrative.

Pirandello's first novel *L'esclusa* (*The Outcast*) was written, at Capuana's instigation, during a late summer holiday in 1893 and it shares with its successor *Il turno* (*The Merry-Go-Round of Love*), at least superficially, the *verista* or realist aesthetics of his friend and patron. Outside Italy, the development of the novel had run parallel through the eighteenth and early nineteenth centuries with philosophy's increasing interest in questions of individuality, identity, and consciousness. The development in Europe of a realist movement turned the novel's natural propensity for representations of individual rather than collective experience into narratives whose construction was determined more by character than plot; but in Pirandello's case what started as part of the literary landscape was to become a character-led aesthetics that was eventually to contribute to his move away from narrative and into drama.

Arte e scienza is made up of nine of his earlier articles and a substantial new piece, 'Soggettivismo e oggettivismo nell'arte narrativa'[8] ('Subjectivism and Objectivism in Narrative Art') which draws on some dozen articles written between 1890 and 1905. It is clear from this collection that Pirandello found his voice early and that his theoretical writing was, from the start,

---

[7] Luigi Pirandello, 'Lettera autobiografica', *Le lettere* (15 Oct. 1924). Repr. *Spsv* 1286. Pirandello's poetry is not on the whole character-based and will not therefore be discussed in this book.

[8] For an account of the evolution of this essay see Giorgio Pullini, 'Poetica di Pirandello: Soggettivismo e oggettivismo nell'arte narrativa', in *Tra esistenza e coscienza: Narrativa e teatro del '900* (Milan, Mursia, 1986), 138–56.

guided by his approach to his creative writing; indeed, the very term 'poetics' does not signify for Pirandello a set of philosophical and aesthetic questions in an abstract sense, but relates before all else to his own concrete interests as a working writer. Every literary work, he argued, should be guided by the same principle—that it is the literary character who must be free to take the initiative—and once that is established, the writing of the text can organize itself around it. So the primacy of the literary character was the cornerstone to his work, both as creative writer and literary critic. Literary languages and rhetoric, artistic schools and movements, and literary tradition itself were all seen as obstacles to the freedom that characters must be allowed to exercise if their authors are to produce the masterpieces which, as will become clear later, will buy them their eternal life. With this in mind, I shall look briefly at each of these potential impediments before turning to how Pirandello's respect for the alterity of character also informed his views on genre.

Pirandello was unambiguous in his declaration of war on rhetoric—synonymous in his lexicon with imitation—directing his criticism both at those writers who try to follow in the footsteps of their indigenous literary tradition and at those who look for guidance elsewhere in Europe, and in particular the then current Italian fascination with French realism.[9] It is clear that already in the early essays he felt that Italian literature laboured under a linguistic disadvantage, inhibited by the

---

[9] In an earlier essay, 'Un critico fantastico', *Nuova antologia* (16 Mar. 1905), repr. *Spsv* 366–87, Pirandello uses 'rhetoric' and 'imitation' interchangeably. Ibid. 367: 'Il male proviene da questo: che noi, per quanto si voglia credere il contrario, siamo ancora dominati dalla Retorica e seguiamo tuttavia, senza avvedercene, le sue regole e i suoi precetti, non in letteratura soltanto, ma anche in tutte le espressioni della nostra vita: Retorica e imitazione sono, in fondo, una cosa sola [. . .] Il retore quasi sempre insegnò da noi al poeta secondo quali norme, secondo quali precetti egli dovesse costruire l'opera d'arte, come se l'opera d'arte fosse un ragionamento.' 'The harm comes from this: that, however much we want to think the opposite, we are still dominated by Rhetoric and still follow its rules and precepts without being aware of it, not only in literature but also in all the ways in which we express ourselves in life: Rhetoric and imitation are fundamentally the same thing [. . .] Our rhetoricians almost always taught our poets the norms and precepts which they should follow in order to make a work of art, as if the work of art were an argument.') *L'umorismo*, pt. 1, Ch. 4, is also directed against Rhetoric, presented as 'il guardaroba dell'eloquenza' ('the wardrobe of eloquence') where naked thoughts go to dress themselves up.

literary tradition that preceded it and insecure about its own position within it. With his intellectual formation in the field of romance philology, it is not surprising that he traced the problems back to language, arguing that, in the absence of a common spoken language, the language of literature is often heavy, artificial, and imitative. In an essay written while he was preparing his thesis on the Girgenti dialect, Pirandello argued that the problem with Italian novels had nothing to do with plot or storyline, and everything to do with the weakness of the form—from the choice of individual words to style. He attributes the fault to the authorial practice of taking their words not from the spoken language they hear about them, but from the written tradition, so that the reader is left studying a book instead of experiencing it.[10] Here the call for a written language born of the spoken tongue is linked to his view that the individuality of the author's voice within the text remains buried under the anonymity of a language that is imposed by literary tradition. Pirandello did not know the Sicilian writer Giovanni Verga well (their first meeting in 1904 is a classic of the genre: it took place at the printers where, as Pirandello stood watching his novel *Il fu Mattia Pascal* (*The Late Mattia Pascal*) come off the presses, Verga explained why he had decided to stop writing), but he had read Verga's work very attentively and had dedicated several articles to it. With the arrogance of youth, Pirandello was quite harsh on the older writer, criticizing him in his review of *Mastro-don Gesualdo* (*Master-don Gesualdo*) for what he argued was an excessive use of dialect, but when he came to make a

---

[10] 'Prosa moderna: Dopo la lettura del *Mastro don Gesualdo* del Verga' ('Modern Prose. After a Reading of Verga's *Master Don Gesualdo*'), *Vita nuova* (5 Oct. 1890), repr. *Spsv* 878–81. Pirandello was very eloquent on why, in his view, contemporary Italian narrative was so poor (Ibid. 879): 'Se letteratura, o meglio, tradizione letteraria ha mai fatto impedimento al libero sviluppo d'una lingua, questa più d'ogni altra è l'italiana. Dirò di più, la lingua nostra, che a volerla cercare, non si saprebbe dove trovarla, in realtà non esiste che nell'opera scritta soltanto, nel campo cioè della letteratura. [. . .] I letterati non conoscono altra lingua che quella dei libri; mentre gl'illetterati continuano a parlar quella a cui sono abituati, la provinciale; ossia i varii dialetti natali.' ('If a literature, or more accurately a literary tradition has ever stood in the way of the free evolution of a language, then this has happened to Italian more than to any other. I will go further, if you wanted to find the Italian language you would not know where to look for it; in fact it only exists in written works, that is to say in works of literature. [. . .] Those who write know only the language of books; while the illiterate continue to speak the provincial tongue to which they are accustomed; that is to say their various different native dialects.')

commemorative speech in honour of Verga in 1931, he spoke with admiration of his work and praised Verga for being the most 'anti-literary' of writers.[11] His own interest in the spoken language comes from *verismo* and in particular Verga's concept of *prosa parlata* ('spoken prose'), which provided Pirandello with the evidence he needed to support his argument that the gap between written and spoken Italian was too great, the written too tied to literary tradition, for an author to be able to give expression to his or her own voice by means of it. In his own book on contemporary literary movements called *Gli 'ismi' contemporanei* (*Contemporary 'isms'*) of 1898, Luigi Capuana attributes Verga's artistry to his realization that the artist must disappear, obliterate himself by living the life of his characters.[12] But where for the *verista* Verga, authorial silence guaranteed the objectivity of the representation, for Pirandello it signalled the disappearance—but as we shall see later, not the death—of the author, a prerequisite for the birth of the character.

Lined up, in his essays, face to face with rhetoric and a literary language made venerable by tradition, are sincerity and spontaneity, sister virtues that Pirandello used both of the artist in the act of creation and of the work itself. 'Sincerity' in this context is produced by the freedom that an artist must exercise in respect of schools, movements, precepts, and formulae; of anything in short that limits or curtails the autonomy of the creative moment, allowing for a creativity which is itself unmediated and spontaneous; a *lived* experience where the work is allowed to come into existence free of preconceptions and unhampered by tradition.[13] From the very beginning of his literary career Pirandello rejected wholesale all literary schools and movements; in one of his earliest essays, 'La menzogna del sentimento nell'arte' ('The Deceptiveness of Feeling in Art'), written at 23, he describes a summer day in Rome when, feeling bored and at a loose end, he began a desultory reading of

[11] Pirandello delivered two speeches in honour of Giovanni Verga. The first on 2 Sept. 1920, on the novelist's eightieth birthday, the second on 3 Dec. 1931, at the Reale Accademia d'Italia to commemorate the fiftieth anniversary of the publication of his novel *I Malavoglia* (*The House by the Medlar Tree*). Repr. *Spsv* 391–426.

[12] Luigi Capuana, *Gli 'ismi' contemporanei*, ed. Giorgio Luti (Milan, Fabbri, 1973).

[13] Sincerity is a key word in his discussion of Verga's work. See M. Lorena Maddaloni, *Pirandello e la crisi dell'estetica contemporanea* (Poggibonsi, Lalli, 1988), 8–9.

Poliziano's *Orfeo*. At first he enjoys the book, then he falters once or twice, his sensibility offended by what he sees as a lack of psychological realism, and finally he is pulled up short by the absence of verisimilitude when what he feels would be the 'natural' response to the death of a loved one is sacrificed at the altar of literary convention. That it is an episode taken from Greek mythology—Orpheus reacting to the news of Eurydice's death—does not influence his argument, which sees Pirandello subject a late fifteenth-century courtly verse drama to the same rules of psychological verisimilitude that one might expect of a piece of realist fiction:

Rammento ancora. La prima volta, in cui m'indusse l'animo d'iniziar le indagini per tale studio, fu un'estate, a Roma; e mi trovavo in una di quelle condizioni di spirito non singolari oggidì e pienissime di miseria, in cui un freddo e calmo disamor d'ogni cosa pigramente c'invade; e il senso del buono e del bello è come inaridito, e tutto ci par vuoto, insulso, senza scopo. Leggevo l'Orfeo di messer Angelo Poliziano, tolto così a caso, senza pena di scegliere, di tra gli altri libri dello scaffale [. . .] Ma non potei tollerare il terzo, *heroicus*, e mi sentii cader l'animo e il libro di mano ai versi di Mnesillo dopo l'annunzio della Driade:

> Vedi come dolente
> Se parte quel tapino . . .

Non saprei dire, mi parve così contro natura e inverisimile un amante, il quale, all'annunzio della morte della sua bella, ti volta le spalle senza aprir bocca, e che per dolersi del suo crudo destino aspetta di trovarsi in una ripa sola, e che quivi giunto accorda la lira e comincia. [14]

I can still remember it. The first time that my spirit induced me to begin research for such a study was one summer in Rome; and I found myself in one of those miserable states that are not uncommon these days in which a cold calm disenchantment with everything slowly creeps over us: and our sense of the good and beautiful seems to have dried up, and everything appears to us empty, dull and without purpose. I was reading Master Angelo Poliziano's *Orpheus* which I had

---

[14] *Luigi Pirandello*, 'La menzogna del sentimento nell'arte', *Vita nuova* (29 June and 6 July 1890). Repr. *Spsv* 868–78. Pirandello is in fact confusing two (and possibly three) works here. His reference is not to the original *Fabula di Orpheo* by Poliziano, which has no Mnesillo, no Dryads and very few *settenari*, nor to the edn. by Cardinal Gonzaga's circle, but to the anonymous *Orphei Tragoedia*, a five-act drama once attributed to Poliziano. See Antonia Tissoni Benvenuti, *L'"Orfeo' del Poliziano, con il testo critico dell'originale e delle successive forme teatrali* (Padua, Ed. Antenore, 1986).

selected at random from among the books on my shelves [. . .]. But I could not tolerate the third act, the *heroicus*, and I felt my spirits fall and the book drop from my hand as I read the lines spoken by Mnesillo after hearing what the Driad had told him:

> See how sad
> The wretch departs . . .

Somehow it seemed to me so unnatural and unlikely that a lover on hearing of the death of his beloved should turn around without saying a word and should wait before lamenting his cruel destiny to find himself in a lonely place in which to tune a lyre and begin.

In the years between 'La menzogna del sentimento nell'arte' (1890) and 'Soggettivismo e oggettivismo nell'arte' (1908) Pirandello often returned in essays and in book reviews to the question of sincerity (understood as an unfailing, rigorous, and unmediated honesty on the part of the artist), but his early impatience with movements and schools gradually gave way to a more moderate position, where he neither denied nor objected to their importance, but suggested that they should take their place alongside other influences bearing on the creative process.

Pirandello's theory of creativity received its fullest elaboration in 'Soggettivismo e oggettivismo nell'arte narrativa', where his presentation of the artistic act as spontaneous, intuitive creation in which mind, spirit, and emotion work in unison to transform perceptions into images, owed a profound intellectual debt to the writings of the spiritualist and psychologist Gabriel Séailles and the thinker he in turn influenced, Henri Bergson.[15] Pirandello had first coined the neologism *sincerismo* ('sincerism') in 1898 to add to Capuana's collection of -isms when, with a group of mainly Southern writers, he had launched a cultural journal called *Ariel*, described with a hint of exasperation by Pirandello's biographer, Gaspare Giudice, as being short on critical acumen but having 'una grande volontà di esseri sinceri'[16] ('a great desire to be sincere'). He also took

---

[15] For an account of the contribution Séailles's 'Essai sur le génie dans l'art' (1883) made to Pirandello's thought see Gösta Andersson, *Arte e teoria: Studi sulla poetica del giovane Luigi Pirandello* (Stockholm, Almquist and Wiksell, 1966), 142–226. For a clear and scrupulous study of Pirandello's essays, see Claudio Vicentini, *L'estetica di Pirandello* (Milan, Mursia, 1970).

[16] Gaspare Giudice, *Luigi Pirandello* (Turin, UTET, 1963), 152.

the opportunity to modify his earlier position slightly and allow that a sincere writer could draw on cultural movements, 'a patto però che non siano voluti a forza da un preconcetto teorico o tirati su la falsariga d'una data formula di scuola'[17] ('on condition though that they are not forcibly introduced because of a theoretical prejudice or follow slavishly the pattern of a school'). In his subsequent and final contribution to the short-lived journal, Pirandello applies this principle to Zola's *Paris*, arguing that the French author is writing too closely to his naturalist rule-book. Drawing on a metaphor that he often used to describe the difference beween originality and imitation, he rebuked Zola for having looked at the world 'attraverso gli occhiali d'un preconcetto. Un metodo prestabilito regola le sue osservazioni che perciò non sono nè spontanee nè sincere'[18] ('through his spectacles of preconception. A pre-established method rules his observations which for that reason are neither spontaneous nor sincere'). A few years later Pirandello began a review of a collection of stories by Alberto Cantoni with an attack on fellow critics who, instead of reading with their own eyes, borrow spectacles that have been modelled in Paris;[19] when he later revised the essay for inclusion in the collection *Arte e scienza* he added the story of an illiterate peasant who, on overhearing his parish priest say that he was unable to read because he had left his spectacles at home, decided to go into town to buy himself a pair of spectacles so that he too would be

[17] Luigi Pirandello, *Ariel*, 19 (24 May 1898). Tommaso Gnoli writing in *Leonardo* (Mar. 1935) said of the group that formed around *Ariel* that it 'auspicava in letteratura l'avvento del Sincerismo' ('hoped for the coming of Sincerism in literature'). He added: 'Ricordo che il Pirandello si riscaldava per questa parola da lui coniata, e diceva fra il serio e il faceto, che bisognava bandire una crociata in nome di questa nuova insegna, e aver il coraggio di proclamare il nuovo *ismo*, da mettere in coda o in testa agli altri (naturalismo, simbolismo, verismo ecc. ecc.) che il Capuana aveva esaminato e smontato nei suoi *Ismi contemporanei*.' (Andersson, *Arte e teoria*, 105–6.) ('I remember that Pirandello used to get excited by this word he had coined and he used to say, half-seriously and half-facetiously, that they should launch a crusade under the new flag, and have the courage to proclaim the new *ism* to put at the top or the bottom of the others (naturalism, symbolism, realism etc. etc.) which Capuana had taken apart and examined in his *Ismi contemporanei*').

[18] Andersson, *Arte e teoria*, 136.

[19] First publ. in *Nuova antologia* (16 Mar. 1905) as 'Alberto Cantoni', later included in *Arte e scienza* under the title 'Un critico fantastico', *Spsv* 363–87. He reuses the anecdote which follows to open 'Teatro nuovo e teatro vecchio', a lecture he delivered in Venice in July 1922 (ibid. 227–43.)

able to read. He tries on pair after pair without success until in desperation the oculist asks him if he is able to read. Astonished at the question, the protagonist responds by asking: 'E se sapessi leggere, sarei venuto da voi?' ('And if I knew how to read, would I come to you?'). The world of literature, Pirandello adds, suffers from a surplus of spectacles and a paucity of eyes. Seeing with one's own eyes without the assistance of spectacles became, for Pirandello, 'sincerity'.

Although an aesthetics structured around sincerity and spontaneity could easily fall into the idealist trap or, in its more extreme form, take a solipsistic turn, Pirandello's sceptical empiricism saved him from any such excess. In 'Sincerità e arte' ('Sincerity and Art', 1897), which was his response to an article by his friend, Ugo Ojetti, Pirandello had argued that sincerity is not only the product of an artist freeing himself of the constraints of tradition so that he can give free rein to his own ideas, but comes about when the artist gives his characters the space to think and talk for themselves. A writer who is guided by sincerity knows he has to respect both the inner world that he brings to the work and, as importantly, the outer world as it is in itself, without recourse to previously elaborated forms:

Per me il mondo non è solo un'idealità, non è cioè limitato all'idea che io possa farmene: fuori di me il mondo esiste per sè e con me; e nella mia rappresentazione io debbo propormi di *realizzarlo* quanto più mi sarà possibile, facendomene quasi una coscienza, in cui esso viva, in me come in se stesso; vedendolo come esso si vede, sentendolo come esso si sente. E allora più nulla di simbolico e di apparente per me, tutto sarà reale e vivente. E non farò pensare, sentire, parlare, gestire gli uomini a un modo, cioè a modo mio, come fanno gli scrittori che tu, secondo me, hai il torto di predilegere; ma a ciascuno m'ingegnerò di dar la sua voce, a ogni cosa il suo aspetto e il suo colore; la sua vita, insomma, non la mia maniera, lo stile attemprando al soggetto, guardando senza gli occhiali del pregiudizio, domando l'ingegno con l'esperienza.

E allora soltanto mi parrà di esser sincero.[20]

For me the world is not only an ideality, that is, it is not limited to the idea that I make of it for myself: outside of me the world exists for itself and with me, and in my representation I must determine *to realize it* as

---

[20] Luigi Pirandello, 'Sincerità e arte', *Il Marzocco* (1897, not republ.) Quoted Andersson, *Arte e teoria*, 127.

much as I can, creating for myself something like a consciousness of it in which it lives, in me as it does in itself, seeing it as it sees itself, feeling it as it feels itself. Then there will be no need for symbol or appearance: everything will be real and living. And I will not make characters think, feel, act in one way, that is to say in my way, as the writers do whom you, I think, mistakenly favour; but I shall endeavour to give each his own voice, each thing its own appearance and colour, its life in short, not my manner, fitting the style to the subject, looking without the blinkers of prejudice, taming intelligence with experience.

And only then will it appear to me that I am being sincere.

Pirandello's defence of the inimitable uniqueness of the individual creative voice is of course not in itself so singular; as long as there have been artists and critics, there has been resistance from the former to attempts by the latter to categorize according to schools, class, gender, or any other potentially unifying factor. Among his close contemporaries, Flaubert is one who on learning that he was a realist, exploded in a letter to a friend of Zola's: 'Down with Schools, whatever they are, down with empty words' and, in an irate letter to Turgenev, explained:

Reality, in my view, ought to be no more than a spring-board. Our friends believe that to it alone belongs the Kingdom! This materialism makes my blood boil, and nearly every Monday I feel a wave of anger as I read old Zola's literary articles. After the Realists, we have the Naturalists and the Impressionists. What progress! A gang of humbugs trying to make themselves believe, and us with them, that they have discovered the Mediterranean . . .[21]

In a similar spirit Joseph Conrad, in 1905, commented witheringly that 'to try voluntarily to discover the fettering dogmas of some romantic, realistic, or naturalistic creed in the free work of its [the novel's] own inspiration, is a trick worthy of human perverseness'.[22] Where Pirandello is different is that for the most part he is writing in these essays from the position of a literary critic, before his own talents as creative writer had come to fruition, while Flaubert and Conrad are protesting at the critical reception of their work.

In his published response to Ojetti, Pirandello moves swiftly from an acknowledgement of the autonomy of the world about

---

[21] Gustave Flaubert, letter to Ivan Turgenev, 8 Nov. 1877. See Miriam Allott, *Novelists on the Novel* (London, Routledge and Kegan Paul, 1959), 69.

[22] Joseph Conrad, 'Books' (1905), repr. *Notes on Life and Letters* (1921). Allott, *Novelists*, 132.

him to a recognition of the alterity of the people who inhabit it. He argues that this recognition places the onus on the creative writer to respect their identities as unique to them. Two years later in his first article on drama, 'L'azione parlata' ('Spoken Action'), he argues through the consequences of this position, blaming the lamentable state of contemporary Italian theatre on playwrights who think first of the event (the 'fatto') and only then of the characters who might best represent it.[23] It should, he says, be the other way round; the characters must be free and independent of their author so that the story is *born* of them:

Non il dramma fa le persone; ma queste, il dramma. E prima d'ogni altro dunque bisogna aver le persone: vive, libere, operanti. Con esse in esse nascerà l'idea del dramma.[24]

It is not the drama that makes the characters, but the characters who make the drama. And so before all else one must have the characters: living, free, and active. With them in them the idea for the drama will be born.

Pirandello went on to distinguish between contemporary plays—usually reworkings of a story or novel—and the subject of his essay which he describes as a *dialogo drammatico* ('dramatic dialogue'). The difference between the two, he explains, is that a 'dramatic dialogue' has no narrative substructure, the event depends entirely on the characters. The action is in their words. He illustrates his point with a story taken from a poem by Heinrich Heine, in which the troubadour Jaufré Rudel and his lady Melisenda each night bestir themselves and, together with other figures stitched into the tapestries which line the walls at the Castle of Blaye, step down to take a stroll around the great hall. And similarly, Pirandello says, characters should 'step out' ('staccarsi vivi') from the written pages of the drama and come to life.

Ora questo prodigio può avvenire a un solo patto: che si trovi cioè la parola che sia l'azione parlata, la parola viva che muova, l'espressione immediata, connaturata con l'azione, la frase unica, che non può esser che quella propria a quel dato personaggio in quella data situazione: parole, espressioni, frasi che non s'inventano, ma che nascono,

---

[23] 'L'azione parlata', *Marzocco* (7 May 1899). *Spsv* 1017.
[24] Ibid. 1016.

quando l'autore si sia veramente immedesimato con la sua creatura fino a sentirla com'essa si sente, a volerla com'essa si vuole. [25]

Now this miracle can happen only on one condition: that you find the word that is the spoken action, the living word that moves, the immediate expression at one with the action, the one which alone is appropriate to that given character in that given situation: words, expressions, turns of phrase that are not invented but are born when the author feels really identified with his creation to the point of feeling it as it feels itself and of wanting it to be as it wants itself to be.

In the balance between author and characters, too much of the author results in a work that is *fatta* and *scritta* where it should be *nata* or *viva*. By neatly sidestepping the difference between theatre as text and theatre as performance, and directing his discussion at the *azione parlata* of the written *dialogo drammatico*, Pirandello extends his insight to written narrative in general, and the boundaries between the written and the spoken become blurred with, as we shall see, interesting results.

From the admiring description of a troubadour and his lady who step down from a wall tapestry to take a turn around the great hall to the reprimand delivered to the author of a late fifteenth-century courtly pastoral drama for his mythological protagonist's unnatural reaction to the death of his loved one, we have seen how Pirandello's essays champion the autonomy of the literary character. In the second part of *L'umorismo*, a study bristling with scholarly references (it was written not out of choice, but to obtain a tenured post at the Magistero, a women's teacher-training college), when Pirandello turns his attention to literary characters—Marmeladoff in *Crime and Punishment*, Don Quixote in the novel named after him, and especially Don Abbondio in *I promessi sposi* (*The Betrothed*)—he discusses them as though they were living beings. His use of the present tense only serves to heighten our sense of them as self-determining creatures, with moral choices yet to be made and decisions to be taken. The case, for example, of Don Abbondio, the frightened and easily intimidated village priest in Manzoni's great historical novel, is presented in a familiarly comfortable tone; the sort of register one may well use when gossiping about

---

[25] 'L'azione parlata', *Marzocco* (7 May 1899). *Spsv* 1015–16. The thought is repeated verbatim in 'Illustratori, attori e traduttori', *Nuova antologia* (16 Jan. 1908). *Spsv* 209–24.

a third party who is not around to defend him or her self—'Ora, io non nego, don Abbondio è un coniglio . . .'[26] ('Now, I do not deny that Don Abbondio is a rabbit')—but, Pirandello continues, we know that the threats made against him were real enough so what else could he do? The pleasure of such an exercise is that it affords reader and critic the opportunity to discuss others as though we really do, or indeed can, know them. With the characters frozen into the eternal present, the same moral dilemmas and the same life choices facing them each time we pick up the book, it is we the readers who change, grow old, learn wisdom, or sometimes not. Unlike our own lives which are subject to the vagaries of passing time, a literary character is not going to deprive the reader of the satisfaction of being able to 'know' somebody else, a desire that can never be fully satisfied in the world beyond the story.

Talking about character as Pirandello does in *L'umorismo* presupposes that they are independent and fully realized creatures who have the capacity to make their own choices, and therefore also take responsibility for their actions. This recognition of their self-determination underlines the realist project (and indeed marks it off from the naturalist novel where responsibility is, to a much greater extent, displaced on to environment and circumstance). It is a matter of degree rather than approach. Many of Pirandello's contemporaries likewise experience their characters as beings who simply and intractably are themselves: to try to make something else of them leads to a deeply flawed work. Here is Anthony Trollope writing in his autobiography about how important it is for an author to take the trouble to really get to know his characters:

and he can never know them well unless he can live with them in the full reality of established intimacy. They must be with him as he lies down to sleep, and as he wakes from his dreams. He must learn to hate them and to love them. He must know of them whether they be cold-blooded or passionate, whether true or false, and how far true, and how far false. The depth and the breadth, and the narrowness and the shallowness of each should be clear to him. [. . .] It is so far that I have lived with my characters, and thence has come whatever success I have attained.[27]

---

[26] *Spsv* 143.
[27] Anthony Trollope, *Autobiography* (1883; Oxford, OUP, 1980), 232–3.

And this warning came from a writer who prided himself on the number of words he produced before lunch each day. Another novelist of an altogether different social and geographical milieu from Pirandello's, Henry James, recalled in his preface to *The Portrait of a Lady* Turgenev's description of the creative process:

I have always fondly remembered a remark that I heard fall years ago from the lips of Ivan Turgenieff in regard to his own experience of the usual origin of the fictive picture. It began for him almost always with the vision of some person or persons, who hovered before him, soliciting him, as the active or passive figure, interesting him and appealing to him just as they were and by what they were. He saw them, in that fashion, as *disponibles*, saw them subject to the chances, the complications of existence, and saw them vividly, but then had to find for them the right relations, those that would most bring them out; to imagine, to invent and select and piece together the situations most useful and favourable to the sense of the creatures themselves, the complications they would be most likely to produce and feel.

'To arrive at these things is to arrive at my "story",' he said, 'and that's the way I look for it. The result is that I'm often accused of not having "story" enough. I seem to myself to have as much as I need—to show my people, to exhibit their relations with each other; for that is all my measure. If I watch them long enough I see them come together, I see them *placed*, I see them engaged in this or that act and in this or that difficulty. How they look and move and speak and behave always in the setting that I have found for them, is my account of them—of which I dare say, alas, *que cela manque souvent d'architecture*.' [...]

So this beautiful genius, and I recall with comfort the gratitude I drew from his reference to the intensity of suggestion that may reside in the stray figure, the unattached character, the *image en disponibilité*. It gave me higher warrant than I seemed then to have met for just that blest habit of one's own imagination, the trick of investing some conceived or encountered individual, some brace or group of individuals, with the germinal property and authority. I was myself so much more antecedently conscious of my figures than of their setting [...] I could think so little of any fable that didn't need its agents positively to launch it; I could think so little of any situation that didn't depend for its interest on the nature of the persons situated, and thereby on their way of taking it.[28]

[28] Henry James, Preface to *The Portrait of a Lady* (1881; Oxford, OUP, 1981), pp. xxvii–xxviii.

Pirandello's own description of creativity is one which not only recognizes, but is indeed posited on the alterity, or otherness, of the world and its inhabitants. In the crossover between the artistic self and the world outside it, it is the self that has to make the first move. Creativity is preceded by the attempt to absorb into one's own consciousness that which is external to it. But internalization is only a first stage in an artistic process which will see the writer struggling to maintain the essential alterity of his characters and the realities they inhabit. Artistic consciousness is therefore based on the recognition of otherness. In the relation between the artistic self and the other that is delineated here, Pirandello describes a process that is very similar in its conception to Mikhail Bakhtin's exploration of multiplicity in human perception, which is also posited on the non-centered position of the 'I' and the alterity of the other: 'I *actively* enter as a living being into an individuality, and consequently do not, for a single moment, lose myself completely or lose my singular position outside that individuality. It is not the subject who unexpectedly takes position of a passive me, but *I* who actively enter into him.'[29] For understanding to occur, Bakhtin argues that the author must always retain his one-sidedness, remain off-centre. Only in this way can he recognize the integrity (which Bakhtin understands as the potential) of the literary character. Such independence from their author confers on characters a capacity to exceed expectation, they are robust enough to be released as genuine creators in their own world. The result for Bakhtin is the polyphonic work which admits to dialogic truth by allowing the consciousness of a character to be truly someone else's consciousness. As a theory of creativity, polyphony is remarkably similar to Pirandello's own representations of the artistic process.

In *Problems of Dostoyevsky's Poetics* Bakhtin imagines his hero's creative process as one where he had no structure or plan, but instead imagined specific voices, integral personalities with their own ideas and sense of the world. The monopoly enjoyed by characters in this scenario is very similar to Pirandello's view on the matter expressed in 'L'azione parlata':

[29] Mikhail Bakhtin, 'Toward a Philosophy of the Act', quoted in Gary Saul Morson and Caryl Emerson, *Mikhail Bakhtin: Creation of a Prosaics* (Stanford, Calif., Stanford University Press, 1990), 93.

Che se egli ha creato veramente caratteri, se ha messo su la scena uomini e non manichini, ciascuno di essi avrà un particolar modo di esprimersi, per cui, alla lettura, un lavoro drammatico dovrebbe risultare come scritto da tanti e non dal suo autore, come composto, per questa parte, dai singoli personaggi, nel fuoco dell'azione, e non dal suo autore.[30]

For if he has really created characters, if he has put men and women on stage and not puppets, each of them will have his or her own particular way of speaking, so that, on reading it, a dramatic work should give the impression of being written by many and not by its author, as if it were composed in this respect by the individual protagonists in the heat of the action and not by the author.

The writer's function would be to devise situations which can bring characters together to talk. The theory develops out of circumstances that, as we can see from Henry James's preface, would be familiar to many novelists. So what the reader encounters is not, in Bakhtin's words, a 'stenographer's report of a *finished* dialogue, from which the author has already withdrawn and *over* which he is now located as if in some higher decision-making position', but a situation where the author addresses characters, taking them as people who are 'actually present . . . and capable of answering him.'[31] In his writings Pirandello recognizes that the writer does not play God, he is an equal among equals, de-centred, his writing is the product of his recognition of the alterity of others:

Bisogna innanzi tutto non presumere che gli altri, fuori del nostro io, non siano se non come noi li vediamo. Se così presumiamo, vuol dire che abbiamo una coscienza unilaterale; che non abbiamo coscienza degli altri; che non realizziamo gli altri in noi, per usare un'espressione di Josiah Royce, con una rappresentazione vivente per gli altri e per noi.[32]

First of all one must not presume that other people, outside of ourselves, are only as we see them. If that is what we presume, it means that

---

[30] *Spsv* 1017. Pirandello praised Verga's *I Malavoglia* for the way it is written to appear, in Salvatore Farina's words, 'essersi fatta da sè' ('to have created itself') because, he adds, the essential unity does not dominate from outside 'ma si transfonde e vive nei singoli attori del dramma' ('but enters and lives in the single actors of the drama'). *Spsv* 405.

[31] Mikhail Bakhtin, *Problems of Dostoyevsky's Poetics*, ed. and tr. Caryl Emerson (Minneapolis, University of Minnesota Press, 1984), 64.

[32] 'Illustratori, attori e traduttori'. *Spsv* 242.

our awareness is one-sided; that we are not aware of others; that we do not make others real in ourselves, to use an expression of Josiah Royce, through a representation that is living for others and for ourselves.

The most far-reaching consequences of this will, however, eventually take him, not to Bakhtin's polyphonic novel, but to the stage. In *Sei personaggi in cerca d'autore* (*Six Characters in Search of an Author*, 1921) the theatre becomes the last resort for a group of characters at loggerheads with Pirandello, who has refused to take up their case after they have been ill-served by another writer. The breakdown in their relationship is re-enacted, not only on stage, but also in three short stories that were written before the play and a twenty-page preface added later. On each of these occasions Pirandello presents the events from a different point of view. The conflict between author and characters only increases their determination and independence, or what Bakhtin calls 'integrity'. They have come to him complete with their own tale to tell, but Pirandello refuses them, and eventually, in the hope that they will stop hounding him, he suggests they go it alone. The problems raised when a group of characters are let loose on the stage intent on representing themselves, refusing the mediation of author, director, or actors becomes one of the subjects of Pirandello's best-known play.

Sei personaggi in cerca d'autore emerges from the collapse of any viable collaboration between an author and a group of characters, but it also develops out of the failure of communication between the protagonists themselves. It is a work born of antagonism. Long before its conception Pirandello's recognition of the alterity of his literary characters was to lead him away from the realist fictions of his early work to first person narratives where characters become self-determining subjects no longer mediated by an authorial presence. One of the consequences is that the characters appear bearing their own plot around their necks like an albatross. The intellectual watershed comes in about 1908 when *L'umorismo* and the title essay of *Arte e scienza* were both published; they reveal a shift towards a position which, while recognizing that there is an irrepressible objective world outside, accepts that it can only be reached through our own subjective apprehension of it. For the author to mediate reality on behalf of his character is a bit of a cheat; the novel's subjectivity should belong to the character, not to the author. Gradually, in the short stories that Pirandello wrote between 1900 and 1914, dialogue and monologue come to occupy the entire narrative space, sometimes with strange results. For example, the story 'La morte addosso' ('Living with Death') is pure dialogue which, when it is turned into a one-act play under the new title *L'uomo dal fiore in bocca* (*The Man with the Flower in his Mouth*), becomes, because of the addition of stage directions, more of a narrative text than the original story.

Pirandello's belief in the literary character's right to self-determination, defended by him in his essays, and developed in his fictions, also feeds into his approach to narrative genres. I wish to consider one particular statement of his position before going on to look at how the views expressed impact on his own short stories. In 1897 he published a book review whose title, 'Romanzo, racconto, novella' ('Novel, Tale, Story'), is a reference to the odd mismatch between the differing lengths of the three fictions that make up the volume, and the terms that are employed to describe them.[33] The longest of the three, 'Nelle tenebre' ('In the Shadows') by Boffico, is referred to as a *racconto*; Neera's 'L'amuleto' ('The Lucky Charm'), which is just a little shorter, is called a *romanzo*; and Capuana's contribution is described as a *novella*.[34] Pirandello seizes upon the opportunity provided by this discrepancy to discuss the relationship between narrative genres. While happy with the practice of defining the novel and the short story (*romanzo* and *novella*) in terms of their respective lengths, he draws the reader's atten-

---

[33] 'Romanzo, racconto, novella', *Le grazie* (16 Feb. 1897). Paolo Mario Sipala discusses the article in his *Capuana e Pirandello: Storia e testi di una relazione letteraria* (Catania, Bonanni, 1974), 35–7.

[34] At the time Pirandello wrote the review, *romanzo* was used, as now, of the novel, *novella* of the short story, and *racconto* of narratives that fell mid-way in length between novel and short story. In contemporary Italian usage *novella* and *racconto* are used interchangeably of the short story irrespective of length, and *racconto* is more commonly used of the contemporary short story. In both Niccolò Tommaseo's *Dizionario della lingua italiana* (1879) and Salvatore Battaglia's *Grande dizionario della lingua italiana* (1921) the *novella* is associated with the *fiaba* or *favola* and the *racconto* is linked to tales of realist derivation. Only Battaglia includes length and complexity as characteristics of the *racconto*, which he describes as 'generalmente collocato per ampiezza e complessità fra la novella e il romanzo' ('because of its breadth and complexity it is generally placed between the story and the novel').

tion to the way that the length of a given piece exercises an influence over not only its subject-matter, but also its presentation. To illustrate his point, Pirandello appropriates a definition provided by Niccolò Tommaseo in his *Dizionario estetico*, where it is argued that the brevity of the short story and the unities of classical theatre determine an approach to subject-matter that is common to both genres:

La novella e la tragedia classica invece pigliano il fatto, a dir così, per la coda; e di questa estremità si contentano: intese a dipingerci non le origini, non i gradi della passione, non le relazioni di quella con i molti oggetti che circondano l'uomo e servono a sospingerla, a ripercuoterla, ad informarla, in mille modi diversi, ma solo gli ultimi passi, l'eccesso insomma.[35]

The story and the classical tragedy, on the other hand, take the event so to speak by its tail and are happy with that: intending to paint for us not the origins, not the gradations of passion, not the relation of passion with the many objects that surround human beings and serve to drive it on, feed it, shape it in a thousand different ways, but just the last few steps, the excess in short.

Where Pirandello strikes out on his own is over the definition of *racconto*; he sees little point in using the word to refer to a narrative that falls short of a novel but is too long to be called a story. He argues instead that the term should not indicate the length of the piece, but quite simply refer to any piece of narrative in which the implied author or narrating subject speaks in the first person. As we shall see, it means that the narrating protagonist controls the story to an extent which will make him the envy of his peers who find themselves in plays or, even more disablingly, in third person narratives—be they *novella* or *romanzo*.

---

[35] 'Romanzo, racconto, novella', in Sipala, *Capuana e Pirandello*, 56–7. The later 'Soggettivismo e oggettivismo nell'arte narrativa' includes this passage in full, with quotation marks to acknowledge that it is borrowed and the name of the author is included. The two additional sentences included in the later essay are (*Spsv* 223–4): 'La novella sta al romanzo, [. . .] a un dipresso come la tragedia osservatrice delle unità al dramma storico. E la novella e la tragedia classica condensano in piccolo spazio i fatti, i sentimenti, che la natura presenta o dilatati o dispersi.' 'The novella is to the novel [. . .] approximately as tragedy which observes the three unities was to historical drama. The novella and classical tragedy are the condensation in a small space of facts and feelings which in nature are spread out or dispersed.')

Racconto insomma diventa il romanzo, quando la favola in essa racchiusa venga esposta per dir così descrittivamente, o riferita dall'autore o da un personaggio che parli in prima persona, più che rappresentata o messa in azione: e racconto breve, la novella, nelle identiche condizioni.[36]

The novel in sum becomes a tale when the story contained within it is expanded so to speak descriptively, either related by the author or by a character speaking in the first person, rather than performed or put into action: a *novella* becomes a short tale in the same circumstances.

In making this claim, he also rejects the positivist, progressive view of literary history which sees the then current espousal of objectivity, articulated in *verismo* or realism, as representing a higher level of artistic achievement. In the later 'Soggettivismo e oggettivismo nell'arte narrativa' which incorporates and develops the argument, Pirandello prefaces his comments by noting that the distinction to be drawn between *racconto* and its sister genres is based on a different attitude or approach to narrative art. For Pirandello it is a question of where, in the cognitive act, the emphasis falls—whether it is on the external world with its separate and distinct reality or on the subject's own conscious efforts to apprehend it:

La differenza tra rappresentazione obiettiva e rappresentazione subiettiva deriva, in fondo, semplicemente dal diverso valore che noi attribuiamo all'atto dello spirito nella rappresentazione della realtà esteriore: valore obiettivo se ci sforziamo di cogliere e di rappresentare il mondo esteriore nella sua composizione reale; valore subiettivo se impieghiamo un'attività cosciente nel coglierlo. [. . .] non si tratta insomma della separazione impossibile tra soggetto e oggetto; ma soltanto del valore intenzionale che attribuiamo all'atto della rappresentazione.[37]

The difference between an objective representation and a subjective one derives quite simply from the different value that we attribute to the act of the spirit in its representation of external reality: an objective value if we make the attempt to apprehend and to represent the external world as it really is; a subjective value if we literally use a conscious activity in order to apprehend it. [. . .] it is not a matter of an impossible separation between subject and object; but only of the intentional value that we attribute to the act of representation.

[36] 'Romanzo, racconto, novella', in Sipala, *Capuana e Pirandello*, 56–7.
[37] *Spsv* 219.

So the *racconto* catches the action in its making, the story is related from within its own frame of reference. From the last few lines of the quotation it is clear, however, that Pirandello is reminding us that all writing is subjective, that it only appears more or less objective according to where the author lays the stress. (If the story is the genre closest to classical theatre, then the *racconto*, according to Pirandello's definition, is allied to the dramatic monologue.)

By dividing narrative genres into two groups—third person narratives (made up of the *romanzo* and the *novella*) and first person narratives (*racconto*)—Pirandello develops a working model similar to the French linguistician Emile Benveniste's own categories of 'discourse' (*racconto*) and 'narrative' (*romanzo* and *novella*) where the distinguishing features of 'discourse' are the presence of the pronoun 'I' (which contains an implicit reference to a 'you'), adverbial indicators of time and space (such as 'here', 'now', 'yesterday') and certain tenses: the present, future, and present perfect. 'Narrative' on the other hand is identified by its exclusive use of the third person and such forms as the preterite and the pluperfect. Where 'discourse' displays subjectivity and reveals something of the personality of the mediator, 'narrative' displays objectivity and impersonality; here the events appear to narrate themselves regardless of who is doing the narrating. Hayden White has more recently pointed out that:

the distinction between 'discourse' and 'narrative' is, of course, based solely on an analysis of the grammatical features of two modes of discourse in which the 'objectivity' of the one and the 'subjectivity' of the other are definable primarily by 'a linguistic order of criteria'. The subjectivity of the discourse is given by the presence, explicit or implicit, of an 'ego' who can be defined 'only as the person who maintains the discourse'. By contrast 'the objectivity of narrative is defined by the absence of all reference to the narrator'.[38]

He is reminding us that what purports to be the text's greater objectivity, or subjectivity, is the product of nothing more than what he calls the 'grammatical features' of the text. The concern expressed refers to the ideological implications of the

---

[38] Hayden White, 'The Value of Narrativity in the Representation of Reality', in W. I. T. Mitchell (ed.), *On Narrative* (Chicago, University of Chicago Press, 1981), 3.

'authority' an impersonal narrative carries and Pirandello made a similar point to emphasize his scepticism about the cultural prestige then enjoyed by realism. Pirandello's discussion is motivated throughout by his argument that all writing, all forms of representation, are subjective, but they appear more or less objective according to how far the author wishes to conceal or reveal his own part in the textual construction of reality. The narrator either 'comes out' to the reader, making him or herself visible (and audible), or remains hidden behind the screen provided by the cast of characters. Pirandello, for his part, is concerned to keep within the reader's sight the link between the originary subject and the object of representation.

What is at stake is more than purely a question of literary aesthetics for, with his insistence upon the subject's role in the construction of reality, Pirandello is outlining a position that is as much philosophical, in the broadest sense of the term, as it is literary. His scepticism over how far any of us can 'know' reality in a disinterested way was in fact fuelled by idealist thinkers, in particular Immanuel Kant, who while never denying the existence of a world beyond us, independent of our cognition of it, 'appears to insist that the limitations are limitations just *because* they have their roots in human sensibility and understanding and therefore make it impossible to achieve knowledge of reality *as it is in itself*'.[39] By reminding us that all writing is of necessity subjective, Pirandello is bent on revealing what realism was equally committed to concealing—namely the link between what is said and who is saying it. The *racconto*, or *rappresentazione subiettiva* ('subjective representation'), with its foregrounding of narrative voice, is a highly efficacious way of showing readers that what is before them is the expression of one point of view among others.

At the time Pirandello was arguing his case in Italy, in Germany the critic Käte Friedemann was challenging in similar terms the then current creed that the novel should avoid the personalized narrator. Her argument is based on an analogy between the narrator's role in literature and the way the reader

---

[39] P. F. Strawson, 'Echoes of Kant: How and When We Know What We Know', *TLS* (3 July. 1992), 12. Claudio Vicentini has charted the evolution in Pirandello's thinking, whereby the role of the subject becomes increasingly important to the cognitive process, in *L'estetica di Pirandello*, 15–40.

functions in life: ' "The narrator" is the one who evaluates, who is sensitively aware, who observes. He symbolizes the epistemological view familiar to us since Kant that we do not apprehend the world in itself, but rather as it has passed through the medium of an observing mind'.[40]

In his writing, Pirandello moved with apparent ease across genres, but if, for a moment, we put the traditional definitions aside, to turn to Pirandello's own narrative categories, we find that the impersonal realist writing that dominates in his earlier work gradually gives way to first person narratives in his later, better known, writing. Four of his seven novels are written in the third person: *L'esclusa* (1901), *Il turno* (1902) and *Suo marito* (*Her Husband*) (1911), and a fourth, historical, novel, *I vecchi e i giovani* (*The Old and the Young*) published in 1909. The remaining three, which are also the most innovative, are first person narratives: *Il fu Mattia Pascal* (1904), *Si gira . . .* (*Shoot*, 1915; to become *Quaderni di Serafino Gubbio operatore* (*The Notebooks of Serafino Gubbio, Cameraman*) in 1925), and the monologue of a madman sustained for over 150 pages that we saw Pirandello read aloud from at the opening of this chapter, *Uno, nessuno e centomila* (1925–6). Apart from these long narrative fictions, Pirandello also completed 200 of the 365 short stories that he had hoped to accomplish, one for each day of the year, as their collective title *Novelle per un anno* (*A Year's Worth of Stories*) suggests. Of these about fifty are written in the first person, beginning with 'Le tre carissime' ('The Three Loved Ones') which was first published in 1907. His interest in the *racconto* or *rappresentazione subiettiva* becomes apparent between 1904 and 1908, the years when his essays are indicating a philosophical shift towards a more relativist approach to the world about us. By allowing a literary character to speak for her- or himself in a monologue, or characters to debate between themselves in dialogue, in other words by giving the narrative space to the character, Pirandello's *racconti* acquire a dramatic form which is heightened by the pervasive use of the present tense and the spoken aura he gives to the written text.

Until now our attention has been on the primacy of character in Pirandello's essays and fictions, but literary characters are

[40] Käte Friedemann, *Die Rolle der Erzählers in der Epik* (Darmstadt, 1965), 26, quoted in F. K. Stanzel, *A Theory of Narrative* (Cambridge, CUP, 1984), 4.

phantasms put together with words. In fiction characters acquire selfhood through language and Pirandello's protagonists are, of course, no exception. Only in their case it is the spoken rather than the written word that gives them access to the narrative stage. Everything is invested in the spoken word. It is language that propels events. His characters are born in and through speech. Direct speech implies the present tense with all its potential for open-endedness. The author 'immedesimato con la sua creatura fino a sentirla come'essa si sente, a volerla com'essa si vuole'[41] ('truly identified with his creature to the point at which he feels as the character feels, wishes her as she wishes herself') returns us to the opening cameos of this chapter where we saw Pirandello as he composed his work and as he read aloud from it.

In the next chapter we shall be looking at Pirandello's representations in stories, novels, and plays of the moment that gives rise to the creative work: the meeting between author and character. But here I want to turn to some examples of what develops out of those encounters by turning initially to tales from the *Novelle per un anno* where the character is storyteller. We shall look at how Pirandello develops the relationship between the short story, orality, and performance through characters who are engaged in telling their own life-stories.

First a word about the stories as a collection. From 'Capannetta' ('The Little Hut'), which was written in 1884 when its author was only 17, to 'Il buon cuore' ('A Kind Heart'), published posthumously in 1937, Pirandello remained loyal to the short story throughout his long and productive career.[42] His grand plan to write 365 stories,[43] many of which underwent one or more revisions, gives an indication of his commitment to the genre. Some thirty-four of the stories were to provide the crea-

---

[41] See n. 24.

[42] Pirandello's last volume of poetry, *Fuori di chiave*, appeared in 1912, while his last novel, *Uno, nessuno e centomila*, written between 1909 and 1925, was published in 1926. His career as playwright began in earnest in 1916.

[43] It was however left unrealized: of the projected 24 vols., Pirandello saw the publication of 14 vols. with a 15th appearing after his death. As his *Avvertenza* included in the edns. published between 1922 and 1928 makes clear, he had hoped to publish the collection in a single very large volume, 'di quei monumentali che da gran tempo ormai per opere di letteratura non usano più' ('one of those massive ones which have not been used for literary works for a long time'). *Novelle per un anno*, ed. Mario Costanzo (Milan, Mondadori, 1985), vol. i/2. 1071.

tively economical Pirandello with ideas, situations, and characters for his plays, but it would be wrong to see the short story as a literary equivalent to the artist's sketch pad; these tales stand on their own, fully realized in their own right.

All narrative is the outcome of somebody somewhere with a tale to tell and Pirandello's tales are alive with characters who press to tell their story from their own standpoint. Indeed the overall impression that the reader gets from Pirandello's tales is that they belong more to the characters who tell them or inhabit them than to the author under whose name they appear. This impression is reinforced by the absence of a framing device. From the instructions that Pirandello gave, it is evident that he wanted his *Novelle per un anno* to be seen as having a collective identity; he even concedes that to some he may appear to be overreaching himself, 'se si pensa che per antica tradizione delle *notti* o delle *giornate* s'intitolarono spesso altre raccolte del genere, alcune delle quali famosissime'[44] ('if one considers that by venerable tradition *Nights* or *Days* appeared in the titles of other collections of this sort, some of which are very famous'), but unlike his prestigious predecessors he himself never considered using a frame. Although one can only speculate, its absence none the less is consistent with his representation of a literary process where the first move comes from a character who hopes to gain entry into the house of fiction. Without a *cornice* or a framing device that attaches the tales to some reality external to them (as the author's *Avvertenza* ('Foreword') makes clear, there is no link with the reader's world either), these stories belong firmly within the ambit of the characters who tell them and the characters they are told about.

A distinguishing characteristic of the short story itself is that it comes directly from an oral tradition. While the novel has its roots in a written culture, the story was originally spoken aloud in the presence of one or more listeners. Walter Benjamin reminds us in 'The Storyteller' of a fundamental difference between story and novel: 'A man listening to a story is in the company of a storyteller; even a man reading one shares this companionship. The reader of a novel, however, is isolated,

---

[44] Ibid. 1071.

more so than any other reader'.[45] To read Pirandello's own collection of tales is to be reminded at every turn of the origins of the genre, for the reader is greeted by a cacophony of voices—many pressing to tell their own story. Taken as a whole, the collection gives an overwhelming impression of a society that dedicates much of its time and energy to talk in all its varieties. In the midst of this are characters whose lives are marked by a silence that is often equated with helplessness and despair. Their silence makes them the victims of society. But here I want to turn to three stories where the relationship between the short story, orality, and performance is used for a first person narrative with a narrator who recounts her or his life-story.

The protagonist of the first story, 'L'altro figlio' ('The Other Son') is an illiterate beggar who lives her life in conditions of deprivation that are extreme even by the standards of the impoverished Sicilian community, decimated by the emigration of its men, that she belongs to. Mariagrazia is unusual among Pirandello's storytellers in that she is reluctant to communicate her own life history; she has agreed to do so only because her interlocutor, a young doctor dispatched to this desolate outpost, will then write a letter on her behalf. It is to be addressed to her two sons who had left for America many years earlier and have never since been in touch. Before putting pen to paper, however, the doctor learns that a third, deeply caring son lives close to hand, and yet she refuses to acknowledge his existence, let alone accept his help. The doctor discovers that even in this closed community, Mariagrazia's story is not known because she has never spoken it; nobody, not even her rejected son, can tell her story other than herself.

Before Mariagrazia speaks she is introduced to the reader through a portrait so physically repellent as to deny her any vestige of dignity. A figure of derision and wretchedness, she crouches, like a dog, on other peoples's doorsteps, ignored except for the odd scraps of food thrown in her direction. But as soon as this festering bundle of rags starts to speak our perception of her changes dramatically. The doctor by contrast is presented as the villagers see him; although still so young 'era

[45] Walter Benjamin, 'The Storyteller', *Illuminations* (London, Fontana, 1992), 100.

proprio vecchio di senno, e dotto: faceva restar tutti a bocca aperta, quando parlava'[46] ('he was old when it came to wisdom and learning: he astounded everyone when he spoke'). In this story, though, it will be the silent beggarwoman who through speech will gain first dignity and then power over the doctor, so that the tale ends with him transcribing the letter dictated by her.

Her illiteracy reminds us that storytelling is amongst the least élitist of all cultural forms of communication. It is not restricted to any social class—it needs neither familiarity with literature, nor access to a print culture—it is as free as the air it travels on. All it requires (and Mariagrazia unhampered by any cultural baggage has it in abundance) are sincerity and spontaneity: prerequisites, as we saw earlier, for the professional writer. Mariagrazia and the doctor between them represent many of the characteristics of an oral-based society as opposed to a literate culture. She is, in the purely conventional sense of the word, ignorant—she has never moved beyond her immediate surroundings, she has no knowledge of any other form of social organization, she cannot conceptualize—while he has studied, he has travelled, and he can make deductions from his reading. But she is old and can speak with the wisdom of experience: he is young and can speak only with the abstract knowledge of book learning. At the beginning of her tale, she prefaces her account with a reminder that experience has taught her things that he cannot so much as begin to imagine; 'n'ho viste! n'ho viste! Ho visto cose, signorino mio, che vossignoria non si può nemmeno immaginare [. . .] e io le ho viste con questi occhi che hanno pianto da allora lagrime di sangue'[47] ('I have seen such things! such things! I have seen things that your lordship cannot even imagine [. . .] and I have seen them with these eyes of mine that since then have cried tears of blood'). She then tells of her husband's murder at the hands of brigands who were newly released from gaol by Garibaldi's men, of a region terrorized by the barbarism and bestiality of the 'patriots', and

---

[46] *Novelle per un anno*, ed. Mario Costanzo (Milan, Mondadori, 1987), ii/1. 39. The story was first published in 1905 during the period when Pirandello was gradually moving away from realism. He turned the story into a one-act play with the same title in 1923.

[47] Ibid. 50.

of how they used the severed heads of local men to play bowls with. Her story continues with an account of her own imprisonment and impregnation by the man who raped her, followed by her release several months later and the birth of the child her mother farms out to relatives so that she need never see him. Here lies the reason for her physical and psychological revulsion for this now grown man, so overwhelming that it has not diminished with the passing years. The tale is chilling; its content determines its own telling and there are no rhetorical embellishments. When she falters, overwhelmed by these memories, the doctor urges her on. It is a personal tale of her own life experiences, but it also belongs to the history of Sicily and the Unification of Italy. It illustrates graphically how people's lives can be caught up in public events over which they have no control.

In oral transmission much depends on how the tale is told. Telling inevitably involves performance. Mariagrazia tells the tale effectively, her pacing is instinctive because she relives the story as she tells it. By contrast, in another story, 'Acqua amara' ('Bitter Water'), written by Pirandello in the same year, there is no holding back the garrulous, overweight protagonist from launching into his story for the benefit of a sickly young man who is new to the spa-resort. On learning that his companion does not as yet know his life-story, Bernardo can hardly believe his good fortune that here is an opportunity for him to get it in first. After all he has been the talk of the town for some thirteen years now!

Stia pur sicuro che oggi, a tavola da Rori, le narreranno la mia storia. Ci prendo avanti, se permette, e glielo narro io, filo filo.[48]

You can be certain that today, at Rori's restaurant, they will tell you my story. I'll get in ahead, if you don't mind, and I'll tell it to you, down to every last detail.

What follows is a Boccaccian tale of marital misery with its *coup de grace*—Bernardo's unexpected good fortune in being able to trap a handsome young doctor into taking over responsibility for his wife—generously interspersed with references to his own home-spun philosophy of life ('Sarà che io mi trovo in corpo un

---

[48] *Novelle per un anno*, ed. Mario Costanzo (Milan, Mondadori, 1990), i/1. 269. First published 1905.

certo spiritaccio . . . come dire? fi . . . filosofesco, che magari a lei potrà sembrare strano; ma mi lasci dire';[49] 'It may be that there's a wicked little spirit . . . of how can I say? phi-philosophy in me, that may seem odd to you; but let me speak'), of women, and of the battle between the sexes. Where the power of Mariagrazia's tale in 'L'altro figlio' rested in the material itself, the inexorable and damning accumulation of fact, free of comment or speculation, Bernardo's story in 'Acqua amara' is the product of an accomplished storyteller, attentive to the needs of his interlocutor and in no hurry to reach the end of his story. Where Mariagrazia's story was part of an exchange, here Bernardo is entertaining his companion for his own pleasure. Using delaying devices where he can, his narrative makes frequent appeals to a common *doxa*—one that unites men at the expense of women—interspersed with rhetorical questions whose only aim is to ensure that he continues to hold the attention of his listener. Unlike 'L'altro figlio', whose content and structure is such as to make any questioning of the content misplaced and insensitive, Bernardo's narrative is clearly told from his own partisan viewpoint and leaves the reader wondering what tale his wife would tell if given the opportunity to speak in her own voice, instead of being represented by her far from impartial spouse.

In both 'L'altro figlio' and 'Acqua amara', the protagonist's tale is embedded within a frame story. In 'Acqua amara' the frame provides the opportunity to describe the storyteller and contextualize the story, while at the same time introducing the listener who will be the reader's surrogate. In 'L'altro figlio' the frame and Mariagrazia's story are interdependent, for the cruelty described by her would be much less credible if it were not embedded in a narrative that goes to some lengths to describe conditions of life in a post-Unification Sicilian community. Not all the characters in *Novelle per un anno* who have a tale of their own are introduced to the reader from the external perspective that an impersonal narrator can provide however; sometimes the entire narration is entrusted to a storyteller. In my third example, 'La carriola' ('The Wheelbarrow'), the highly respectable and respected protagonist uses the narrative space to

---

[49] Ibid. 270.

reveal himself to an interlocutor, the reader, who exists somewhere beyond the confines of the society he moves in, who is
never going to meet him, and in respect of whom he may
therefore feel free of constraint, 'Guaj, dunque, se il mio
segreto si scoprisse!'[50] ('Imagine what would happen if my secret were discovered!'). In other words this is a confession, not
of a crime or of a sin, but of a daily ritual so absurd that it would
defy the respect family, colleagues, and friends hold him in; a
moment of pure rebellion conducted behind locked doors
when, lifting the old family dog by her hind-legs, he wheels her
around the room like a wheelbarrow. Although the dog understands the 'terribilità dell'atto che compio' ('the horror of the
deed I'm committing'), the need to confess it, to share it with
'quei pochissimi, a cui la vita si sia rivelata come d'un tratto s'è
rivelata a me'[51] ('those few to whom the world has shown itself
like it suddenly did to me') proves overwhelming. It is not
enough to perform the liberating gesture, it has to be translated
into words, described and discussed with an ideal interlocutor.
When our anonymous protagonist begins his account it is unclear whom he is addressing, he could be talking to himself; it is
the acknowledgement of an external listener or audience that
marks the beginning of the story. One may try to reason with
oneself, or talk to oneself, but telling one's own story requires
the implicit or explicit presence of another person.

All three examples of storytelling are characterized by the
presence of a 'personalized narrator who performs audibly
and visibly before the readers'.[52] Be it explanation, obsession,
or confession, Pirandello's characters *tell* their stories—their
rhythms and cadences are those of the spoken word. In the first
two stories the reader listens in on a tale told to a third party
whose narrative function at that point is to listen. In 'La
carriola' the storyteller addresses an interlocutor who is neither
present, nor part of his community; in other words although he
'tells' his story, he is free to do so only because his 'listener' is
absent. The short story as a literary genre allowed Pirandello to
extend the narrative act across time and space, conferring on
the work the possibility of permanence, while its brevity and

---

[50] *Novelle per un anno*, iii/1. 554,
[51] Ibid. 554.
[52] Stanzel, *Theory of Narrative*, 17.

links with orality assure an immediacy, a sense of 'hereness', characteristic of tales orally transmitted. What Pirandello tries to retain is the reader's sense of being apart from and yet participant in the storytelling process. His stories go a long way towards recreating the conditions of oral performance where the audience is excluded from the performance area itself, but included in the circle as one of the group of hearers. Like the audience at the theatre we are both set apart from and participating in a framed space which stands in contrast to the reality, our reality that lies outside it.[53]

In the examples we have discussed so far, the protagonists have been free to tell their own tales unchallenged by others. In his accounts of creativity, Pirandello's characters will go to considerable lengths to ensure that their account is fixed in writing in case somebody else comes forward with a different version. Where the control exercised by the first person narrator over the *racconto* does not hold, and an impersonal or third person narrator fails to maintain order between rival factions and interpretations, the narrative can become unwritable. This is the fate of the unrealized *romanzo*, forerunner to *Sei personaggi in cerca d'autore*, whose author, to the great reluctance of two of the participants, can only escape the protagonists by releasing them on to the stage to battle it out between themselves.

What unites the two most famous figures in Italian literary modernism, Italo Svevo and Luigi Pirandello, is the demise of authorial, real or implied, omniscience, and with it the questioning of the possibility of uncontested authority. Even Zeno's magnificently obsessive monologue in *La coscienza di Zeno*

[53] See Marie Maclean, *Narrative as Performance: The Baudelairean Experiment* (London, Routledge, 1988), 51. Another form of first person narration in the *Novelle per un anno* is one where the speaker appeals over the heads of his own community to a separate and distinct public. In 'Difesa del Mèola' (Defence of Mèola)—published in 1909, it is the first of three tales with the subtitle 'Tonache di Montelusa' (The Habits of Montelusa)—having failed in his bid to get his fellow citizens to listen to him, the speaker makes an appeal to the judgement of all liberal-minded Italians, *Novelle per un anno*, i/1. 109. In the tales of Montelusa, the narrator belongs entirely to the world he describes, whereas in the two stories about Milocca, Pirandello writes in his own persona as narrator (ibid. i/1. 849): 'La mia fama di scrittore era volato fino a Milocca, dacchè in un giornale s'era letto non so che articolo che parlava di me e d'un mio libro, dove c'era un uomo che moriva due volte.' 'My reputation as a writer had travelled as far as Milocca for someone had read in a newspaper some article about me and one of my books where there was a man who died twice.' His confidence that his name is known even in Milocca is soon shown to be misplaced.

2

The Rise of the Character: Six Characters and the Drama of Creativity

> We have, each of us, a life-story, an inner narrative—whose continuity, whose sense, *is* our lives. It might be said that each of us constructs and lives a 'narrative', and that this narrative *is* us, our identities.
>
> (Oliver Sacks, *The Man Who Mistook His Wife for a Hat*)

Pirandello's storytellers in *Novelle per un anno* do not have a selection of tales to draw from like Scheherazade of *The Arabian Nights* or the *brigata* in the *Decameron*. Instead they appear before their audience with just the one tale, and their wish to hold their listeners' attention by telling a good story well (and who, after all, wants to be found uninteresting?) is equalled only by their concern to establish their own version of what is usually either a sequence of events that makes up their life history, or an axiomatic moment in that life. As we have seen, the reasons for this unburdening vary from character to character, occasion to occasion, but it always includes an urgent need to put the record straight. In other words, for them the success of the tale depends on their getting us to see it from their point of view. They know that by telling their story they will neither change the past nor exorcize it.

The two lead protagonists of the first of Pirandello's plays that we shall be looking at, *Sei personaggi in cerca d'autore*, are no different in this respect from their peers in the *novelle*. The play itself is the first, and remains the most performed, of a trilogy of experimental works that Pirandello wrote for the stage between 1921 and 1930. The version that has come down to us today is the result of important changes the author made to the text in 1925, by which time he was a well-known name in the theatre with four critically acclaimed plays to his credit, among them

Enrico IV (1922) and the second play in the trilogy *Ciascuno a suo modo* (1924). The 1925 revisions were stimulated by his experience of seeing in Paris George Pitoëff's innovative production of April 1923. The six characters of the title refer to the members of an extended family who invade a theatre where another play by Pirandello (*Il giuoco delle parti* (*The Rules of the Game*), of 1918) is in rehearsal. Dominating the family are two rival storytellers, a Father and his Stepdaughter, who implore the theatre director to abandon the rehearsal and give their own story a hearing, in the hope that he will be persuaded that their story merits a public performance—a not unreasonable aspiration given the marked lack of enthusiasm exhibited by the entire company, including the Director, towards the play they are rehearsing. Although Father and Stepdaughter concur over the events they want to re-enact, they are locked into disagreement when it comes, in particular, to interpreting the Father's role. The combination of antipathy and dependency which binds them together is of an intensity which can arguably only be generated within families, but overriding this is their shared bitterness towards the anonymous author who had rejected them. (Concealed, and as we shall later see for good reason, behind the mask of anonymity is Pirandello himself.) It is a work born of antagonisms; the play itself purports to be the product of an earlier failure to create an artistically viable collaboration between the Characters and their original author, while the events within the play are motivated by the family's internal feuds. Even the actors in the provincial theatre company are constantly squabbling among themselves. One antagonism, though, Pirandello may not have foreseen—and that was the uncomprehending hostility that greeted the play on its first night in Rome, when the playwright had to shepherd his daughter out of the theatre to the accompaniment of the taunts and jeers of the audience.

Sei personaggi in cerca d'autore takes Pirandello's recognition of the alterity of the literary character discussed in Chapter 1 to the stage, which provides a circumscribed and separate physical space in which the unhappy Characters can enact and re-enact their variant of a domestic drama, one which lurches between melodrama and tragedy. What the characters in the play illustrate, and are victims of, is Pirandello's unshakeable belief that people—be they literary or living—cannot be separated from their life-story. In terms of literary aesthetics it means that an author who detaches the characters from their life-story and provides them with a new biography or autobiography (in the light of Pirandello's propensity for first person narration) more consonant with the needs of the text, condemns that work to artistic failure and the characters in it to literary extinction. We have already seen Pirandello's argument that an important aspect of the characters' alterity is that the author must also accept that their life history originates with them: to try to impose a narrative on them is to produce a deeply flawed work. It is a view whose inception can be traced back to the article, 'L'azione parlata,' written in 1899, in which Pirandello criticized contemporary playwrights who 'concepito il *fatto*, pensano ai personaggi, cercano i più idonei a dimostrarlo' ('having thought of the *fact*, [. . .] set about devising the characters most suited to reinforce the fact').[1] Now, nearly thirty years on, he finds himself the victim of his own beliefs, trapped by six characters:

presi in un dramma terribile, che mi vengono appresso, per esser composti in un romanzo, un'ossessione, e io che non voglio saperne, e io che dico loro che è inutile e che non m'importa di loro e che non m'importa più di nulla, e loro che mi mostrano tutte le loro piaghe e io che li caccio via . . . —e così alla fine il romanzo da fare verrà fuori fatto.[2]

caught in a terrible drama, who approach me asking to be made into a novel, it's an obsession, and I don't want to have anything to do with them, and I tell them it's useless, I'm not interested in them, I'm not interested in anything, and they show me all their wounds and I send them away . . . and so in the end the novel in the making will emerge complete.

Character and plot are inseparable, the author cannot adopt the one without the other, and by rejecting the story the characters bring with them, he has barred their way to a literary existence. At the same time, unable to free himself of the hold they have on his imagination, he remains in their thrall.

---

[1] Luigi Pirandello, *Spsv* 1016.
[2] Leonardo Sciascia, *Almanacco Bompiani*, 1987 (Milan, Bompiani, 1986), 47 (tr. S. Bassnett and J. Lorch, *Luigi Pirandello in the Theatre: A Documentary Record* (Reading, Harwood Academic Publishers, 1993), 56).

The passage above, which is taken from a letter Pirandello wrote in 1917 to his son Stefano, reveals that though the finished work was a play, *Sei personaggi in cerca d'autore* started out as a novel. Pirandello's account of the behind-the-scenes struggle between author and characters which led to their eviction on to the stage is described in an extended preface of some twenty pages that he added to the 1925 edition of the play. There are also three short stories written between 1906 and 1915 which, while having no bearing on the Characters' story, describe the sometimes delicate meetings that took place between author and characters as part of a process of deciding who to adopt for his own writings. Aside from these materials, we have the benefit of a very brief fragment of what was to be the novel of *Sei personaggi*, together with the letters describing the project which Pirandello wrote to his son Stefano who was a prisoner of war in Austria at the time. So the different stages in the play's gestation are well-documented—in letters, stories, a preface and, finally, the play.

The play-text itself, like a palimpsest, retains the traces of its original narrative status. It is the Capocomico (theatre director), much maligned by actors and characters alike, who soon after the Characters have invaded the stage where he is wearily attempting to stir up some enthusiasm for one of the playwright's earlier works, identifies the technical difficulties the Characters present to anyone seeking to make a play out of their story. The six Characters, led by the Father and the Stepdaughter of the *commedia da fare* (the play-in-the-making), have just launched themselves into a description of the events that have given rise to the present tragedy: in other words they are describing the *antefatto*, the events that have taken place before the start of the action that falls within the frame of the drama. The difficulty lies in the relationship between the 'telling' (*raccontare*) of narrative and the 'showing' (*rappresentare*) of drama. The Director breaks into the battle of words that is being fought between Father and Stepdaughter over what happened, in which each of them is struggling to ensure that his or her own version of events is the one that will be remembered, and points out the artistic problem their particular case presents to someone who is trying to translate it into theatre:

IL CAPOCOMICO. Ma tutto questo è racconto, signori miei!

IL FIGLIO [*sprezzante*]. Ma sì, letteratura! letteratura!

IL PADRE. Ma che letteratura! Questa è vita, signore! Passione!

IL CAPOCOMICO. Sarà! Ma irrepresentabile!

IL PADRE. D'accordo signore! Perchè tutto questo è antefatto. Ed io non dico di rappresentar questo.[3]

THE DIRECTOR. A bit discursive this, you know!

THE SON [*contemptuously*]. Literature! Literature!

THE FATHER. Literature, indeed! This is life, this is passion!

THE DIRECTOR. It may be, but it won't act.

THE FATHER. I agree. This is just background. I don't suggest this should be staged.

Such a point can only be raised at all because the play is posited on the pretence that what the audience is watching is a rehearsal in which there is no (paying) audience present. In other words the lines quoted above are delivered within the frame of a play which denies its own status as a play in performance. It creates the conditions for a very convenient solution which allows the Father to continue to deliver the story that makes up the *antefatto*, while at the same time claiming that this part can be omitted on the night. Although the Father provides a neat answer to the Director's professional reservations about the artistic feasibility of the project, there is a further problem that is embodied in the persona of the Father himself. He comes from Pirandello's stable of domineering, monologic males who, while perfectly at home in first and even third person narratives where they can indulge their garrulity, find themselves in difficulty with the verbal give-and-take of theatre. He is unable, or unwilling, to enter into dialogue with either his family or the Capocomico, whose task he suggests, with some asperity, is to keep order so that he, the Father, can speak; 'Imponga un po' d'ordine, signore, e lasci che parlo io, senza

---

[3] Luigi Pirandello, *Maschere nude*, ii (Milan, Mondadori, 1993), 697. I have adapted the first English translation of the play here because current translations are too far from the original to throw light on the point I am making. Theatre censorship was strict in Britain in the 1920s and the play was refused a licence because of its incestuous content, although the Lord Chamberlain did allow it to be performed in the original language, thus limiting access to the few who understood Italian. Shortly before this exchange the Stepdaughter had commented to the Father (ibid. 692): 'Qui non si narra! Qui non si narra!' ('We don't want to hear any of your stories', to which he replied somewhat disingenuously, 'Ma io non narro! Voglio spiegargli!' ('But I'm not telling a story. I want to explain things to them.').

prestare ascolto all'obbrobrio'[4] ('Why don't you impose some order, so that I can have my say, without your listening to these insults'). He has the temerity to suggest, once a tentative consensus has been established, that the Director assume the function of the writer; that is to say that he transcribe as best he can the words he hears:

IL CAPOCOMICO. Lasciamo andare, lasciamo andare!—Capirà, caro signore, che senza l'autore . . .—Io potrei indirizzarla a qualcuno . . .

IL PADRE. Ma no, guardi: sia lei!

IL CAPOCOMICO. Io? Ma che dice?

IL PADRE. Sì, lei! lei! Perchè no?

IL CAPOCOMICO. Perchè non ho mai fatto l'autore, io!

IL PADRE. E non potrebbe farlo adesso, scusi? non ci vuol niente. Lo fanno tanti! Il suo compito è facilitato dal fatto che siamo qua, tutti, vivi, davanti a lei.[5]

DIRECTOR. Maybe, maybe . . . But you do see, don't you, that without an author . . . I could give you someone's address . . .

FATHER. Oh no! Look here! You do it.

DIRECTOR. Me? What are you talking about?

FATHER. Yes, you. Why not?

DIRECTOR. Because I've never written anything!

FATHER. Well, why not start now, if you don't mind my suggesting it? There's nothing to it. Everybody's doing it. And your job is even easier, because we're here, all of us, alive before you.

Behind this brief exchange lies the assumption, which we saw first presented in 'L'azione parlata', that it is the character, and not the author, who is the generative force behind the creative act. The Father notes that on this occasion the whole exercise is made much easier by the fact that the protagonists are all physically present—the one missing person, Madama Pace, will be summoned at the point in the story when her presence is required—in what is, as yet, an unwritten drama. We, audience

---

[4] Luigi Pirandello, *Maschere nude*, 692.

[5] Ibid. 705. The play reveals an interesting division of roles along gender lines, for whereas the Father is the voice of the *racconto*, it is the presence of the Stepdaughter that makes the play-within-the-play happen. She relives the events by performing them, hurrying the others on so that she can reach the point where reenaction or performance takes over from words. 'Mi muojo [. . .] della smania di viverla' ('I am dying to do that scene'). It throws an interesting light on his choice of women protagonists for many of his later plays, while his protagonists in the first person narratives are all male. I shall discuss this further in Ch. 8.

and readers, have already been informed by the Director that the Characters have interrupted the rehearsal of a play that has been previously performed and so the author is not present ('Ma qui non c'è nessun autore, perchè non abbiamo in prova nessuna commedia nuova.' 'But there isn't an author here because we are not rehearsing a new play.'). The Father's confidence that, as protagonist of the story that the Characters bring with them, he will be able to recreate it himself, as a work of literature, and without so much as the creative collaboration of the author, establishes him as an even more autonomous figure than the literary characters who appear in the three meta-tales which are antecedents to the play, each of which stages the difficult relationship the author has to negotiate with his characters.

I shall begin by tracing the evolution of the figure of the Father through the short stories, where although the encounter between character and author is presented from the author's point of view, the character is allowed to speak in his own voice and describe his circumstances for himself without authorial mediation. The representation of an encounter between author and character first appeared in a little-known story 'Personaggi' ('Characters') of 1906; it was followed by 'La tragedia di un personaggio' ('A Character's Tragedy') in 1911; and four years later 'Colloquii coi personaggi' ('Interviews with Characters').[6] Although written over a period of sixteen years the stories share markedly similar characteristics. Each of the three tales has its own male protagonist, but differences in name and circumstance are undermined by the way in which they speak as one; words, phrases, indeed entire paragraphs, are transmitted from one character to another so that they stand together as a distinctive group. Each of these stories stages a confrontation between a character and the author, understood to be Pirandello, in which it is the character who is eventually the loser and who leaves with his request unfulfilled. The setting is always the same: the author's study where every Sunday morning

---

[6] 'Personaggi' was published in the Genoese periodical *Il Ventesimo*, 30 (19 June 1906). 'La tragedia si un personaggio' first appeared in the Milanese newspaper *Corriere della sera* (19 Oct. 1911) and 'Colloquii coi personaggi' was published in *Giornale di Sicilia* (17–18 Aug. 1915). 'Personaggi' is not included in collections of Pirandello's stories published during his lifetime.

Pirandello 'holds audience' with the characters waiting to be seen. The description of the room and of the procedures adopted, remind one of the provincial lawyers' offices, like the one belonging to the anonymous protagonist of 'La carriola' ('The Wheelbarrow'), that appear so often in Pirandello's work. On the closed door is a brass plaque which informs clients of the opening hours when the author is available for consultation; outside the characters queue, waiting their turn. In the early piece 'Personaggi', which Pirandello published once and then abandoned, the author seems to have little control over his unruly young servant, called 'Fantasia', and the characters that she searches out in secret for him. But 'La tragedia di un personaggio' suggests that in the five years separating the two stories organization has improved quite markedly. Once summoned, characters are questioned closely and note is taken of their personal details; so that although the status and trappings align the writer's activity with a lawyer's, the proceedings within the office suggest something else again—a doctor perhaps, or a psychiatrist. The characters who dominate the stories are more determined than their peers: in the first two, a spiritualist called Leonardo Scotto and a philosopher called Dr Fileno force their way to the front of the queue. In the third story, the author's attention is seized by a partially sighted individual who ignores a sign on the door which announces in a pastiche of bureaucratic Italian that audiences have been suspended 'for an indeterminate period' because of the war and invites those unable to wait to collect their letters of application before seeking assistance elsewhere. The three male protagonists resemble each other closely in character traits too; they are all obsessive, insistent, garrulous, and humourless, just as the Father is in *Sei personaggi in cerca d'autore*. With the arrival of each new character Pirandello draws attention to the bad company he, as writer, is condemned to keep: 'tutti i malcontenti della vita' ('all the disgruntled', in 'Personaggi') turn up, 'a cattiva compagnia' ('bad company') with whom it is 'veramente una pena trattare' ('truly painful to have dealings' in 'Tragedia di un personaggio'), and ungrateful too—no matter the care he takes, the characters from these stories go around calling him a 'scrittore crudelissimo e spietato' ('a really cruel, ruthless writer', in 'Tragedia di un personaggio').

In the previous chapter we saw examples of writers, particularly of realist novels, who share Pirandello's experience of their literary characters being, in a profound way, living independent beings, and so refuting vigorously both the suggestion that their protagonists are copied from life, and, equally, the implication that they are their author's creation. What unites these very disparate writers is a common insistence upon the alterity and integrity of the inhabitants of a fictional world. The more singular aspects of Pirandello's descriptions of his encounters with his characters are echoed in the memoirs of another author of that period. When Pirandello was acting as host to future characters who visited him in his study in Rome, the front sitting-room of a furnished apartment in London's Pimlico Square saw the arrival of a very different group of people. In his memoirs, which were published in 1912 under the title 'Some Reminiscences', Joseph Conrad describes the beginnings of what was to become *Almayer's Folly*:

Unknown to my respectable landlady, it was my practice directly after my breakfast to hold animated receptions of Malays, Arabs and half-castes. They did not clamour aloud for my attention. They came with silent and irresistible appeal—and the appeal I affirm here, was not to my self-love or my vanity. It seems now to have had a moral character, for why should the memory of these beings, seen in their obscure sun-bathed existence, demand to express itself in the shape of a novel, except on the ground of that mysterious fellowship which unites in a community of hopes and fears all the dwellers on earth.

I did not receive my visitors with boisterous rapture as the bearers of any gifts or profit or fame. There was no vision of a printed book before me as I sat writing at that table, situated in a decayed part of Belgravia.[7]

---

[7] Joseph Conrad, *Some Reminiscences* (Oxford, OUP, 1988), 9. The passage was written in 1908–9. The title was later changed to 'A Personal Record'. Pirandello's literary mentor, Luigi Capuana, believed strongly that characters have an existence and a will-power that allows them to resist their author: 'Anche i personaggi delle creazioni d'arte si ribellano alla nostra volontà, e noi siamo costretti a seguirli nella logica dei loro errori, senza poter farli deviare. Io ne soffro ma essi resistono, proprio come nella vita.' 'Even the characters of artistic creation rebel against our wishes, and we are have to follow them through the logic of their mistakes without being able to set them right. I suffer from this but they resist me, just as happens in life.' *Rassegnazione* (Milan, Treves, 1907), 313. For a post-modern twist to the autonomy of the literary character see Italo Calvino's story 'Il conte di Montecristo' where the two protagonists of the Dumas novel burst through the page onto the author's desk and start rifling the many variants in their impatience to find out what

Like Pirandello, Conrad represents the meeting between himself, as author, and the creatures who were to be his future protagonists, as an occasion when they presented themselves to him in person. More bashful, less pushy than the Italian author's subjects, they none the less share the same sense of urgency, the same need to be translated into a written work. Conrad's characters are no less real, no less inopportune than Pirandello's, but unlike the Italian writer, Conrad does not come to feel that the stage is a more suitable habitat for them than the pages of a narrative. Before asking how it is that Pirandello, who considered himself to be a narrative writer, found himself, contrary to both expectation and inclination, writing for the theatre, I want to return to the short stories to see what the characters themselves have to say, not so much about their material circumstances, as about the terms within which they exist. Until now the discussion has focused on the rights of literary characters; rights that have to be respected on aesthetic rather than ethical grounds—if the work is to be an artistic success, the character's autonomy is paramount. What has not as yet been broached is the question of why these characters so ardently desire literary representation for themselves when their lives are for the most part such misery. (It would be more comprehensible if they could use the opportunity fiction provides to recreate themselves in another persona.)

The literary characters that present themselves to Pirandello begging to be written up, have the same emotions, experiences, and histories as living people. They may seem extreme but their experiences are of the same order as ours. All similarities though end here. In every other way their lives are not circumscribed by the constraints that we experience. To begin with they live in an atemporal dimension, outside the reach of passing time, and so they are immune to the vagaries of history; living outside real time, they live beyond the reach of history. This point is brought home to us in 'Colloquii coi personaggi' when the character, described as a 'creatura chiusa nella sua realtà ideale, fuori delle transitorie contingenze del tempo' ('creature enclosed within his ideal reality, outside the transi-

---

is going to happen to them next. See Italo Calvino, 'Il conte di Montecristo' in *Romanzi e racconti* (Milan, Mondadori, 1992), 344–56.

tory contingencies of time'),[8] asks impassively of the author who is anxiously perusing the newspapers for reports on Italy's declaration of war against Austria, '—La guerra? Che guerra?' ('War! What war?'). Untouched by the contingent, they are inaccessible to change—they are fixed, immutable presences. In one way it makes it even more difficult to comprehend their motives, for not only are their lives painful but they also have no possibility of moving on. They are trapped, condemned to existences where they can only relive or re-enact their past.

To understand the urgency with which they clamour for an existence in literature, one has to understand that on it rests the chance of eternal life. Where artistic failure means the death of a character, success creates the conditions for its immortality.[9] Dr Fileno, the protagonist of 'La tragedia di un personaggio' and precursor to the Father in *Sei personaggi*, sees the rivalry between culture and nature in terms of a struggle between masculine and feminine creativity and he extols the condition of eternal life offered by a literary paternity over the fugacity of mortal life afforded by maternal nature:

noi siamo esseri vivi, più vivi di quelli che respirano e vestono panni; forse meno reali, ma più veri! Si nasce alla vita in tanti modi, caro signore; e lei sa bene che la natura si serve dello strumento della fantasia umana per proseguire la sua opera di creazione. E chi nasce mercè quest'attività creatrice che ha sede nello spirito dell'uomo, è ordinato da natura a una vita di gran lunga superiore a quella di chi nasce dal grembo mortale d'una donna. Chi nasce personaggio vivo, può infischiarsi anche della morte.[10]

we are living beings—more alive than those who breathe and wear clothes. Less real perhaps, but more alive! One is born into life in so many ways, my dear sir, and you know very well that nature avails herself of the instrument of human fantasy in order to pursue her work of creation. And the man who's born as a result of this creative activity which has its seat in the spirit of man, is destined by nature to a life greatly superior to that of anyone born of the mortal womb of woman. The man who is born a character, the man who has the good

---

[8] Pirandello, *Novelle per un anno*, iii/2. 1138.
[9] The claim on immortality is made only by Pirandello's male characters, the Stepdaughter's desire to re-enact the scene is unrelated to any aspirations in the direction of eternity.
[10] Luigi Pirandello, *Novelle per un anno*, i/1. 821 (Pirandello, *Short Stories*, tr. Frederick May (New York and London, OUP, 1965), 99).

fortune to be born a living character, may snap his fingers at death even. He will never die!

Pirandello's own writings on creativity abound in metaphors of conception, gestation, and birth. While never denying that women also have both the right and the capacity to be artists,[11] it is clear from the plot of *Suo marito*, a novel which takes a woman playwright as its protagonist, that he could not entertain the idea that a woman can both 'mother' children and 'father' texts. In a cruelly vindictive conclusion to the novel, its protagonist, Silvia Roncella, is punished for the triumphant première of her new play with the death of her young son. There is, though, another more complicated problematic at work. Although Dr Fileno extols the condition of the literary character whose author is capable of bestowing on him eternal life, in contrast with the 'creatures of mortal woman' for whom birth is the beginning of a life that will resolve itself in death, there is a terrible price to be paid for this privilege. Where a life born of nature is fluid, entry into the realm of art ensures a deathly fixity of form, an immutability that in *Sei personaggi in cerca d'autore* is communicated, in the first instance, visually through the characters' masks.

But existence outside time and history has other benefits. Only when we compare their lives to the human condition do we see what they are spared. Injustice, incomprehension, misunderstanding are their lot as much as it is ours, but living in an immobile reality, the impending catastrophe is always foreknown. For those of us who live in real time, as Pirandello never tires of showing, life is a concatenation of arbitrary events as unpredictable as they are far-reaching. Typical of the Pirandellian hero is the eponymous *Enrico IV*, an unidentified young aristocrat living in Rome in the 1920s, who falls from his horse during a cavalcade and for the next twelve years believes himself to be the Holy Roman Emperor of some six hundred years earlier, whose role he had temporarily assumed.

---

[11] Pirandello did write a very supportive review of Sibilla Aleramo's autobiographical novel *Una donna* (1906) which he had some difficulty in getting accepted. It was eventually published in *Gazzetta del popolo* (27 Dec. 1906) after Orvieto at *Il Marzocco* had rejected it. The first person narrative describes the protagonist's life up to the point when she decides to leave her husband; a decision which entails her also leaving her young son over whom she had as a woman no juridical rights.

Pirandello's work is not about evolutionary processes, the slow unfolding of a life in time, but about change that is as arbitrary as it is capricious. There were personal reasons for which Pirandello should view life with such fatalistic pessimism; his own economic well-being had been snatched from him over-night with the flooding and subsequent collapse of the family's sulphur mines in January 1904. His wife, whose dowry had been invested in machinery for the mine, learnt about it when she opened a letter addressed to her husband; the news precipitated a partial paralysis, a physical manifestation of the mental instability she was to suffer for the rest of her life. But it cannot be explained in terms of personal circumstance alone, for it is a *Weltanschauung* that Pirandello shared with his fellow Sicilian, Giovanni Verga, whose own brand of 'realism' (*verismo*) carries no message of belief in progress; on the contrary, it suggests that attempts at self-improvement or self-advancement will meet only with adversity: natural disaster, like the storm that ship-wrecks the vessel carrying the Malavoglias' hopes for a better future in the novel of that name, or emotional misery and betrayal, such as that endured by the eponymous hero of *Mastro-don Gesualdo* after an ill-fated marriage that he had hoped would unite social class with wealth.

So far we have looked at the encounter between author and character from the point of view of the character's needs, but none of this explains why, unlike Conrad or James, Flaubert or Trollope, Pirandello felt compelled to abandon narrative in favour of drama. To understand the mechanisms that lie be-hind the transition we will put the short stories with their repre-sentation of encounters between characters and author to one side, and turn to the specific case of *Sei personaggi in cerca d'autore* and a work that has a direct bearing on the play—the preface—to see what light it throws on its inception and its evolution.[12] In 1925, after having written a further five plays since the inauspi-cious première of *Sei personaggi*, Pirandello took the opportunity provided by a fourth reprinting to add a preface which explains

---

[12] Unfortunately the English edns. of the play rarely include the preface, al-though it is an essential and integral part of the work. There are two exceptions: translations by Felicity Firth (London, Calder, 1988) and Eric Bentley (New York, Dutton, 1952). The experience of the play's disastrous first night led Pirandello, whenever possible, to publish plays he wrote before they were performed.

a posteriori the circumstances in which this 'play in the making' (*commedia da fare*) came into being. Why did he decide to do this? In view of his, by now, international reputation, it is not unnatural that he should wish to make some kind of public statement about it, particularly in the light of so much misinterpretation in the intervening years.[13] But the preface is in practical terms far too long to add to the programme notes to a production, which raises the issue (discussed later) of the relationship in his work between the play as text and the play in performance. Here I will be putting to one side aesthetic considerations, to look instead at other unspoken and more shadowy motives for the preface which focus on the textual and extra-textual relationship between author, situation, and character.

It is here in the preface that readers are presented with the author's version of events told entirely from his own point of view. In the play-text itself the authorial voice is limited to the stage directions, although one should bear in mind that a noticeable feature of Pirandello's plays is the length and detail contained in the directions, rivalled only, perhaps, by George Bernard Shaw. The characters represent themselves directly through speech. Pirandello's tendency to invest everything in the spoken word is vindicated in theatre where speech is of necessity the principal mode of representation.[14] Furthermore by giving the prompter[15] the role of stenographer whose task it

---

[13] The preface was first published in *Comoedia* (Milan), 7/1 (1 Jan. 1925) under the title 'Come e perchè ho scritto i *Sei personaggi in cerca d'autore*' ('How and why I wrote *Six Characters in Search of an Author*'). The preface was then added to the 1925 edn. of the play. The 4th edn. makes the most far-reaching changes to the original text, including the addition of masks for the Characters, the extension of the action into the auditorium and the concluding moments with the reappearance of the Characters with back lighting. Georges Pitoëff's ground-breaking production in Paris in Apr. 1923 had important repercussions not only for French theatre but also for Pirandello's textual revisions. For a full account see Jennifer Lorch, 'The 1925 Text of *Sei personaggi in cerca d'autore* and Pitoëff's Production of 1923', *The Yearbook of the British Pirandello Society*, 2 (1982), 32–47.

[14] 'L'azione parlata' ('Spoken Action'), the title Pirandello gave his first essay on theatre, shows his awareness that speech in drama is performative; it makes things happen.

[15] When Pirandello began work with theatre, the prompter still spoke the whole play in a voice that was often perfectly audible to the audience as well as to the actors. (Actors in early 20th-cent. Italy continued to have very little time to learn or rehearse scripts.) One of the most important reforms Pirandello sought to introduce with his own theatre company, the Teatro d'Arte, was that actors should know

is to take down the lines as the characters speak them, the illusion that the play is the product of its characters is complete. But, interestingly, when he comes to write the preface to the play, Pirandello not only puts himself into the script, but he also asserts an authority over the text and its meanings that he had apparently relinquished. He does this both by writing in the first person, and also by barring the characters' access to direct speech. Their thoughts and words are channelled through his narrative voice. Where there is direct speech, apart from one quotation which is taken from the play, it gives unmediated access only to the author's own thought processes. So while at the level of content the narrative describes the situation of an author under siege from characters who, at this stage, are not even in any sense 'his', at the same time by retaining control of the narrative voice the manner of its delivery communicates to the reader the authority of authorship. Although the silencing of his characters in the preface is natural enough, given that it is part of what Roman Ingarden has called the 'para-text' of a play (those areas, such as introductions and stage directions where the author can speak for her or himself), it is none the less in Pirandello's case an unusual narrative choice.[16]

First of all it should be made clear that the preface does not

their parts well enough to be the part (see Ch. 7). It therefore changed quite radically the prompter's role. I am grateful to Jennifer Lorch who has pointed out that the practice has continued into the second half of the 20th cent. She was present at a production of T. S. Eliot's *The Confidential Clerk*, in Naples, in which the prompter spoke all the lines of the play throughout the performance.

[16] In his early 'realist' novels and short stories, Pirandello already favoured the soliloquy over free indirect discourse. Marziano Guglielminetti, *Il romanzo del Novecento italiano: strutture e sintassi* (Rome, Riuniti, 1986), 59: 'Anche quando Pirandello giunge a scoprire nella sintassi narrativa la possibilità del discorso indiretto libero, non riesce ad arrestarsi e a valorizzare la scoperta; forse non ne avverte nemmeno la capacità di rompere la sintassi naturalistica. Predomina in lui la necessità di scendere più o meno gradatamente dal discorso indiretto libero al discorso diretto, svevianamente di uscire dal 'monologo interiore' per entrare nel soliloquio, forse perchè l'autonomia di comportamento dei suoi personaggi, e quindi la loro esemplarità deve risultare evidente, quasi essere percepita uditivamente.' ('Even when Pirandello came to discover the possibility of free indirect speech within narrative syntax, he was unable to stop himself and make the most of the discovery; perhaps he was not even aware of its capacity to break with a naturalistic syntax. What dominates in him is the need to descend more or less gradually from free indirect speech to direct speech, in the manner of Svevo to come out of the 'inner monologue' in order to enter the soliloquy, perhaps because the autonomy of his characters' behaviour and their exemplarity must show itself as evident, almost as though it were perceived aurally.')

discuss the play-within-a-play, its only apparent concern is the creative process itself. It opens with the author's *servetta* ('servant girl') Fantasia still hard at work, searching out for him new subjects among 'la gente più scontenta del mondo' ('the most disgruntled people in the world'). On this occasion motivated by either 'la cattiva ispirazione o il malaugurato capriccio' ('poor inspiration or unfortunate caprice') she returns to her employer accompanied by an entire family of uncertain provenance, from whom she believes he could 'cavare il soggetto per un magnifico romanzo'[17] ('extract the subject for a magnificent novel'). What is interesting in this representation of the author at work is how, from the outset, Pirandello depicts the situation in a way designed to distance him from the story that is about to be unleashed on stage. His servant, Fantasia, is presented in the guise of an unruly and insubordinate creature who brings to her master whatever takes *her* fancy, while he remains at her mercy, not knowing from one day to the next who is going to turn up. While not in itself an inaccurate description of the processes by which the mind fills with characters and incidents, it is revealing for the way in which Pirandello develops a scenario describing the workings of the imagination which places him as the text's author at one remove from the characters and story which will form the text's subject; feeling, perhaps, that the distancing devices employed within the play do not afford him sufficient protection. He divides the act of writing (where the author does exercise some control) from the workings of the imagination (where he does not). On two occasions he uses 'mi trovai davanti' ('I found before me') to refer to how the characters present themselves to him—so alive, he goes on to say, he can reach out to touch them, so audible, he can hear them breathe. The implied parallel with their stage appearance is also made explicit; they appear before him 'come ora si vedono apparire sul palcoscenico, al principio della commedia'[18] ('as now they appear on stage, at the beginning of the play'). After listening to their unhappy story, Pirandello decides that they are not for him and he tries to dismiss them, for as we know he cannot accept them while rejecting their story. But the more insistent he becomes, the more tenaciously

[17] Pirandello, 'Prefazione', *Sei personaggi*, 653–67.   [18] Ibid. 654.

they hold fast; the battle the characters wage for a literary existence has hardened them not only in their resolve, but also in confirming their autonomy. They will not quit but the author will not accede to their demands. The situation is impossible to sustain, for having ensnared him, they now haunt him, until eventually in desperation he hits upon a method to free himself of their presence. It is his resistance to them and the conflict that ensues that brings them the autonomy they need, to break away from him altogether, and so he releases them on to the stage where they can fight for self-realization. He suggests that the characters who are released on to the stage have a more marked autonomy in relation to their author than their peers in narrative texts. The author the characters have seized upon is Pirandello but he has rejected them, and now, unable to slacken their hold on him, he takes them in as rejects. They are brought into a literary existence as 'rifiutati: in cerca d'altro autore' ('rejects: in search of another author'). In other words Pirandello accepts the characters and rejects their story, not by suggesting that the story can be suppressed (which is not seen as a viable option) but by accepting them (hence their presence in his play), while at the same time refusing the drama they have brought with them (which then becomes their sole responsibility and makes up the play-within-a-play).

The preface also provides us with an explanation of why Pirandello considers them unsuitable for his own literary needs. As a statement it merits attention if only because it has been adopted by many critics to define Pirandello's writing as a whole. He argues that there are two types of writer: there are writers who present a character, tell a story, or describe a landscape for the pure pleasure the narration brings, and these he calls 'scrittori di natura più propriamente storica' ('writers who are by nature more strictly historical'). Then there are those who experience a deeper spiritual need, who do not allow into their writings characters, events, or scenery which do not partake of a particular awareness of life, and with it a sense of universality. These are 'scrittori di natura più propriamente filosofica'[19] ('writers who are by nature more strictly philosophical') and he claims to have the misfortune, as he puts it, to

---

[19] Ibid. 655.

belong to this second category. Leaving to one side its value as
an insight into Pirandello's presentation of his work, it is also in
this context something of a red herring, given that the character who presents himself as the Father in the play, shares so
many of his characteristics with the playwright's other male
protagonists. The solution to the quandary presented by
Pirandello in his preface is that he will superimpose the struggle
of the characters to find a literary existence (the play's frame)
on the story which they bring with them, the play-within-the-
play or the *commedia da fare*.

Although the underlying idea behind the three earlier stories
had been of a character in search of an author, the startling and
paradoxical assumption that a character can exist without an
author and, even more aggravatingly, without a text, emerges
only with the play. Pirandello seems to suggest that the autonomy of characters on the stage is more marked than that of
characters in narrative texts. As the author has declined to
represent the characters' drama, it is the Father within the play
who takes over the work of the Author; 'esprime come proprio
un travaglio di spirito che è riconosciuto essere il mio'[20] ('expresses as his own a spiritual torment which is recognized as
being mine'). Pirandello is adamant that the anguish experienced by the Father has causes 'che non hanno nulla da vedere
col dramma della mia esperienza personale'[21] ('that have nothing to do with the drama of my personal experience'). So the
Father 'authors' the text, and the experiences described hold
true only for him.

In the earlier meta-tales it is unclear how far the characters
who present themselves have their story ready and how far they
are looking to the author to help shape it. Their problem is that
they feel that their original author has not done them justice,
and they come to Pirandello effectively seeking a rewrite. Dr
Fileno of 'La tragedia di un personaggio' is a typical case in this
respect. The author tells of how he arrived late in his office one
Sunday morning, having stayed up the night before to read a
novel whose only 'real' character ends up the victim of the
book's weak denouement, only to find that the novel's protagonist is there waiting for him. What is interesting is that

---

[20] Pirandello, 'Prefazione', *Sei personaggi*, 660.   [21] Ibid. 660.

Pirandello assesses the work purely in terms of human psychology, without allowing any other aesthetic consideration to influence his judgement; by refusing to relinquish control of the narrative, the unknown author has denied the literary character a life of his own. The characters who appear on stage are in an even worse situation than their predecessors in the stories for they have been refused a textual existence by their original author. They are literary outcasts or rejects, kept going by their determination to find an author 'who would let them into the world of art':

O perchè—mi dissi—non rappresento questo novissimo caso d'un autore che si rifiuta di far vivere alcuni suoi personaggi, nati vivi nella sua fantasia, e il caso di questi personaggi che, avendo ormai infusa in loro la vita, non si rassegnano a restare esclusi dal mondo dell'arte? Essi si sono già staccati da me: vivono per conto loro; hanno acquistato voce e movimento; sono dunque già divenuti di per se stessi, in questa lotta che han dovuto sostenere con me per la loro vita, personaggi drammatici, personaggi che possono da soli muoversi e parlare; vedono già se stessi come tali; hanno imparato a difendersi da me; sapranno ancora difendersi dagli altri. E allora, ecco, lasciamoli andare dove son soliti d'andare i personaggi drammatici per aver vita: su un palcoscenico. E stiamo a vedere che cosa ne avverrà.[22]

Why—I said to myself—don't I represent this novelty of an author who refuses to bring to life some of his characters, who were born alive in his imagination, and the fate of these characters who, having by now had life infused into them, cannot resign themselves to remaining excluded from the work of art. They have already split off from me: they live on their own account, they have acquired voices and movement; through the battle for existence that they have fought with me, dramatic characters, characters who can all on their own move and speak; they already see themselves in this light; they have learnt how to defend themselves against me; they will soon know how to defend themselves against others. And so, well, let us leave them to go where dramatic characters are in the habit of going to come alive: on to the stage. And we will wait and see what happens.

In one sense the characters win, since the author can only find release by creating for them a context in which they can realize themselves, in another sense the author wins, for the unstated but none the less inevitable conclusion is that literary characters

---

[22] Ibid. 656.

need an authorial figure to organize them to avert a descent into chaos. So writing becomes the art of controlling the potentially uncontrollable.

So far we have looked at Pirandello's presentation of his relationship to the characters he has authored without distinguishing between the individuals that make up the family group. Before leaving his authorized version of the history of the play's conception, I should like to turn to his presentation of the Stepdaughter. The preface puts her on a par with the Father in terms of the degree to which she is a realized and self-aware character, but then says very little else about her, choosing instead to focus on the persona of the Mother. It remains silent on the tactics employed by the Stepdaughter to persuade him, the author, to adopt their case. This contrasts with the references within the play to the Stepdaughter's sexuality, which she directs also at him in an attempt to induce him into following their wishes:

È vero, anch'io, anch'io, signore, per tentarlo, tante volte, nella malinconia di quel suo scrittojo, all'ora del crepuscolo, quand'egli, abbandonato su una poltrona, non sapeva risolversi a girar la chiavetta della luce e lasciava che l'ombra gl'invadesse la stanza e quell'ombra brulicasse di noi, che andavamo a tentarlo.[23]

It's true, I would go, would go to tempt him, time after time, in his gloomy study, just as it was growing dark, when he was sitting quietly in an armchair not even bothering to switch a light on but leaving the shadows to fill the room: the shadows were swarming with us, we had come to tempt him.

She is also depicted exhibiting a flirtatious seductiveness that those who gather around her when she arrives on stage find difficult to resist. There is an interesting variant at this point between the 1921 and the 1925 versions. Where in the first she performs a song-and-dance routine that wins her laughter and applause from the watching actors on stage, in the definitive edition the same performance draws the onlookers to her 'come attratti da un fascino strano' ('as though attracted by a strange fascination')—they even reach out almost as though they were trying to seize hold of her: 'leveranno appena le mani quasi a ghermirla'.[24] But she eludes their grasp. The playwright

---

[23] Pirandello, 'Prefazione', *Sei personaggi*, 734–5.   [24] Ibid. 962.

and the theatre company are not alone in succumbing to her
allure; in a more disturbing, shadowy way the Father too is
drawn to her.

The Stepdaughter is the firstborn of the new family that has
been set up, with the Father's collusion, between his wife and
his secretary. Two further children will follow, both of whom
will die in tragic circumstances: deaths that will be re-enacted in
a shocking episode on stage. The Father explains how he took
an interest in the new family and how he followed their lives
'con una incredibile tenerezza' ('with incredible tenderness').
When he turns to the Stepdaughter to corroborate his story, she
adds a more disturbing note to his fond memories, whose implication is not lost on him:

LA FIGLIASTRA. Eh, altro! Piccina, piccina, sa? con le treccine sulle
spalle e le mutandine più lunghe della gonna—piccina così—me lo
vedeva davanti al portone della scuola, quando ne uscivo. Veniva a
vedermi come crescevo . . .
IL PADRE. Questo è perfido! Infame![25]

STEPDAUGHTER. Oh yes, I can indeed. I was a pretty little girl, you
know, with plaits down my shoulders and my little frilly knickers
showing under my dress—so pretty—he used to watch me coming
out of school. He came to see how I was maturing.
FATHER. That's shameful! It's monstrous!

The suggestion that his 'fondness' for his new family and in
particular his Stepdaughter was not as innocent as he would
have his listeners believe, is pursued in his Stepdaughter's description of how he would follow her home from school: on one
occasion 'un involtone di carta tra le mani. Mi s'avvicinò, mi
carezzò' ('with a paper bag in his hand. He came close and
petted me'), and then pulled out of the bag a straw hat which he
gave to her as a gift. We also learn that the Mother, after having
responded on the first occasion by keeping her daughter at
home for a few days, then moves her family away altogether to
another town. But all this is, in the words of the impatient
Director, 'racconto' and as such unrepresentable.

We now come to the kernel of the play, the play-within-the-
play, which the preface insists is entirely the family's responsibility. Not only has Pirandello argued that he has had no hand in

---

[25] Ibid. 696.

the story's origins, but by dispatching the family to the stage he distances himself from the artistic representation of the episode in which the Father, some years later, visits a brothel where he inadvertently buys the sexual services of his Stepdaughter who is working there in an effort to supplement the family income. If the autonomy of the theatrical text did not afford the author sufficient protection against the psychological implications of the bleak sexual scenario that unfolds, the formal properties of meta-theatre—a play-within-a-play—create a second barrier between author and subject. A parallel can be drawn between the theatrical device and a similar mechanism that occurs in dreams. In *The Interpretation of Dreams* Freud suggests that a dream-within-a-dream is a means by which heavily censored materials can be returned to the consciousness of the dreamer:

Dreams occur from which we do not awaken—for instance, some in which we dream that we are dreaming. [. . .] It seems probable [. . .] that the first portion of the dream-work has already begun during the day, under the control of the preconscious. Its second portion—the modification imposed by the censorship, the attraction exercised by the censored sins, and the forcing of its way to perception—no doubt proceeds all through the night.[26]

The family drama that the Characters take with them to the stage is a curious combination of the tragic and the melodramatic. In many of its aspects, the story *Sei personaggi* tells is a familiar one to readers of nineteenth-century popular fiction: narratives which fed off contemporary economic and social realities that drove families off the land and into the rapidly expanding cities in search of work and that saw young girls, often seamstresses as here, driven to prostitution in an effort to provide for a destitute family. (There is an added poignancy in the Characters' story in that the same woman, Madama Pace, who employs the mother as seamstress also employs her daughter to work as a prostitute for her. What the mother does not know is that she is not being paid for her own labour, which according to her employer is substandard, but for her schoolgirl

[26] Sigmund Freud, *The Interpretation of Dreams* (Harmondsworth, Penguin, 1977), 731.

daughter's sexual services.) What may then strike us as an implausibly melodramatic climax, namely the Father's meeting with his Stepdaughter in the brothel (that is, if, in the light of what has preceded, we do believe that it is pure coincidence) may have had a different resonance for Pirandello. The concern in the early Christian Church that anonymous, purchased sex could also turn out to be incestuous sex was such that prominent theologians had argued that men should not visit brothels or have recourse to prostitutes for fear they could unwittingly commit incest with a child they had fathered. The practice of abandoning unwanted children was still common in the Sicily that Pirandello grew up in; one example is provided by his close friend, Luigi Capuana, who fathered several children with a family servant, all of whom were deposited at the orphanage in Caltagirone.[27]

Pirandello is adamant in the preface that he and the Father have absolutely nothing in common, and he spells out very clearly that the Father's anguish comes 'da cause e per ragioni che non hanno nulla da vedere col dramma della mia esperienza personale' ('for causes and reasons that have nothing to do with the drama of my own personal experience'). He has had to endure him (in the play the Father will become surrogate Author), he says, but he has not created him. The point of this denial becomes clearer when one turns to the last outstanding document associated with the manuscript for the play—the very brief fragment of the original narrative later abandoned by Pirandello. Given Pirandello's concern in the preface to put as great a distance as possible between the figure of the Father and himself, it is interesting to see in the projected novel how closely the narrative voice identifies with the Father. Although written in the third person, the focalizer in the extract is the Father. The narrative opens with the Father on his way to the brothel where he has requested a schoolgirl. The text is explicit and emphatic on this point. He has to arrive at the

---

[27] The practice was not restricted to Sicily: in Florence in the early 19th cent., the figure rose as high as 43% of all baptized infants. Traces can still be found today in the number of Florentines bearing the surname Innocenti—name of the foundling hospital. See John Boswell, *The Kindness of Strangers: The Abandonment of Children in Western Europe from Late Antiquity to the Renaissance* (Middlesex, Allen Lane, 1988).

establishment at three o'clock in the afternoon because the girl in question is available only for an hour at a prearranged time because she is still at school:

perchè andava a scuola, lei, alla terza normale, vi stava fino alle tre, e dopo le quattro doveva studiare, farsi i còmpiti, per poi andar verso le sette al Pincio in carrozza con mammà.[28]

because she was still at school in the fifth form until three, and then after four she had homework to do and then at seven she had to accompany her mother in the carriage to the Pincio.

The passage makes it clear that the protagonist expressly desires to have sex with a young schoolgirl, an aspect of the encounter which the play will subsequently neither suppress nor spell out. The name of the brothel-keeper and the front for the establishment ('Tailleuses pour dames') enter the play unaltered. From the extract it is not absolutely clear whether the protagonist has frequented the same brothel before, but the implication from the opening of the third paragraph is that he is a regular visitor: 'Eppure, ogni qual volta da lontano ne avvistava il portiere' ('And yet each time he saw the doorman in the distance'). The narrative focuses on his sense of 'scottante vergogna' ('burning shame') with which he 'sentiva stridersi dentro grottesco il desiderio inverecondo che tra poco lo avrebbe cacciato in quel portone' ('could feel that grotesque shameless desire shrieking within him that would shortly push him in through that doorway') and carry him up to the third floor. What is described is a dilemma common to Pirandello's male *personaggi*; they share a self-consciousness that allows them to see themselves through the eyes of others, while at the same time they are victims of inner desires that completely undermine the respectable public persona. Here the Father endures the conflict between a self that is serious, well-respected, and middle-aged, and the ageless and humiliating gnawing at his body of sexual desire. But when he actually enters the building, the story breaks off abruptly; and Pirandello comments instead on how the narrative suddenly transmogrified into performance before his eyes:

Il bello è questo, che han lasciato me e si sono messi a rappresentare tra loro le scene del romanzo, così come dovrebbero essere. Me lo

---

[28] 'Foglietti' in *Spsv* 1256–8 (tr. Bassnett and Lorch, *Pirandello in Theatre*, 57).

rappresentano davanti, ma come se io non ci fossi, come se non dipendesse da me, come se io non potessi in alcun modo impedirlo.[29]

The interesting thing is that they left me and started acting out the scenes of the novel among themselves, just as they ought to be acted. They performed in front of me, but as though I was not there, as though they did not depend on me, as though I could not stop them at all.

The narrative breaks off at the point when the Father arrives at the brothel, when it comes dangerously close to being a transcription of a phantasy of censored desire. Its translation into a play-text 'performed in front of me, but as though I was not there' where multiple viewpoint is one among a number of devices[30]—which include the play-within-a-play structure—to put as great a distance as possible between the Father as protagonist and Pirandello as author, suggests that the switch to theatre is the product of an aesthetic choice that is itself motivated by a complex psychological tissue of factors.

It is impossible to date the inception of *Sei personaggi in cerca d'autore* with any certainty. What we do know from one of Pirandello's 'foglietti' is that the idea was present *in nucleo* in 1910–12, and as is clear from the letter to his son Stefano by July 1917 the project had taken shape in his mind, although he still thought of it as a novel. We do not know when he decided to turn the material into a play and abandon the narrative, but certainly before October 1919 (it was announced in the first number that year of the journal *Il primato*). The gestation and writing of the work occurred during a period of profound tension and unhappiness for Pirandello. The death of his beloved mother, Caterina, in 1915 (she appears to him in the second part of 'Colloqui coi personaggi', which he published on 11–12 September 1915) was followed in November of the same year by the capture at the front of his son Stefano, who then remained a prisoner of the Austrians until the end of the war. At home in Rome, the first signs of his wife Antonietta's

---

[29] *Spsv* 1256 (tr. Bassnett and Lorch, p. 57).

[30] While focalization, understood as being 'the relationship between the "vision", the agent that sees, and that which is seen' (Mieke Bal, *Narratology: Introduction to the Theory of Narrative* (Toronto, University of Toronto, 1985), 105), can switch from one character to another in a narrative text, a dramatic text lends itself more easily to the representation of a conflict of points of view.

uncertain mental health had become apparent shortly after the birth of their first child, followed by a rapid deterioration between 1912 and 1913. She appears to have suffered from a form of schizophrenia in which she manifested an acute delusional jealousy. At first it was directed at her husband, but by 1916 she had made her daughter and carer Lietta the subject of her delusions. In the belief that her daughter wished to poison her so that she could continue an incestuous relationship with her father, Antonietta insisted that her daughter tasted the food that she had prepared for her. It was Lietta's attempt to shoot herself and unsuccessful attempts to run away from home that made Pirandello realize that he would have to do something, but nevertheless he waited for Stefano's return before incarcerating Antonietta in a private asylum just outside Rome. There is no suggestion that Antonietta's delusions had any foundation, and I am not intimating that the transgressive sexual desire of the play has any basis in material reality. But the effect on father and daughter of living with a wife and mother who will not be shaken in her conviction that they are enjoying an incestuous sexual relationship must have been devastating. At least Pirandello could, as he admitted in his correspondence with his son, escape into his work, but for his shy withdrawn daughter there was no way out. Where Lietta tries physically to escape from the home environment, Pirandello reworks the raw materials into his fictions.

This is the family situation during the time of Pirandello's 'obsession' with the six Characters. In his paper on *Repression* (1915), Freud describes the repressed as being straightforwardly that which is kept away from the conscious, 'the essence of repression lies simply in turning something away, and keeping it at a distance, from the conscious'[31] and it may be that Pirandello's *personaggi* are the vehicles whereby the unacceptable and the censored can return to the surface. They play out a drama that Pirandello, by insisting on their alterity, disowns but cannot cast out. In *Pirandello's Naked Prompt*,[32] Jennifer Stone

---

[31] Sigmund Freud, 'Repression', *Standard Edition of the Complete Psychological Works of Sigmund Freud*, xiv (London, 1953–73), 147 quoted in J. Laplanche and J.-B. Pontalis, *The Language of Psychoanalysis* (London, The Hogarth Press, 1985), 390–4.

[32] Jennifer Stone, *Pirandello's Naked Prompt: The Structure of Repetition in Modernism* (Ravenna, Longo, 1989), 989. See in particular part 2, 'Rehearsing Psychoanalysis', 79–131.

brings together clinical and stage concepts when, drawing on the French word *répétition* which translates as 'rehearsal', she develops an analogy between the repetition compulsion which Freud sees as an attempt to dominate a trauma and the Characters' need to act out over and over again a scene from their past. *Sei personaggi* is the staging of a repetition/rehearsal, not of a performance. As in the much-debated case of 'seduction theory' where, from the frequency with which patients recalled experiences of sexual seduction in early childhood, Freud came to believe that they were products of unconscious phantasy rather than fact, so in Pirandello's play too what is enacted in these rehearsals is not a real but an imaginary past, created retrospectively. And what is so singularly fascinating about this play is the way in which the defence mechanisms its author has mobilized to protect himself against its implications, real or perceived, are those very artistic practices that put the play at the forefront of modernism. This reading is suggesting neither that Pirandello had an incestuous relationship, nor that he entertained the phantasy; he was living a family life where one member believed this to be the case. Writing can have a therapeutic funtion, it can work as a form of exorcism, but to write out the Father's dilemma in a narrative created an uncomfortable proximity between author and protagonist. At the same time, what Pirandello clearly experienced as an obsession had to be expelled—and the play within the play afforded him a safer way of achieving this. Where in the narrative fragment the boundary between author and protagonist is undermined at the moment when the protagonist becomes focalizer, in the play-text the character is independent and the authorial presence is tidied away in the stage directions.

The creatively productive interplay that exists between psychological expediency and aesthetic experiment is illustrated by the presentation of the Characters themselves. In the 1921 edition, among the strategies the play uses to set the Characters apart, the playwright makes them appear, as a group, from the back of the stage. After seeing the Paris production where Pitoëff has the Characters descend on to the stage in a lift swathed in a green light, Pirandello added his own visual markers in his revised text which emphasize the unbridgeable divide that separates the 'us', the actors, and the 'them', the

Characters; their otherness is emphasized by masks and heavy, stiffened dress:

I *Personaggi* non dovranno infatti apparire come *fantasmi*, ma come *realtà create*, costruzioni della fantasia immutabili: e dunque più reali e consistenti della volubile naturalità degli Attori. Le maschere aiuteranno a dare l'impressione della figura costruita per arte e fissata ciascuna immutabilmente nell'espressione del proprio sentimento fondamentale [. . .][33]

The Characters must not appear as *phantoms* but as *artificial realities*, fantasy's unchanging creations. In this way they appear more real and consistent than the changeable naturalness of the Actors. Masks will help to give the impression of figures created through Art, each fixed unvaryingly in the expression of his or her basic feeling [. . .]

It is a brilliant device, entirely in keeping with the six Characters who, trapped in their drama, are in practice much closer to classical tragedy than to modern concepts of character. Outside their story they are nothing, like classical heroes they cannot be assigned to, or imagined in, another situation. By giving them no name other than their familial role, their identities are bound up in their relationships to each other which confers on them a fixity and a typicality undermining individuality. The very word 'character' as opposed to 'person' suggests, in the words of Francis Jacques, that 'there is no particular expectation of identification, and no need for it either'.[34] Where the actors, in common with the audience, inhabit the present with all the inconclusive open-endedness that entails, the characters occupy a timeless zone where their existence depends on reliving the scene that unites their lives. They have no future: 'Neither an epic nor a tragic hero could ever step out of his own character during a pause in the plot or during an intermission: he has no face for it, no gesture, no language. In this is his strength and limitation.'[35]

Born of phantasy, Pirandello's 'characters' none the less articulate through their literary existence the essential difference between being a literary character and a live character. In *The*

---

[33] Pirandello, *Sei personaggi*, 678.
[34] Francis Jacques, *Difference and Subjectivity: Dialogue and Personal Identity* (New Haven, Yale University Press, 1991), 21.
[35] M. M. Bakhtin, 'Epic and Novel', in *The Dialogic Imagination* (Austin, Tex., University of Texas Press, 1985), 36.

Theory and Analysis of Drama Manfred Pfister explains his preference for the term 'figure' for a literary character, in place of 'character' or 'person', on grounds that it clarifies the distinction between the fictional and the real. He warns of the danger of conflating theatrical codes and codes of everyday life, 'thus underemphasizing the functional and structural aspects of dramatic personages in favour of psychological and social analysis, as if they were living persons in historical matrices'.[36] A fictional 'figure' is deliberately constructed for a particular purpose and exists within the constructed boundaries of a dramatic text. The difference is embodied in the famous distinction that the Father in *Sei personaggi* draws between human beings and characters. In his words: 'Perché un personaggio ha veramente una vita sua, segnata di caratteri suoi, per cui è sempre "qualcuno"'[37] ('a character has really a life of his own, marked with especial characteristics; for which reason he is always "somebody"'). But his very ability to make such an observation makes of him a liminal figure who is capable of mediation between 'our' world and the world of 'art'. Just like his predecessors in the meta-tales, he is not entirely contained by the situation he exists within and he is constantly pushing against the constraints that bind him to it. In the preface Pirandello indirectly acknowledges the dilemma when he rebuffs the perception that the Father has escaped the condition of being a character by making the activity of the writer his own, 'facendo sua l'attività dell'autore'. Pirandello strenuously denies that the Father had any part in the creative activity that brought the play forth.[38]

---

[36] Manfred Pfister, *The Theory and Analysis of Drama* (Cambridge, CUP, 1991), 160–1. Although I disagree with Pfister's premiss that the distinction he draws between figure and character applies not only to dramatic figures, but also holds true for all fictional characters—the novel in particular presents itself as a genre which invites the reader to see literary character, like real character, as separate from the environment they inhabit—he has, none the less, identified the epic quality of Pirandello's six characters.

[37] Pirandello, *Sei personaggi*, 741.

[38] Ibid. 660.

3

Self and Other in Society: Gossip, Shame, and Scandal

Oserei definire la civiltà: la perfetta [arte] di fingere.
E la virtù: il segreto di mascherare tutti i volti,

(I would venture to define civilization: the perfect art of
pretence. And virtue: the art of covering up.)

(Ugo Foscolo, *Il sesto tomo dell'Io*)

In a *Theory of Modern Drama* Peter Szondi begins his discussion of
Sei personaggi in cerca d'autore by noting that the play's 'historical
role hardly corresponds to the occasion that, according to
Pirandello's preface, inspired the play: a breakdown in the
workings of his imagination. The question is, why are the six
characters "in search of an author"; why did not Pirandello
become this author?'[1] In Chapter 2 I suggested that the answer
can be found in the nature and implications of the story that the
characters bring to Pirandello, who then finds himself trapped,
unable either to write the novel, or to reject outright the characters and their story in favour of other subjects. The solution
he finds to his difficulties is to provide the characters with a
context within which they can present themselves to the public.
At the same time the play's aesthetic importance derives
from the battery of highly innovative, imaginative devices designed to maximize the distance between author, characters,
and story.

The drama at the heart of *Sei personaggi* revolves around
family life—the secrets that circulate and the shame it gener-
ates. In Chapter 4 we shall explore the reasons why the family is

[1] Peter Szondi, *Theory of Modern Drama* (Oxford, Blackwell, 1987), 77. He goes on
to argue that there is no reason to doubt Pirandello's explanation that he rejected
them 'because he saw no "higher meaning" in their fate that could justify giving
them form'.

so central to constructions of selfhood in Pirandello's writings, but this chapter will stay with the subject of secrecy and its role in the social construction of identity. The chapter falls into two parts. The first will look at a cross-section of short stories and a novel which share a common Sicilian context and a play, *Così è (se vi pare)* (*Right you are (if you think so)*) which represents an important moment of transition within Pirandello's writing both in terms of genre—from narrative to theatre—and location—from Sicily to mainland Italy. In the second part of the chapter we shall turn to two further plays, both located in large cities on mainland Italy: *Vestire gli ignudi* (*To Clothe the Naked*) (1922) and *Ciascuno a suo modo* (*Each in His Own Way*, 1924). By reading across his fictions in this way and disregarding genre, the themes that in Pirandello's work are in a continuous process of elaboration and re-elaboration are freed to rise to the surface. There are few things that Pirandello as author enjoys more than to revisit scenes or situations in which his characters find themselves trapped and survey them from a different angle, through a different pair of eyes. But just as in a ball game moving the goal-post can change the game and its outcome more effectively than simply bringing on a substitute player, so in a literary text the consequences of changing genre will be more radical in its effects than simply replacing the character who functions as focalizer. As this chapter sets out to demonstrate, secrets and gossip, motivated more often than not by sex—above all, adulterous sex—are, in the author's hands, much more than illustrations or cases for the 'philosophical' writer to draw on. They go to the very heart of how we try to live our lives which, in its turn, is pivotal in determining who we think we are and what we think we are like.

My decision to group the texts according to location perhaps requires a short explanation. A division exists within Pirandello's fictions between those works that are situated in Sicily, and those that are located on the mainland, where the environment is, with few exceptions, urban.[2] It is noticeable that when the author uses Germany as a setting, as happens in *Come tu mi vuoi* (*As you want me*), the two countries are represented as

---

[2] An example of a rural background outside Sicily is provided in the first part of *Il fu Mattia Pascal*. But even here, although the location is ostensibly Liguria, its physiognomy is Sicilian.

broadly similar, whereas mainland Italy and Sicily are presented with very marked social and cultural differences. The significance of location goes much deeper than a simple question of geography, background, or 'local colour'. In his Sicilian writings, where the context is usually provided by small provincial towns or indeed villages, identity is sustained both by and within the given community. The presentation contrasts strongly with the anonymity of the large-scale urban life presented elsewhere. In his now classic study of the city, Lewis Mumford noted that ancient cities did not extend beyond limits which could be covered on foot or even reached by voice; the community extended as far as, and no further than, an effective transmission of information could be maintained. He went on to identify three types of information that were circulated: the private, which was interfamilial, the public, which circulated primarily in town-squares, but also in streets and ports etc., and the official, where news was circulated by means of edicts, assemblies, and so forth.[3] In his Sicilian fictions, Pirandello draws on environments which have the dimensions of Mumford's 'ancient cities' and where news continues to be carried by word of mouth. *Così è (se vi pare)* by contrast is a study of what happens when anonymity and community are brought together within the same environment. The three adults that make up the family unit at the centre of the drama have been forced by an earthquake to leave their Sicilian home town and have moved to a small provincial town whose location is not identified. Unlike the cities that will later provide the context for Pirandello's plays, here the provincial town remains a place where the citizens continue to be fully informed about each other's circumstances. Not only are the newcomers completely unknown to the community, but to make matters worse, they have come with no personal documents that will testify as to who they are or explain their unusual domestic arrangements.

Pirandello's earliest sustained exploration of the ways in which secrets and gossip are used both to maintain the norms of the community and expel, or at least segregate, those who

[3] Lewis Mumford, *The City in History: Its Origins, its Transformations and its Prospects* (Harmondsworth, Pelican, 1973).

transgress them, comes in his novel *L'esclusa*.[4] It is also a work that sets out to show how what people take to be the truth about each other carries far more weight than any approximation of truth, to the point at which events that are shown to have taken place in the narrative are overridden and replaced in people's minds by a fiction of what occurred. Marta Ajala, heroine of *L'esclusa*, watches her life fall apart when her husband accuses her of an adultery she did not commit and hounds her from the marital home. Shunned by her father and the community at large, she eventually leaves Girgenti to begin a new life as a schoolmistress in Palermo. Her husband Rocco's response is guided by his knowledge that his own identity is caught up in her actions. If she is known as an adulteress, he will be known as a cuckold. When he goes to seek help from a teacher, Bill Madden, whose Irish background affords him immunity against the Sicilian code of honour, Rocco's claim that he must seek 'satisfaction' 'di fronte al paese'[5] ('before the community') is challenged by the Irishman who asks him what the community has to do with it. Marta's husband is not alone in experiencing shame, her father's sense of being unmanned is so strong that he relinquishes his successful business and locks himself into his bedroom where he lives out his remaining days in a traditionally feminine position of seclusion, passivity, and isolation. The men's sense of humiliation is aggravated by Marta's own steadfast refusal to capitulate to the role the term 'adulteress' demands of her, and when she decides to maintain herself and the remaining female members of the household by becoming a teacher on the other side of the island in Palermo, her husband goes so far as to propose that he will secretly maintain them, 'come se fare la maestra significasse un disonore per il nome che aveva portato'[6] ('as if being a teacher conferred a dishonour on the name she had carried').

Alongside Marta in the novel is another fallen woman, one who really did commit the act that she stands accused of, who

---

[4] Luigi Pirandello, *L'esclusa*, in *Tutti i romanzi*, i (Milan, Mondadori, 1977). A very early novel, it was written originally with the title *Marta Ajala* in 1893 and published in instalments in *La Tribuna* of Rome between June and Aug. 1901 with the new title of *L'esclusa*. Pirandello revised the text in 1908 and again in 1927, so thirty years passed between the 1st and the last edns.

[5] Ibid. 18.   [6] Ibid. 88.

has so internalized her guilt that although years now separate her from her 'crime', she continues to behave in conformity with her status as social pariah, even to the point of always enveloping herself in a 'lungo scialle nero da penitente' ('long black penitent's shawl'). There is nothing ambiguous or subtle about the role expected of Marta; as visibly as the letter A sewn on Hestor Prynne's clothes in Hawthorne's *The Scarlet Letter*, Marta is marked by her husband's accusation; 'non debbo cancellarmi dalla fronte, qua, il marchio, il marchio con cui ha creduto di bollarmi'[7] ('I must not wipe here from my forehead the sign, the sign with which he thought he had branded me'). Her refusal to act in accordance with the role demanded of her dismays even her loyal mother and sister, as well as her friend, the penitent Anna Veronica, although all three are convinced of her innocence. When she finally commits the adultery she stood accused of, it is easy for the reader to pass over the episode without noticing because in itself it is so devoid of significance. So much so that once her husband deems her innocent of the accusation, even the ineluctable fact that she is now pregnant does nothing to prevent her return to the matrimonial home and the community that hounded her. This paradoxical resolution that sees the protagonist welcomed back as an innocent woman even though in the mean time she has committed the offence of which she had been innocent, is entirely consistent with Pirandello's own view that truth resides in what is taken to be the truth and is not to be confused with what in practice happens. Although on first appearance *L'esclusa* might look like a traditional nineteenth-century novel of adultery, it soon transpires that its concerns lie elsewhere.

Pirandello's stories and novels which are situated in his native Sicily show repeatedly his fascination with the mechanisms by which a community controls its own members. Gossip is one of the most efficacious forms of self-policing, supported in *L'esclusa* by the rituals of religion. Marta finds herself unable to adopt Anna Veronica's advice that she should look to the Church for peace of mind, not least because as she kneels waiting her turn to confess she is aware that her very presence there will, in the eyes of others, confirm her guilt. She rejects

---

[7] Luigi Pirandello, *L'esclusa*, in *Tutti i romanzi*, 95.

the opportunity the Church provides to act the part of the penitent. In another remarkable example of social control we see how festivities such as feast days, or carnival itself, can become vehicles for public shaming and also persecution. To celebrate the day of Girgenti's patron saints, two huge effigies of Cosimo and Damiano are carried high on a platform, surrounded by crowds of people, through the streets to bring protection against illness and epidemics (particularly of cholera) to the town. But on reaching the house where Marta, her mother, and sister, and Anna Veronica stand watching the proceedings, the saints stop, seemingly unable to pass on. In a frightening incident that has been secretly orchestrated by Marta's father-in-law:

ecco di nuovo il fèrcolo arrestarsi improvvisamente; tutti gli occhi allora si volgevano alle finestre, e la folla, minacciando, imprecando, costringeva coloro che vi erano affacciati a ritirarsi, poichè era segno che fra essi doveva esserci qualcuno che o non aveva adempiuto alla promessa o aveva fatto parlar male di sè e non era degno perciò di guardare i Santi.

Così il popolo in quel giorno si rendeva censore.[8]

here once again the litter suddenly came to a stop; everybody then looked up at the windows, and the threatening, cursing crowd forced those who had appeared there to withdraw as it signalled that there must be somebody among them who had either dishonoured a promise or who had acted in such a way as to bring ill-repute upon themselves and for that reason was not worthy to look on the Saints.

So it was that the populace that day stood in judgement.

The episode continues with a powerful description of the terror the women experience as they draw back into the recesses of the house, away from the fanatical crowd gathered below. Three knocks of the saints' heads against the iron balcony brings the incident to a close. Underlying the symbolism at work here is an unspoken alignment between moral and physical pollution—between the contamination and dirt associated with Marta's supposed adultery (she has according to her father 'polluted' the family name: he uses the verb *insudiciare*) and the infectiousness and decay associated with epidemics and illness.

As in most places, much of the gossip in Pirandello's Sicilian

8 Ibid. 70.

communities is about adultery. But he delves further to show
how a rule-book of sorts has evolved to protect the subject of the
gossip, and sometimes the community itself, from the potential
damage that such an efficient form of social control can bring
with it. Gossip involves talking about other people in their
absence. It is not enough that private details are known about
another person, they must be talked about, communicated to
others, before they can take effect as mechanisms of control. If
one turns to gossip's (and literature's) voyeuristic fascination
with other people's sex lives one finds that in Pirandello's communities the flag of a double sexual standard flies high. While
a husband's affair has little or no public interest, the expectation is that when a woman commits adultery, whatever his
private feelings, her husband must make a suitable public response. The protagonist of a short story we shall be looking at
shortly makes this plain to the cuckolded wife of the man who
has been in an adulterous relationship with his own wife: if she
had spoken out about an affair in which the other woman had
been single, there would have been no serious consequences,
but in denouncing her husband's affair with a married woman,
the code of conduct demanded that he, as her husband, respond with what the community would deem to be the appropriate severity.[9]

An adultery can only of course become a matter of public
interest once it is talked about and then it is a question of how
much leeway the husband has to respond in a socially acceptable way. There is no symmetry (or justice) in these arrangements, the woman whose husband is having an affair with
another woman has neither the law nor the community on her
side.[10] On the other hand, one (some might feel) very small
compensation is that the husband of an adulterous wife is himself trapped by the situation. Whatever his private feelings, even
if they are of complete indifference, public honour demands an
active response. In 1912 Pirandello published two contrasting
tales about the consequences of a woman's adultery in circumstances where the bonding between the two men involved, hus-

---

[9] 'La verità', in *Novelle per un anno*, i/1. 751.
[10] The only legal sanction a wife had was when her husband kept a concubine in
the family home or 'notoriously' elsewhere. See Lesley Caldwell, *Italian Family
Matters: Women, Politics, and Legal Reform* (London, Macmillan, 1991).

band and lover, is much more binding than that between the married couple. In both 'Certi obblighi'[11] ('Certain Duties') and 'La verità'[12] ('The Truth') a husband of modest background—the one a lamplighter, the other a peasant—discovers that while he is out at work his wife is having an affair with a local dignitary, a *signore*, with the added complication that the man in question is the protagonist's patron. The lamplighter of 'Certi obblighi' belongs to Pirandello's class of philosophers who have caught 'la cattiva abitudine di ragionare'[13] ('the bad habit of reasoning') which allows him to sidestep fate. (In Pirandello's world, to have a philosophical bent is to be a survivor; with a neat, ironic twist, it is the greatest practical gift one may have.) Among a man's public duties, according to the lamplighter, are the responsibilities he assumes when he marries:

Un marito può benissimo in cuor suo non curarsi affatto dei torti della propria moglie. Ebbene, nossignori, ha l'obbligo di curarsene. Se non se ne cura, tutti gli altri uomini e finanche i ragazzi glielo rinfacciano e gli danno la baja.[14]

A husband can perfectly well in his heart be completely indifferent to the wrongdoings committed by his own wife. Well, that's not how it is, dear sirs, he is obliged to pay attention. If he does not, all the other men and even the children will throw it in his face and mock him.

So on the night he has to abandon his work and return home to an unsuspecting wife and her lover, he plays his role as a wrathful, jealous husband for public consumption, while quietly helping his patron out of an incriminating situation. Honour and reputation are saved. The rules of the game are clarified by Tararà, the less fortunate protagonist of 'La verità'. On trial for the murder of his wife, he fails to deliver the formula that will save him, namely that his was a *crime passionnel* committed in the heat of the moment when he discovered his wife's treachery. What he tells the court instead is the truth, and the truth carries a long prison sentence. The responsibility for what has happened rests, he claims with the *cavaliere's* wife who refused to remain silent.

[11] *Novelle per un anno*, ii/1. 446–55. See too *Il berretto a sonagli*, a two-act play published in 1918.
[12] *Novelle per un anno*, i/1 (Milan, Mondadori 1985), 734–52.
[13] 'Certi obblighi', 449.   [14] Ibid. 446.

Che c'entravo, signore presidente, andare a fare uno scandalo così grande davanti alla porta di casa mia, che finanche il selciato della strada è diventato rosso dalla vergogna a vedere un galantuomo, il cavaliere Fiorica, che sappiamo tutti che signore è, scovato lì [. . .][15]

It was hardly my place, your honour, to go and create such a scandal outside my house when even the street cobbles blushed with shame when a gentleman, a nobleman such as the *cavaliere* Fiorica, and we all know that he is man of distinction, was discovered there [. . .]

As long as the affair is passed over in silence, no action need be taken. It was not Tararà's wife who transgressed by committing adultery, but the *cavaliere's* wife who broke the rules by speaking out. (In either case it is noticeable that it is a woman who is causing havoc in a world whose structures are established and maintained by men.) Tararà had always taken the greatest care not 'to know' and when asked by the judge to give answer to the question of whether he was or was not aware of his wife's affair, he struggles to explain himself:

E la verità è questa: che era come se io non lo sapessi! Perchè la cosa . . . sì, Eccellenza, mi rivolgo ai signori giurati, era tacita, e nessuno dunque poteva venirmi a sostenere in faccia che io lo sapevo.[16]

And this is the truth: it was as if I did not know! Because the thing . . . yes, Your Excellency, I address the members of the jury, was unspoken, and nobody therefore could come to me and maintain to my face that I knew about it.

As long as silence was maintained, Tararà could know about it while maintaining the appearance of one who does not know, and so face was saved. With the spoken word, here delivered by the wife of the *cavaliere*, a private matter becomes a public issue, obliterating the distinction between personal and social, private and public, and putting the unwritten code of conduct into motion. The story illustrates all too clearly the double sexual standard at play here; while the offended wife has no right to redress for her husband's behaviour, a husband in the same situation has a social obligation to resolve it and punish the miscreant.

Gossip in general is storytelling in the making. It is talking

---

[15] 'La verità', 750.   [16] Ibid. 750

about people in their absence and what else is third person
narrative if not the exchange of information, much of it unreli-
able, about absent parties? Gossip thrives on diverging points of
view; it feeds off speculation and contested interpretation. For
all their sociological, geographical, and anthropological differences, the communities that Pirandello draws on in his stories
have the same underlying traits as those that can be found in
the novels of Jane Austen. These are small worlds: news, which
within the community seems to travel at the speed of light, slows
to snail's pace beyond; entire social classes with little to occupy
them while away their idle hours in small talk. Although gossip
is sometimes dismissed as 'idle talk', both Jane Austen, with
what she refers to as 'a neighbourhood of voluntary spies' in
Northanger Abbey,[17] and Luigi Pirandello with his many references to men's gatherings in social and political *circoli*, are
sensitive to the forms of social control exercised by gossip. Its
power lies in the way it blurs the boundaries between hearsay
and fact.

As the subject of gossip has to be absent for it to take place,
talking about oneself does not constitute gossip. All the victim
of other people's attention can do is engage in a damage-
limitation exercise by inserting his or her own voice into the
conversations that circulate. Many of Pirandello's first person
narratives, the *racconti*, do this. In Chapter 1 we saw how in the
short story 'Acqua amara' gossip has the power to bring a
modest fame to an otherwised undistinguished protagonist; it is
sufficient to lure Bernardo repeatedly back to the community
where he claims to have been the centre of attention for some
thirteen years.[18] But his interlocutor in the tale and we, the

[17] Jane Austen, *Northanger Abbey* (Harmondsworth, Penguin, 1974), 199. The
heroine Catherine Moreland is reprimanded by Mr Tilney for allowing her
overactive imagination too much freedom. He enquires of her how the Gothic
scenario she envisages could ever occur 'in a country like this, where social and
literary intercourse is on such a footing; where every man is surrounded by a
neighbourhood of voluntary spies, and where roads and newspapers lay everything
open?'
[18] 'Ma sì, come mi conoscono tutti, qua. Sono famoso! Guardi, alla Piazza
dell'Arena, in tutti gli alberghi, in tutte le pensioni, al Circolo, da Pedoca, in
farmacia, da tredici anni a questa parte, e stagione per stagione, non si parla che di
me. Io lo so e ne godo e ci vengo apposta.' ('Just as everybody knows me here. I am
famous! Look, in the Piazza dell'Arena, in all the hotels, in all the boarding-houses,
at the Pedoca Club, in all the chemists' shops. For the past thirteen years in these
parts, season after season, nobody ever talks of anybody other than me. I know and

readers, are not party to the gossip in the spa town, as we hear only his version of events, and so he remains in our eyes largely untarred by the brush of ridicule. It again demonstrates the unassailable position of a first person narrator. By contrast Don Cirincìo, the unfortunate, indeed tragic protagonist of 'La maschera dimenticata'[19] ('The Forgotten Mask') illustrates what happens if one falls victim to other people's talk. Fate has struck at him with a most appalling series of blows: the death of his wife followed by that of his two children, the loss of his sulphur mines, and as if that were not enough, a shooting accident that has left him with a limp. But none of these events has had consequences equal to those brought about by the public perception of him; such is the extent of his misfortunes that he is seen by others as a grotesquely comic figure. As often happens in Pirandello's third person *novelle*, the protagonist is introduced to us at the beginning of the tale through a mixture of information and hearsay; wagging tongues constitute the free indirect discourse of the community as the object of their attention limps on to the narrative stage:

sciagure che avrebbe fatto meglio a portare in pubblico con dignità meno funebre, perchè non si spiccasse agli occhi di tutti i maldicenti del paese quel sigillo particolare di scherno con cui la sorte buffona pareva si fosse spassata a bollargliele, se era vero che la moglie gli fosse morta per aver partorito su la cinquantina non si sapeva bene che cosa: chi diceva un cagnolino, chi una marmotta.[20]

disasters that he would have done better to bear in public with less mournful dignity, so that that particular mark of ridicule which mocking fate had amused itself by stamping on him would not have been so obvious to all the village gossips, assuming it were true that his wife had died on him after giving birth at fifty years of age to who knows what: some said a little dog, others a marmot.

To the community's surprise he has come forward to participate in the next elections. An intrepid campaigner for one of the

---

I like it and I come expressly for that reason.') 'Acqua amara', in *Novelle per un anno*, i/1. 269.

[19] 'La maschera dimenticata', in *Novelle per un anno*, ii/1. 103–11. First published in 1918 under the cumbersome but telling title 'Come Cirincìo per un momento si dimenticò d'esser lui' ('How Cirincìo Forgot for a Moment who he was'), its title was changed in 1923.

[20] Ibid. 103.

Human conduct is oriented towards the reactions of others. In his *The Presentation of Self in Everyday Life* the sociologist Erving Goffman exhaustively analysed the conventionalizing influence that others exercise over us and our behaviour, and we in turn over others. The self is continuously engaged in a practice of self-regulation in accordance with the expectations of others, indeed we go further and take our cues from others. Gossip has an important part in the process—it is used both as a strategy to ensure that the social self behaves in a way that is consonant with the community it is part of, and as a way of transmitting information about the attitudes of others that is internalized to become a part of self-identity. Pirandello explores both aspects in his fictions. To see oneself one has to resort to borrowing the eyes of others, for they are in a position to draw boundaries around us, while we for ourselves remain unfocused and blurred. When Mikhail Bakhtin turned to the problematics of self-knowledge in his early writings, he drew on the language of visual perception to argue that as we are unable to perceive ourselves we must turn to others to complete us. Each individual's sense of self is therefore imbricated with images from others. Only the other has the 'outsidedness', the surplus of vision necessary to the completion of selfhood. The very capacity to have self-consciousness is therefore founded on otherness. When at the victory dinner in 'La maschera dimenticata', the uninvited guest restores to Cirincìo his earlier identity, he first steps back and just looks: 'e s'allontanava rivoltandosi a guardare di sfuggita e di sbieco, con quegli occhietti puntuti'[22] ('and he moved off, turning around to catch another sideways glimpse with those little piercing eyes') before he finally nails him with the epithet *Quello del mulino* ('the one from the mill'). Bakhtin, though, is not alone in insisting on what Michael Holquist has neatly dubbed his 'just-so story of subjectivity [. . .] how I get myself from the other',[23] Lacan too defines in *Seminar II* the unconscious as the discourse of the other: 'This discourse of the other is not the discourse of the abstract other, of the other in the dyad, of my correspondent, nor even of my slave, it is the discourse of

---

[22] *Novelle per un anno*, ii/1. 109.
[23] Michael Holquist, *Dialogism: Bakhtin and his World* (London, Routledge, 1990), 28.

the circuit in which I am integrated. I am one of its links'.[24] This insight is picked up by John Forrester and considered in the context of the relationship between analyst and analysand:

'Gossip' may not be a very grand name for Lacan's grand vision, but we are referring to the same thing: the phenomenon in which the discourse of the other, which is what the analyst says to me, is my unconscious—in the end the analyst only echoes back the gossip that inhabits the subject without his knowing it. And it is the specific circuit of discourse that analysts inhabit in their gossip about their forebears that is the unconscious of analysis.[25]

We all function as subjects, what we have to remind ourselves of is that we also perform as the other—the movement is in both directions. We both gossip and are gossiped about. We need to project identity in order to confirm our own. I shall turn now to a *novella* which became a play in the same year, where there is a short circuit in the process described above and where the self-validating function of gossip fails because the gossip itself cannot construe a coherent account of otherness.

Published in 1917 as a short story, 'La signora Frola e il signor Ponza, suo genero' ('Mrs Frola and Mr Ponza, her son-in-law') was turned into a play with a new title, *Così è (se vi pare)* (*Right you are (if you think so)*), which directs the audience's attention to the question of the relativity of perception, in relation both to the activities of the characters on stage and to their own processes of assimilation and interpretation. Its teasing juxtaposition of the opening assertion and questioning parenthesis reminds us that while perception and understanding are as relative as they are subjective, they none the less present themselves as masquerading as objective truth. The subtitle 'parabola in tre atti' ('parable in three acts') underlines the general impression of enigmatic indeterminacy, hinting at the presence of a conundrum or riddle. What is lost in the change of title is the sense of an identifiable, individualized humanity powerfully conveyed by 'La signora Frola e il signor Ponza, suo genero', with its intimation that the story will be about the relationship between two people linked by marriage. The way in which the two titles pull

---

[24] Jacques Lacan, *The Seminar*, ii. *The Ego in Freud's Theory and in the Technique of Psychoanalysis 1953–II*, tr. Silvana Tomaselli (Cambridge, CUP, 1988), 89–90.
[25] John Forrester, *The Seductions of Psychoanalysis: Freud, Lacan and Derrida* (Cambridge, CUP, 1988), 256.

in opposite directions reminds one of the tension between Stepdaughter and Father in *Sei personaggi in cerca d'autore*; the one demanding that they should represent the events, re-enact what took place between them, the other arguing that they should concentrate on the philosophical questions raised by their story.

Così è (se vi pare) marks an important moment in Pirandello's literary career, for it prefigures the concerns that will dominate his theatre in the 1920s. The central character is the forerunner of a succession of women protagonists who, as we shall see in Chapter 8, will be indecipherable and unsettling presences on stage, but, unlike her successors, her identity and social role remain bound up within the family unit where she is presented in the context of her role as daughter and as wife. As she has no children, however, she lacks the fundamental biological function by which a married woman is, in Pirandello's work, defined. In this family the parts fail to make a whole.

By the beginning of the play every tragedy that could possibly happen to a family appears to have happened to them—death, insanity, illness, and the loss of all they possessed. The three (daughter, mother, and son-in-law) arrive to make a new start in an unfamiliar provincial town after an earthquake devastated their home town. All their possessions have been lost in the ruins, so there is no way of confirming who they are, or clarifying what exactly the circumstances are which led to such an unconventional, and in the eyes of the community, unnatural lifestyle. The domestic arrangements whereby the mother-in-law is lodged in an apartment in an affluent part of town while her daughter lives in much reduced circumstances on the outskirts become a source of endless aggravation for the townspeople. Combine the oddity of their living arrangements with the husband's practice of spending stretches of time each day with his mother-in-law, while she in her turn is only allowed to see her daughter from a distance by standing in the courtyard below her apartment, and one can begin to understand why they are the target of such gossip. At the outset of the play, the audience is encouraged to feel similarly intrigued by the irregularity of their domestic arrangements and concur with the townspeople's curiosity to know more.

Even allowing for the difference in social codes between

eighteenth-century provincial life in England as articulated by Jane Austen and early twentieth-century small town communities in Sicily as represented by Luigi Pirandello, the patterns of behaviour depicted are remarkably similar. Newcomers arrive in the district, and social calls are paid both to extend a welcome and also, less charitably but more imperatively, to satisfy what one of the characters, a young woman called Dina, describes as 'la curiosità naturalissima di tutto il paese'[26] ('the very natural curiosity of the community'). (Dina at 19 is old enough to be part of an adult world, but young enough not to identify fully as yet with its practices; she still has insight—an attribute that is palpably absent from her mother. A few lines earlier Dina had referred to her mother's circle as being 'cortesi per curiosità' ('courteous out of curiosity'), a curiosity that soon turns to suspicion.) Respectable members of the small town community assiduously visit each other at home, urged on by their thirst for enlightenment, while snobbery provides a further stimulus to their curiosity, for Signora Frola has taken an apartment next door to her son-in-law's superior, the consigliere Agazzi. But what begins as a slightly uneasy, but none the less not unreasonable attempt at sociability soon degenerates, as it becomes increasingly evident that the newcomers do not to wish to comply with the unwritten social code. By refusing to engage with the normal exchange of courtesies, the family cannot be assimilated into the community and the townspeople adopt a correspondingly hostile and inquisitorial role. Worse still, mother and son-in-law not only refuse to explain their behaviour, but each offers, on separate occasions, different versions of the family's recent past that would, if they were true, cancel each other out. While we learn from Signor Ponza that his mother-in-law is mad and does not realize that her daughter is dead and he is now living with his second wife, Signora Frola tells us that it is her son-in-law who is mad and she and her daughter have agreed between them on the fiction that she is his second wife, so as not to upset his belief that he was previously married to a woman now dead. Drawing-room chat in Act I soon gives way to a more inquisitorial approach— adding a new sinister dimension to that word 'confession' that

[26] Luigi Pirandello, *Così è (se vi pare)*, in *Maschere nude*, i (Milan, Mondadori, 1986), 438.

we will later see used to describe the purpose of the salon in *Vestire gli ignudi*. What has the makings of being a metaphysical thriller slowly transforms before the audience's eyes into a disconcerting exercise in psychological torture. The image of the 'stanza della tortura' ('torture chamber') was later adopted by one of Italy's foremost interpreters of Pirandello, Giovanni Macchia, for the title of his book on the author: 'E il palcoscenico diventa un poliziesco luogo di tortura, ove gli uni si fanno carnefici degli altri'[27] ('And the stage becomes a police-like torture chamber, where one side torments the other').

At the end of the play Ponza tells Agazzi that he wishes to resign from his post, 'perchè non posso tollerare quest'inquisizione accanita, feroce sulla mia vita privata'[28] ('because I cannot tolerate this heartless, ferocious inquisition into my private life'). Using the gossip generated by the arrival of the family and the successive interviews which an inner circle of townspeople conduct with each member of the family one by one, the play traces the decline in their attitude from curiosity to obsession, from the importunate to the persecutory. The small circle of inquisitors widens as others visit them, urged on by a need to know more:

SIGNORA SIRELLI. Ah, signora mia, noi veniamo qua come alla fonte. Siamo due povere assetate di notizie.
AMALIA. E notizie di che, signore mie?
SIGNORA SIRELLI. Ma di questo benedetto nuovo segretario della Prefettura. Non si parla d'altro in paese.[29]

SIGNORA SIRELLI. Ah, Signora, we have come to your house as to the fountain of knowledge. We are two poor beings, thirsty for news.
AMALIA. And what news do you two ladies wish to have?
SIGNORA SIRELLI. Why about this blessed new secretary at the Prefecture. The whole town is speaking of nothing else.

Behind the enigma presented by the newcomers lies another, namely why this irregular but somewhat featureless family grouping should arouse such extremes of curiosity. It is a question that is foregrounded at the outset of the story by the narrator, but it is not directly posed in the play. 'La signora

---

[27] Giovanni Macchia, *Pirandello e la stanza della tortura* (Milan, Mondadori, 1982), 92.
[28] *Maschere nude*, i. 500.
[29] Ibid. 441.

Frola e il signor Ponza, suo genero' has in common with very many of Pirandello's tales all the hallmarks of orality. The narrator speaks to his interlocutors directly over the heads of the community to which he belongs, while at the same time using the full range of ironic devices, from antiphrasis to mockery, to ensure that we understand that he is not party to the distress exhibited by his fellow citizens. In inviting us to resolve the central enigma—what precisely is the relationship between Signora Frola and Signor Ponza? is he or is he not her son-in-law?—he also makes it clear that what perturbs him is not the problem itself, but the effect it is having on the community; 'ma dico di tenere così sotto quest'incubo, un'intera cittadinanza vi par poco?'[30] ('but I ask you, to keep a whole town on tenterhooks, doesn't that seem serious enough to you?'). The reader is made to feel that the degree of consternation these 'forestieri eccentrici' ('eccentric strangers') bring to the community is out of all proportion to the cause. If gossip were concerned only with social control, a glue that holds the community together, the reaction here would have to be read as excessive. The storyteller hints at another reason.

In taking up the gautlet thrown down by the narrator of the short story, the theatre director Massimo Castri and the critic Lucienne Kroha have both argued that the truth that lies at the heart of the play is, in Kroha's words, 'a truth involving a society in which incest and sexual abuse were known to exist, but as unspeakable facts that could only be alluded to in the most veiled of terms'.[31] Such a truth goes to the very heart of what will four years later reappear as a shameful family secret in *Sei personaggi*. But Castri and Kroha give a different weighting to the subject's importance within the overall signifying structure of play and story. In Kroha's reading, the play's apparent problematic, the unknowability of others, is interpreted as being, together with its promulgator Laudisi, a red herring, designed to cover up the 'unspeakable fact' of incest, while Castri includes the incest motif in his production but sees it as insufficient to explain the workings of a play 'che si sottrae

---

[30] 'La signora Frola e il signor Ponza, suo genero', in *Novelle per un anno*, iii/1. 777.

[31] Lucienne Kroha, 'Behind the Veil: A Freudian Reading of Pirandello's *Così è (se vi pare)*', *The Yearbook of the British Pirandello Society*, 12 (1992), 2.

ostinatamente a qualunque lettura in chiave unica'[32] ('that ob-
stinately resists any single reading'). In the event the suggestion
that there could be an incestuous relationship between Signora
Frola and Signor Ponza is raised early in the play by Laudisi: he
draws the obvious conclusion from a comment made by Dina
and her mother, that mother-in-law and son-in-law are always
together (they are defined in relation to each other, not to the
woman they have in common): 'Sospettate forse che facciano
all'amore, suocera e genero?'[33] ('Do you perhaps suspect that
there is a sexual relationship between mother-in-law and son-in-
law?'). Incest provides a solution to the conundrum presented,
but in so doing it goes against the current of a play whose
internal logic would seem to demand a lack of resolution, an
open-endedness that is irritating both to the inner circle on
stage and the outer circle constituted by the audience. I would
agree with Castri's view that incest is present, but is circulating
as just one among many guilty secrets. It is true that story and
play were written in 1917, at a time when Pirandello's home life
was still torn apart by his wife's accusations of incest, but even in
Sei personaggi in cerca d'autore, incest is arguably the most important, but not the only aspect of an encounter that reeks of
squalor and compromise—both sexual and economic. Disgust
for the body and its proclivities that is so compellingly communicated in *Sei personaggi* is quite absent in *Così è (se vi pare)* which
must count as being amongst the least physical, or the most
metaphysical, of Pirandello's plays. The possibility of incest
is referred to and there is nothing in the play that rules it out,
but it is present in a curiously abstract way as no more than
a potential explanation for the newcomers' unconventional
behaviour.

Another reading would be to suggest that the newcomers are,
in that wonderfully appropriate word, 'misfits', because they will
not allow themselves to be assimilated within the body social.
Their inexplicable domestic arrangements threaten the ordinary, accepted conventions of daily life. In *Modernity and Self-*

---

[32] Castri, *Pirandello ottanta*, 135.

[33] *Maschere nude*, i. 440. Where the daughter considers Laudisi's intervention, and
then rejects it on the grounds that Signora Frola is a 'povera vecchietta' ('poor old
woman'), her mother Amalia appears not to have heard.

Identity, Anthony Giddens comments on the intimate link between mundane everyday practices and self-identity in the following terms:

> On the other side of what might appear to be quite trivial aspects of day-to-day action and discourse, chaos lurks. And this chaos is not just disorganisation but the loss of a sense of the very reality of things and other persons. [. . .] The chaos that threatens on the other side of the ordinariness of everyday conventions can be seen psychologically as *dread* in Kierkegaard's sense: the prospect of being overwhelmed by anxieties that reach to the very roots of our coherent sense of 'being in the world.[34]

The circumstances which led to their arrival in a new community mean that they can be known only in terms of their position and role within the family, and what so perturbs the citizens is that the newcomers' behaviour does not conform to what one might expect from their familial roles. One aspect of incest is that it defies the definition of who one is. To be a father is to preclude any right to a sexual relationship with one's daughter or stepdaughter, and similarly to be known as a son-in-law implies a non-sexual relationship with the mother of one's wife. Incest upsets the fundamental assumption that family bonds, with the exception of husband and wife, are not sexual and empties straightforward labels, such as mother and father, of one set of associations and fills them with another. In the case of the three newcomers in *Così è (se vi pare)* their behaviour is at variance with the position each of them occupies within that family. The philosopher Alistair MacIntyre has commented on how role and identity were seen in pre-modern society as being one and the same:

> In many pre-modern, traditional societies it is through his or her membership in a variety of social groups that the individual identifies himself or herself and is identified by others. I am brother, cousin, and grandson, member of this household, that village, this tribe. These are not characteristics that belong to human beings accidentally, to be stripped away in order to discover 'the real me'. They are part of my substance, defining partially at least and sometimes wholly my obligations and my duties. Individuals inherit a particular space within an

---

[34] Anthony Giddens, *Modernity and Self-Identity: Self and Society in the Late Modern Age* (Oxford, Polity, 1991), 37–8.

interlocking set of social relationships; lacking that space, they are nobody, or at best a stranger or an outcast.[35]

MacIntyre's point reflects well a statement Laudisi makes to the servant in Act II, Scene iii, of the play. Two ladies have called on his sister and on hearing that she is out visiting Signora Frola, ask the manservant if anybody else is at home. On learning of Laudisi's presence, they say they would like to see him. Laudisi asks the servant how he can be so certain that the person he is addressing is the same person requested by the visitors. A now perplexed servant responds by saying that they have asked to see Signora Agazzi's brother: it is only at this point that Laudisi concedes that it is indeed he the ladies are asking after.

To return to the original question: why does the failure to tease out the mystery surrounding the newcomers bring such perturbation in its wake? Whereas in the other narratives of identity referred to in this chapter, the protagonists are, for better or for worse, affected by the gossip that circulates about them, in *Così è (se vi pare)* they appear to be immune to public opinion. Bound up in the network of identities they have created for each other, they do not require further validation and refuse to enter the normal processes of social interaction by which each of us comes to know ourselves. But, by the same token, it suggests that there is nothing noble about being an outsider, nothing heroic.

Pirandello's theatre, like much of his narrative, is concerned with the individual as a social being. Whatever the lengths his characters go to to try to divest themselves of the imprint other people, families, and whole communities have left on them (and some, like Mattia Pascal in *Il fu Mattia Pascal* and Vitangelo Moscarda in *Uno, nessuno e centomila*, as we shall see in the next chapter, will go to extraordinary lengths to do so), his characters remain saturated in the social. Pirandello's work, both drama and narrative, is taken up with questions of how we talk with each other, why we talk about each other, what we do to each other when we talk in these ways, and what we do to ourselves.

Before turning to *Ciascuno a suo modo* (*Each in His Own Way*), the second of Pirandello's meta-theatrical trilogy in which, I

---

[35] Alistair MacIntyre, *After Virtue: A Study in Moral Theory* (London, Duckworth, 1990), 33–4.

shall argue, both structure and content provide an exemplary illustration of how gossip circulates, I want to refer briefly to a play that preceded it by two years and in which Pirandello creates for the first time the fiction of an unbroken continuum between events within the theatre and city life in the streets outside. The events that unfold in *Vestire gli ignudi* (*To Clothe the Naked*, 1922) are contained within the spatial and temporal parameters of the play, but the playwright asks in the stage-directions that the performance be punctuated by sudden inter-ruptions from the world outside the theatre where life goes on. Sudden bursts of intrusive street noise are scripted into the play, loud enough at times to drown the voices on stage, so it appears as if life in the city has penetrated into the theatre and threatens to disrupt the smooth running of the drama. The writer's room which makes up the set, is also designed to remind the audience of urban life by appearing to have its natural light blocked by high buildings that line the narrow street outside where, during the performance, a street accident leading to the death of an elderly man will mark the unpredictability and chanciness of life. Outside, 'la strada c'è, con la gente che vi passa, i rumori della vita; la vita degli altri, estranea ma presente, che frastorna, interrompe, intralcia, contraria, deforma'[36] ('there is the street with people going up and down, the sounds of life: of other people's lives, remote but present, which distracts, disrupts, interrupts and entangles us'). Meanwhile, inside, the principal protagonists have been brought together by a common desire to create out of the life history of one of them 'una bella favola' ('a beautiful story'). A newspaper report is the catalyst for what happens. The play hinges on an important aspect of city life, where the often unwelcome intimacy of small communities is replaced by the anonymity of large urban communities. It has fallen to the press to take on the role of keeping its readers informed about the lives of other, often—but by no means always—public figures, with the result that new ways of 'know-ing' people have come into being.[37] Now a reader can know

[36] *Vestire gli ignudi, Maschere nude, Opera omnia*, iii (Milan, Mondadori, 1947), 23. The play, which was first performed in Rome on 14 Nov. 1922, has no source in earlier work by Pirandello.

[37] It has to be remembered that newspapers in Italy are regional and have traditionally given substantial space to local news (predominantly in the form of 'cronaca nera' or crime-reporting) along with national and international news.

intimate details about somebody wihout actually knowing the person in question.[38] (Nor it does it stop here, for protagonists of these newspaper reports can also, more oddly, find out about themselves; it is through the local newspaper picked up at a railway station that Mattia in *Il fu Mattia Pascal* first learns that he is thought to have committed suicide; with that knowledge comes rebirth.)

In the case of *Vestire gli ignudi*, a young nanny called Ersilia Drei has agreed to allow her life-story to be used as the subject of a forthcoming novel, later changed into a play, by an established writer called Ludovico Nota. His interest in her has been stirred by a series of newspaper articles that appeared in the wake of her attempted suicide after a succession of mishaps had culminated in the death of a child in her care. But as different men from her past appear, each with his own version of events, so the pieces that make up her history start to come apart, and Ersilia turns with increasing despair to the writer Nota to provide her with a coherent and acceptable narrative of her life thus far. The weaker the sense of identity, the greater the dependence on others to construct it and reflect it back to us, so the distraught Ersilia tells the writer that whatever he imagines her to be is how she wants to be. There is a finely balanced exchange of needs between the ageing writer and the young woman: he needs her life (but does not actually require her presence) for his next novel, while she needs him for the biography he can provide and which she can then appropriate and rewrite as autobiography.

ERSILIA. [. . .] Sì, ma almeno—almeno fammi esser 'quella'!
LUDOVICO. Quella, chi?
ERSILIA. Quella che tu immaginasti. Dio mio, se fui, almeno una
   volta, qualche cosa, per come tu hai detto, voglio essere io, nel tuo
   romanzo; io 'questa' come sono![39]

ERSILIA. [. . .] Yes but please at least—at least let *me* be *her*.
LUDOVICO. Her! Which 'her' do you mean?
ERSILIA. The girl you imagined in my story. My God, if, at least once,
   I was something, the way you told it, I want to be me, in your novel;
   this 'me' that I am!

---

[38] Søren Kierkegaard in *The Present Age*, trs. Alexander Dru (New York, Harper and Row, 1962) worried about the obliteration of what he called the 'vital distinction between what is private and what is public'.
[39] *Vestire gli ignudi*, 28.

When their attempt to construct, retrospectively, a past for her fails, she again tries, this time successfully, to kill herself. Ersilia's story is framed by two suicide attempts and, perversely, her death marks her out as one of the few protagonists in Pirandello who succeed in their choice of action.

The practice that provides the catalyst for both *Vestire gli ignudi* and its successor *Ciascuno a suo modo* of a writer taking his story from a newspaper report is not uncommon; two of the greatest nineteenth-century novels, Stendhal's *Le Rouge et le noir* and Dostoevsky's *Crime and Punishment* originated in this way. There is a problem, however, inherent in projects that take their stories from life, as Pirandello wryly notes in his afterword to *Il fu Mattia Pascal*, 'Avvertenza sugli scrupoli della fantasia' ('Notes on the Scruples of the Imagination'). Here he describes the kind of sexual misadventure that his own work abounds in; the incident is taken, he claims, from the New York newspapers of 25 June 1921, but it is one that could very well function as a parody of his own domestic dramas. A husband, his wife, and his lover agree to a collective suicide pact to resolve the intractable and tragic situation in which they find themselves, but after the wife has shot herself, it dawns on the other two who are about to follow her action that her death, by her own hand, has resolved their problem. As he goes on to point out, the inherent absurdity of this tale precludes any writer from using it. Life need not feel restrained by the demands of verisimilitude, but literature does:

Perchè la vita, per tutte le sfacciate assurdità, piccole e grandi, di cui beatamente è piena, ha l'inestimabile privilegio di poter fare a meno di quella stupidissima verosimiglianza, a cui l'arte crede suo dovere obbedire.

Le assurdità della vita non hanno bisogno di parer verosimili, perchè sono vere. All'opposto di quelle dell'arte che, per parer vere, hanno bisogno di esser verosimili.[40]

This is because life, with all the shameless absurdities, both small and large, with which it is blissfully full has the inestimable privilege of being able to do without this ridiculous verisimilitude that art seems obliged to adhere to.

The absurdities of life are not obliged to appear plausible, because they are real. It is the opposite of art where to appear real, they must look plausible.

---

[40] *Tutti i romanzi*, i. 580.

In the world of Pirandello's fictions, life is usually too arbitrary, and events too absurd, to make any discussion of the ethics of public and private behaviour meaningful, but there is one area of concern that appears quite frequently in his writings, and that is the professional use made by writers and artists of other people's lives. Inherent to Ludovico's interest as writer in Ersilia's life is a moral problematic. When he says to her; 'Un romanzo, cara, o si scrive, o si vive'[41] ('One either writes a novel, my dear, or one lives it')—a variant of Pirandello's own much-quoted observation: 'La vita o si scrive o si vive'—he is tacitly acknowledging that he draws on the lives of others for subject-matter. In this case the division of labour sees the male writer write the life that she lives. Nota goes on to observe that he does not even require the subject's presence; the bundle of newspaper clippings collected by him gives him enough material to work on:

non avevo bisogno nè di farti quella profferta nè di venire a prenderti adesso all'uscita dell'ospedale, perchè il romanzo—io— leggendolo su quel giornale i tuoi casi, l'immaginai da me, tutto, da cima a fondo[42]

there was no need to offer you my home, collect you from the hospital. Nothing. The facts of your case I knew from the newspaper—the rest I could imagine for myself, everything, from start to finish

When Ersilia in the play confuses Nota with Pirandello, by attributing *L'esclusa* to him, the link between Nota and Pirandello is made explicit. We never learn why, of all Pirandello's works, it is the early novel *L'esclusa* that Ersilia misattributes to Nota. He responds to her mistake by commenting adversely on both the work, as a bad novel ('un brutto romanzo'), and the author that generated it—thus exhibiting a hostility that is common to all Pirandello's characters who comment on his work. Ersilia's own views of the novel (if she has read it) are not solicited by the author, but it is noticeable that the two protagonists of the respective works are both independent young women trying to make lives for themselves in the face of hostile circumstances.

As we shall see, two years later in *Ciascuno a suo modo*, Pirandello will take the question of the use the author makes of

<hr/>

[41] *Vestire gli ignudi*, 15.   [42] Ibid. 16.

other people's lives a stage further by writing a work which purports to be *à clef*. In *Vestire gli ignudi*, Nota is not alone in appropriating Ersilia's experiences for his own writing: there is also a journalist, Alfredo Cantavalle, who first interviewed her for his paper, giving her story more than three columns, and is now concerned that a case for defamation of character may be brought against him by her former lover. (Nota explains that the media attention is for no better reason than that they have entered the silly season: 'D'estate, capirai, i giornalisti—càpita un caso come il tuo—una bazza: riempono il giornale'[43] ('In the summer when they haven't got much to write about, to get hold of a story like yours—it's a real scoop: they fill the papers with it'). Pirandello's interest in the destructive potential of the relationship between artist and subject is not limited to the written word, as *Diana e la Tuda*, a play written between 1925 and 1926, demonstrates. Here he explores the relationship that develops between a sculptor and Tuda his model, whose most marked characteristic is her extraordinary vitality and exuberance. In a reversal of the Pygmalion myth, as the sculptor (who, unable to bear the thought of her being possessed by another, marries her) nears completion of his statue, so the life is slowly and irreversibly drained out of her. The statue is never completed; he is stabbed to death by another sculptor who loves Tuda and she is left feeling annihilated. Her closing words are: 'Io che ora sono così: niente . . . più niente'[44] ('I who am now like this: nothing . . . nothing at all'). In all these narratives the gendering of artist and subject remain constant; it is a male artist who tries to possess through his work his female subject.[45]

In many ways the two plays, *Vestire gli ignudi* and *Ciascuno a suo modo* complement each other. Both draw on the idea that their subject comes from a 'true-life' scandal which has received many column inches in the press, but where *Ciascuno a suo modo*

---

[43] Ibid. 24.

[44] *Diana e la Tuda, Maschere nude, Opera omnia*, ii (Milan, Mondadori, 1988), 98. It was first performed in Zürich in 1926 followed by a première in Milan on 14 Jan. 1927.

[45] The play is usually read as representing Pirandello's struggle to reconcile the fixity that form imposes on the art work with the fluidity that is characteristic of life. See Adriano Tilgher, 'Life versus Form', in Glauco Cambon (ed.), *Pirandello: A Collection of Critical Essays* (Englewood Cliffs, NJ, Prentice Hall, 1967), 19–34.

dramatizes what happens on the first night, and so purports to refer to a time that comes after the play has been written, *Vestire gli ignudi* dramatizes the processes that lead up to the writing of the play. Both plays point to the difficulties and ultimately the unsustainability of a coherent narrative, be it biographical or autobiographical, of the protagonist and the events that constitute a life. So much of Pirandello's fiction is about the absurdity of trying to construct a narrative of self—be it confession, story, biography, or just anecdote—thus placing him in a position that is diametrically opposed to Freud, whose own work is posited on the conviction that he both can find, and often has found, the psychological determinants that account for a person's behaviour.

The context within which the drama of *Ciascuno a suo modo* unfolds is the Northern Italian city of Turin and, as in *Vestire gli ignudi*, traditional channels of communication—namely, word of mouth—have given way to a print culture that draws on newspapers with their gossip columns for information. The means to communicate innuendo and rumour is scripted into the play at the very outset, with the sale, outside the theatre, of a special edition of the evening paper placed where the audience can see it before they set foot in the theatre foyer. The flier announces 'uno scandalo enorme' ('a major scandal')— namely that the play that is to be premièred that evening has taken as its subject a scandal that shook the city just a few months earlier. It refers to the dramatic suicide in the city of a talented young sculptor, La Vela, who discovered his fiancée, the famous actress Amalia Morello, in the arms of his best friend Barone Nuti, who was himself engaged to La Vela's sister. Instead of turning his gun on the guilty lovers, he chose to shoot himself in their presence. Like a Chinese box there is a scandal within a scandal here: the events themselves and the author's decision to appropriate them, a 'true-life story', for his own artistic ends. Although the original scandal is over and nothing can change it, its resuscitation on stage in the presence of its two remaining participants holds out the promise of an unpredictable outcome. From the outset disorder is carefully scripted into the play. The newspaper report ends with the warning that there are bound to be problems that evening ('È molto probabile che se n'abbia qualche sgradevole ripercussione in teatro questa sera'. The intrusion of the 'real' into the 'imaginary' world of a play is reinforced by the presence in the audience of the two remaining participants in the real-life tragedy, the actress and the baron. The actress in the original tragedy (next to her entry as La Moreno, at the top of the cast-list, is printed 'tutti sanno chi è', 'everybody knows who she is') appears accompanied by three men who are trying to dissuade her from attending the first night. They urge her to move on for fear she may cause a scandal. Meanwhile in the theatre foyer her erstwhile lover Barone Nuti insists to his male friends that all he wants to do is see her: 'non mi fate dare spettacolo qua alla gente che viene a divertirsi alle mie spalle'[46] ('Don't let me make a spectacle of myself with all these people who have come to laugh at me behind my back'). So the audience settles to a story which promises to rerun one scandal while another, lurking in the wings, will eventually succeed in bringing the proceedings to an abrupt close. As the performance progresses so the actress and her former lover in their separate corners of the auditorium, become increasingly agitated and eventually, at the end of Act II, the play is brought to an abrupt, 'unscheduled' halt when Amalia Morello goes backstage and slaps the actress who is playing her. Scripted in among the audience are a few remaining 'spettatori ignari' ('innocent spectators') who are completely bewildered, only realizing as events draw to a close the nature of what they have witnessed: 'A chiave?—Dove? perchè a chiave? Una commedia a chiave?[47] ('A key?—Where? Why with a key? A play with a key?') by which time the scandal has moved from the original event to the author's decision to stage that event. It has transferred from the story enacted on stage to the repercussions in the auditorium.

Ciascuno a suo modo is the second in a trilogy which was completed in 1929 with *Questa sera si recita a soggetto* (*Tonight We Improvise*), a play that was premièred in Germany. In a preface to the trilogy that Pirandello wrote in 1933, when the three plays were for the first time published together, he examined the meta-theatrical issues each of the plays raises. His interpretation, based on his view of theatre as a *locus* of conflict,

---

[46] *Ciascuno a suo modo, Maschere nude, Opera omnia*, i (Milano, Mondadori, 1948), 113–14.
[47] Ibid. 191.

presented each work in terms of the specific struggle it represented: between characters and actors together with the director in *Sei personaggi*; between spectators, author, and actors in
Ciascuno a suo modo; and between actors who have become
characters and the director in *Questa sera si recita a soggetto*. What
he declines to do is enter into a discussion about other aspects
of the trilogy. He is adamant that it is not his role to analyse the
content of his plays, the stories they tell, or the lives they depict:
'Di quanto poi ciascun d'essi contiene in sè particolarmente,
non è qui il luogo, nè il caso, e non spetta a me, di parlare'[48]
('As to what each of them contains in particular, this is neither
the place nor the time to speak, neither am I the person to do
it'). A leading French critic, Jean-Michel Gardair returns to the
incest motif in a psychoanalytic reading of the first two plays
of the trilogy, arguing that their meta-theatrical pyrotechnics
are designed to conceal the concern lurking at the heart of the
two texts:

Il vistoso apparato teorico-critico metateatrale assume sopratutto una
funzione di diversione ideologica, ossia di rimozione dei fantasmi
incestuosi [. . .].[49]

The critical and theoretical meta-theatrical apparatus is spectacular
but its main purpose is to allow Pirandello to cover his ideological
tracks. In other words to keep skeletons of incest shut up in the
cupboard.

[48] Although each play is entirely self-contained with its own plot and characters,
Pirandello intended that they should be published together as a trilogy. This was
finally realized in 1933 when he united the three in his first volume of collected
plays, but subsequent editors have chosen to follow the chronological order of
publication, and so the trilogy has been broken up by the twenty-one other plays
written between 1921 and 1923. It has recently, for the first time reappeared as a
trilogy published by Feltrinelli (1994). *Maschere nude*, ii/2. 935: 'Una trilogia del
teatro nel teatro, non solo perchè hanno espressamente azione sul palcoscenico e
nella sala, in un palco o nei corridoi o nel ridotto d'un teatro, ma anche perchè di
tutto il complesso degli elementi d'un teatro, personaggi e attori, autore e direttore
capocomico o regista, critici drammatici e spettatori alieni o interessati,
rappresentano ogni possibile conflitto.' ('It is a trilogy of all the elements that make
up the theatre as a whole not only because the action is performed expressly on the
stage and in the auditorium, in a box or in the corridors or in the theatre-foyer, but
also because the three plays represent every conceivable element, characters and
actors, author and director or producer, drama critics and alienated or interested
spectators, that make up theatre as a whole.')

[49] Jean-Michel Gardair, 'Vampirismo dell'arte e matricidio', in *Il teatro nel teatro di
Pirandello: La trilogia di Pirandello*, ed. Enzo Lauretta (Agrigento, Ed. del Centro Naz.
di Studi Pirandelliani, 1977), 126.

Pirandello's reticence when it comes to the content of his plays is shared for the most part by his critics, for if one leaves to one side *Sei personaggi in cerca d'autore*, the only one of the three to be frequently performed, written about, and studied, critical attention has concentrated almost exclusively on their meta-theatrical qualities.[50]

Although critical opinion has often claimed that the formal innovations introduced into *Ciascuno a suo modo* are too contrived, I would suggest that the excitement of the play rests in the way it introduces life with all its dangerous unpredictability into the theatre. Inherent to Pirandello's meta-theatre is the sense that any aspect of the performance may, at any moment, fall apart; the audience might rebel, or the actors, or the plot prove to be unperformable, or the fictitious characters might try to take over or, worse still, turn out not to be fictitious at all, or the actors might come to believe that they really are the roles they are playing. More mundanely, the set might not be ready, the curtain may come down at the wrong moment. The production could be brought to its knees and what began as a theatrical performance, self-contained and carefully stage-managed, spill over into confusion, mayhem, or riot. Such an outcome may have been devoutly desired and actively encouraged in their theatrical 'happenings' by Marinetti and his fellow Futurists, but was regarded with fascinated dread by Pirandello. (By the same token, the very structure of the play could be conceived as an invitation to the audience to rebel.) As the critic Claudio Vicentini has pointed out very fairly, by appropriating some of the Futurist practices and scripting them into his own play, he effectively neutralizes the risks that they invite.[51] In *Ciascuno a suo modo* the possibility of an abrupt and premature conclusion to the evening is written into the play, with the following footnote added to the Cast of Characters in the programme notes:

[50] Of the twenty articles included in *Il teatro nel teatro di Pirandello*, only Jean-Michel Gardair (pp. 115–27) discusses this play. For a director's view see Luigi Squarzina, '*Ciascuno a suo modo' di Pirandello e il teatro totale delle avanguardie* (Rome, Bulzoni, 1987).

[51] See Claudio Vicentini, 'La trilogia pirandelliana del teatro nel teatro e le proposte della teatralità futurista', *The Yearbook of the Society for Pirandello Studies*, 3 (1983), 18–32.

Nota bene. Non è possibile precisare il numero degli atti di questa commedia, se saranno due o tre, per probabili incidenti che forse ne impediranno l'intera rappresentazione.[52]

N.B. We are unable to state with any certainty whether the play tonight will consist of two acts or three. It is possible that circumstances beyond our control may prevent the performance from being completed.

The play is divided into four sections, of which two are Acts as traditionally understood, in which the action follows a recognizable story-line and is confined to the stage, and two are what the author refers to as 'intermezzi corali' ('choral interludes'), where, off-stage, theatre critics and public gather together to discuss the events on stage. Pirandello uses two devices to create an appearance of continuity between the reality-effect conjured up by the performance on stage and the reality of the world outside which the audience brings with it into the theatre. He maintains a spatial continuum between on- and off-stage, by extending the theatrical area so that it encompasses the auditorium and the theatre foyer, and later, in the 1933 preface, by also using the space in the street in front of the theatre. ('La rappresentazione di questa commedia dovrebbe cominciare sulla strada o, più propriamente, sullo spiazzo davanti al teatro';[53] 'A performance of this play should really begin outside on the street or better still in the forecourt of the theatre'). In Vicentini's eyes what would appear to be a bold and radical departure from convention is, in practice, a cautious and conservative move. Where the Futurists in their 1915 Manifesto, 'Il teatro futurista sintetico' ('The Synthetic Futurist Theatre'), which carried the signatures of Marinetti, Carrà, and Settimelli, insisted on the urgent need to 'eliminare il preconcetto della ribalta lanciando delle reti di sensazioni tra palcoscenico e pubblico; l'azione scenica invaderà platea e spettatori' ('to eliminate the idea of a barrier between actors and audience at the front of the stage. The acting on stage must invade the auditorium and the audience'), and again in their 'Manifesto del teatro della sorpresa' ('Manifesto for the Theatre of

---

[52] *Ciascuno a suo modo*, 66. The *Nota bene* appeared at the end of the dramatis personae in the 1st edn. It was then moved to the end of the 'Premessa' which Pirandello added to the play in 1933.

[53] 'Premessa', 65.

Surprises') argued the case for a theatre that takes to the streets
and squares of the city, Pirandello starts in the street only to
move back into the safety of the theatre.[54]

Ciascuno a suo modo has a cunningly contrived plot, posited, of
course, on a fiction. No 'true-life' drama lies behind it. There
is no 'commedia *à clef*'; the 'elsewhere' that characters and
events come from is an earlier novel by Pirandello, called *Si
gira* . . . when first published in instalments in 1915, and *I
quaderni di Serafino Gubbio operatore*, when it was republished as a
book the following year.[55] The novel consists of seven notebooks
belonging to a cameraman who works for the film industry in
Cinecittà in Rome. The degree of alienation that his work entails
is forcibly brought home to him when he finds himself continuing with the filming of a scene after it has gone horribly wrong,
with the lead actor being mauled to death by a tiger. Serafino
Gubbio decides from then on to remain mute, confining his
thoughts to the words that he writes down in these *quaderni*.
Contained within his account of life at the studios is a second
story which will later form the nucleus of *Ciascuno a suo modo*.
What in the novel is presented as a succession of episodes in a
life that continues to unfold, becomes in the play a single event
around which everything revolves *post rem*, but the novel also
tells us exactly what happened whereas the play presents it as an
enigma.

When in the 'Primo intermezzo corale' ('First choral inter-
lude') Pirandello introduces and defines the term 'commedia *à
clef*' as 'costruita cioè dall'autore su un caso che si suppone
realmente accaduto'[56] ('that is to say based by the author on an
event that is said to have really happened'), he does not stop to

---

[54] Vicentini, 'La trilogia', 30: 'e infine si risistema entro i limiti convenzionali
e sicuri del palcoscenico dove lo spettacolo è rigorosamente destinato a restare
e a svolgersi fino alla fine. Il riassorbimento del futurismo nei modi dello spettacolo teatrale convenzionale è dunque compiuto.' ('and finally it is rearranged
within the safe conventional boundaries of the stage where the performance is
destined strictly to stay and unfold right up to the end. The reabsorption of
Futurism into the practices of conventional theatrical performance is thereby
achieved.')

[55] *Si gira* . . . appeared in *Nuova Antologia* (1 June–16 Aug. 1915) and was pub-
lished as a book the following year with the same title (Milan, Fratelli Treves, 1916).
The novel is discussed under its 1925 title *Quaderni di Serayino Gubbio operatore* in
Ch. 8.

[56] Pirandello, *Ciascuno a suo modo*, 103.

discuss the moral implications of such a device but hurries on to analyse the meta-theatrical possibilities its adoption presents. Nor in his explanation of the term does he make the point that it is used of a work that claims the status of fiction, but where, none the less, the informed reader can discern the real characters and events that lie behind the pseudonyms. The participants' pleasure therefore stems also from their perception of themselves as members of a select 'knowing' circle which enjoys privileged access to private information about other, often public, figures. The subject of a *roman à clef* whose true identity is concealed behind a pseudonym is more helpless than the subject of a biography where there may be misinterpretation or misinformation on the part of the author but not covert duplicity. Pirandello's silence on the morally dubious appeal of works that draw on an intimate knowledge of living people's lives contrasts interestingly with Sigmund Freud's prefatory remarks to one of his most (in)famous case histories, the analysis of Dora which he wrote in 1901 and published in 1905:

I am aware that—in this city, at least—there are many physicians who (revolting though it may seem) choose to read a case history of this kind not as a contribution to the psycho-pathology of the neuroses, but as a *roman à clef* designed for their private delectation. I can assure readers of this species that every case history which I may have occasion to publish in the future will be secured against their perspicacity by similar guarantees of secrecy, even though this resolution is bound to put quite extraordinary restrictions upon my choice of material.[57]

In his anxiety to clear his name, these remarks achieve exactly what Freud claims he does not wish to happen: they lure the unintended reader into the narrative with promises of revelations about 'real' people which are of a scurrilous and scandalistic nature: 'now I shall be accused of giving information about my patients which ought not to be given'.[58] Like Pirandello, but for very different reasons, Freud has had to bear 'the ill-will of narrow-minded critics',[59] but if he is to reveal the nature of the disorder 'then the complete elucidation of a case of hysteria is bound to involve the revelation of those intimacies

---

[57] Sigmund Freud, *Case Histories*, 1. *'Dora' and 'Little Hans'* (The Pelican Freud Library, 8; Harmondsworth, Penguin, 1977), 37.
[58] Ibid. 35.　　　[59] Ibid. 35.

and the betrayal of those secrets'.[60] It reads like a preface to a novel and nowhere more so than when he seeks to distinguish between the 'man of letters engaged upon the creation of a mental state like this for a short story', who, according to Freud, would simplify and abstract, and what he himself is engaged in doing as a scientist: 'But in the world of reality, which I am trying to depict here, a complication of motives, an accumulation and conjunction of mental activities—in a word, overdetermination—is the rule.'[61] The two texts share other characteristics too: both break off abruptly, unfinished, when their respective women subjects rebel against the attempts being made to write them into narratives that are not of their making, and in which they have difficulty in recognizing themselves. At the level of content as well as frame, both narratives are about gossip, scandal, and the conspiratorial silence that accompanies it.

Pirandello knew about the pain and suffering a *roman à clef* can bring to its unwitting subject from his own experience of having written just such a novel. When in 1911 he published *Suo marito* some readers and critics were quick to see that it was based on the experiences in Rome of the Sardinian writer, later Nobel prize winner, Grazia Deledda. As a satire on the pretensions and greed of Roman *letterati,* and as an analysis of the developing commercialization of culture, it makes an interesting precedent to the much darker study of the nascent film industry in *Quaderni di Serafino Gubbio, operatore.* It is not clear how far Pirandello consciously modelled his protagonist's career and marriage on Grazia Deledda, but his son Stefano recalled that his father recognized the justice of the accusations levelled against him and was sufficiently sensitive to Deledda's reaction to ensure that the book was not republished once the first edition had sold out. It was only more than twenty years later, after Deledda's death, that Pirandello began a very thorough revision of the text, completing four chapters before his own death. Much of the material that was specific to the writer and her life was removed and the title, while retaining the same barbed dig at her husband, was changed to *Giustino Roncella nato Boggiòlo* so removing the genericity of the original *Suo*

---

[60] Ibid. 36.   [61] Ibid. 36.

marito (Her Husband).[62] In an interview he gave in 1924, Pirandello tied himself up in knots as he tried to offer pseudo-psychological explanation as to why, with the exception of Grazia Deledda, he had such a low opinion of women writers:

In generale ne ho poca stima. Ho molta stima di Grazia Deledda. Le letterate poi non bisogna guardarle come donne. La donna è passività e l'arte è l'attività. Ciò non toglie che non ci possa essere uno spirito femminile attivo. Ma allora non è donna.[63]

On the whole I have a low opinion of women writers. I have a very high opinion of Grazia Deledda. Women writers should not be thought of as women. Woman is passivity, art is activity. That is not to deny that there can be an active female spirit. But then it is not a woman's spirit.

Where the scandal of a playwright taking a real-life story to the stage is communicated to the audience in the first instance through the printed word, within the play proper Pirandello dramatizes the processes of the endless ill-informed hearsay or small talk which makes his characters feel able to pronounce on each other. Like the psychoanalyst's case history, Pirandello's play reveals little concern for the truth or otherwise of the different versions of events that circulate and considerable interest in the transmission and circulation of these narratives, illustrating the way opinions are formed, the processes by which hearsay hardens into 'fact'. The very stuff, as John Forrester has persuasively argued, of psychoanalysis:

We all know that psychoanalysis opens up all secrets. We all know that psychoanalysis shrugs off all reticences concerning our opinions of other people. We all suspect that the practice of analysis allows the airing of truths, facts, rumours, fantasies that live only a phantom-like existence elsewhere. From the outset then, the practice of psycho-analysis involves speaking what sounds often remarkably like gossip, rumour and—that extraordinary word so close to the analytic process itself—hearsay.[64]

---

[62] *Suo marito* (Florence, Casa Editrice Italiana, 1911). Pirandello did not allow its republication in his lifetime. His partially revised edn. was published posthumously in 1940 with the title *Giustino Roncello nato Boggiolo*. The novel is more commonly known under the original title. As was his practice, Pirandello refers within the text to other works of his, including a reference to an inscription on the old village church clock which reads *Ognuno a suo modo*. See *Suo marito*, *Tutti i romanzi*, i. 721.

[63] Interview with Giuseppe Villoroel, 'Colloqui con Pirandello', *Giornale d'Italia* (Rome, 8 May 1924).

[64] Forrester, *Seductions of Psychoanalysis*, 10.

On- and off-stage, much of what the spectators watch is a dramatization of gossip. The play opens on a private conversation between two men at a party where the older one is recommending prudence to his companion and tells him that only after he has listened to what others have to say, should he express a view of his own. Their conversation gives way to a group of women gossiping intently about the state of mind of the baron. To facilitate private chat and the exchange of confidences, the stage directions indicate that adjoining the drawing-room there is a small sitting-room where different groups of guests repair: 'Ci verranno dal salone alcuni degli invitati, a due, a tre alla volta, per farsi, appartati, qualche confidenza'[65] ('Some of the guests wander in in two and threes in search of a quiet place to talk discreetly'). The room which accommodates these exchanges of confidences is compared in the stage directions to a 'cappella d'una chiesa', and a few pages on one of the guests refers to it as being 'la cappella delle confessioni' ('the chapel of confessions'). In an interesting reading Susan Bassnett connects what she suggests are the three key verbs in the play; *pensare* ('to think') *sapere* ('to know'), and *dire* ('to speak') to the process of confession,[66] but there are also three nouns that should be added to the list, which put the practice of confession into a more worldly context, and they are *indiscrezione* ('indiscretion'), *scandalo* ('scandal'), and *confidenza* ('confidence'). There is no central episode in the play; the most dramatic event of the evening, the slap that the 'real-life' actress delivers to her stage counterpart, happens after the curtain has come down and news of it filters through to the audience by word of mouth, in a rising tide of information and misinformation that passes backwards and forwards around them. So on all sides, in the auditorium and on stage, the audience finds itself either listening to or overhearing others who observe, chat, express opinions, and take sides:

E prima si formino varii crocchi; e dall'uno all'altro si spicchi di tanto in tanto qualcuno in cerca di lume. Giova e diverte veder cambiare a vista d'opinione, due o tre volte, dopo aver colpito a volo due o tre opposti pareri.[67]

---

[65] Pirandello, *Ciascuno a suo modo*, 68.
[66] See Susan Bassnett McGuire, *Luigi Pirandello* (London, Macmillan, 1983), 52.
[67] Pirandello, *Ciascuno a suo modo*, 104.

4

Configurations of Identity:
the Family's Undoing

> All happy families are alike but an unhappy family is un-
> happy after its own fashion.
>
> (L. N. Tolstoy, *Anna Karenina*)

From what we have seen so far of family life in Pirandello's
fictions, it is an institution that affords little pleasure to its
members. Something has gone seriously amiss in both *Sei
personaggi in cerca d'autore* and *Così è (se vi pare)*, leaving family
members in the one locked in battle and bound to each other
by ties of hatred and self-hatred, while in the other it is the
family's appearance of unity and harmony in the face of their
bizarre domestic arrangements that upsets the community
they have joined. In his short stories too Pirandello presents
characters who are endlessly inventive in the strategies they
adopt and in the lengths to which they will go to lose, mislay, or
isolate themselves from all or part of their family: the husband
who successfully manages to dupe another man into taking on
his wife ('Acqua amara'), the lawyer and family man who locks
himself in his study and plays dubious games with the family dog
('La carriola')—not to mention the unspeakable treatment
adults mete out to children.[1] This chapter will concentrate on
the parental role within the family, but my concern is not so
much for the psychological dimension of child-rearing, as with
the social, legal, and economic function of the parent. Within
Pirandello's fictions there are marked gender differences determining the particular configuration that the parental role assumes. In keeping with this, I have divided the chapter into two
sections: the paternal and the maternal.

[1] See Felicity Firth, 'Fixed for Death: Pirandello on Birth, Babies and Children',
Yearbook of the Society for Pirandello Studies, 14 (1994), 54–60. Firth states categorically
of the *novelle*: 'There are no stories of happy children or happy families.'

The discussion will focus, but by no means exclusively, on *Il fu Mattia Pascal* (*The Late Mattia Pascal*, 1904) and *Uno, nessuno e centomila* (*One, None and a Hundred Thousand*, 1926), narratives both written as fictional autobiographies. The first of the two works was put together in a great hurry against a background of serious financial and domestic worries—the family's fortune had been lost with the flooding and ensuing collapse of their sulphur mines, and Pirandello's wife Antonietta suffered her first crippling bout of psychological illness (see Chapter 2). So it is hardly surprising that the plot takes as its point of departure an escapist fantasy, the stuff of daydreams—to walk out of an oppressive marriage, win a small fortune at the roulette table, and start a new life under an assumed identity. Begun in 1912, *Uno, nessuno e centomila*, on the other hand, had a long and difficult gestation period, and in the event it was only published in its entirety between 1925 and 1926. The crisis undergone by its protagonist and narrator Vitangelo Moscarda, precipitated by an idle comment made by his wife, is different in its nature from Mattia's in that it has its origins in an existential malaise rather than any material hardship or unhappiness. Where Mattia Pascal sets out on a journey that takes him in the first instance abroad, and later to Rome, to escape the material and emotional problems in his life, Vitangelo Moscarda stays put in the provincial town in Sicily where he was born and embarks on a solitary existential crusade to free himself of all the selves or personae projected on to him by his fellow citizens over the years. The source of his anguish lies at the opposite extreme to that experienced by the protagonists of *Così è (se vi pare)* and *Vestire gli ignudi*: where they had to struggle with the consequences of living in a community where no one knows anything, or can find out anything, about their past, Vitangelo, living in his home town, has to contend with the surplus of knowledge and the misplaced intimacy of his fellow citizens, who, having known his family before he was born, presume on that slender basis to know him.

Il fu Mattia Pascal and *Uno, nessuno e centomila* (but more specifically the second) are novels of ideas, weaving together plot and speculation, where the organization of the narrative is often determined not by a pattern imposed by historical time, but by the narrator's own propensity for meditation. (Parallels can be found in two other great twentieth-century narratives of identity: Robert Musil, *A Man without Qualities*, and Samuel Beckett, *The Unnameable*.) Pirandello's own narratives together present a comprehensive account of his literary explorations into the nature and experience of subjectivity, but both thematically and narratologically the subject is given very different treatment. Written on the cusp of the century, *Il fu Mattia Pascal* retains links with the anti-positivist spirit of nineteenth-century literature of the fantastic, sharing its fascination for metempsychosis and the double, but reworking them in a realist frame. *Uno, nessuno e centomila*, on the other hand, is a psychological drama played out entirely within the confines of the protagonist's psyche. If, as Pirandello claimed, he looked on the novel as an introduction to his theatre, then he must have intended Vitangelo to be read as a figure endowed with a universality that would allow him to embody the human condition. In Chapter 5, where I shall be looking more closely at the novel, I will, however, resist the invitation held out by the protagonist himself to draw from his own protracted identity crisis conclusions about the human condition in general. In its place I shall propose a different reading, in which by focusing on the details that we learn indirectly from him about his life, instead of the issues towards which he directs our attention, a different formative model emerges in which gender is a powerful mediating factor.

   Mattia Pascal and Vitangelo Moscarda share an important advantage over other male protagonists we have encountered. They are presented as authors, and therefore masters, of their own narratives. They do not have to contend with dissenting voices or the clamour for attention from other characters. The power they enjoy has a valuable therapeutic function. Given that their stories are of a progressive disintegration of the narrative self—emphasized in Vitangelo's case by the multiplication of speaking/writing subjects—writing their lives brings order to disorder, gives shape to the inchoate, and confers meaning, and above all purpose, on what otherwise might be seen as confused and arbitrary or, worse still, pointless. If, as Paul Ricoeur in his rich and complex work *Oneself as Another*, has argued, 'it is precisely because of the elusive character of real life that we need the help of fiction to organize life retrospectively, after the fact',[2] how much more necessary it is in cases like these where the protagonists are not trying to build a present on the foundations of the past, but a present that springs from a rejection, even a denial, of the past. If, at the end of their respective narratives, Vitangelo Moscarda and Mattia Pascal have each found their own *modus vivendi*, then the reason is to be found as much in the processes associated with writing down their life-story as with the events described therein. Protagonists of their own tales, they each occupy an uncontested space in which they can tell their story from their own viewpoint. It is a privilege that the Father in *Sei personaggi in cerca d'autore* would have given a great deal to enjoy, instead of having continuously to contest narrative space with his Stepdaughter—not only in terms of her version of events but also her own desire to relive the past through the re-enaction of it. As it is, the Father's appearance in the play alongside others means that he can, and indeed does, dominate the narrative space, but he cannot deny others the right to speak. As authors of their own autobiographical narratives, Mattia and Vitangelo can nurture the privileged relationship they enjoy with their readers, whereas a character in a play not only has to contend with being just one presence among others, but stage directions, stage set, and even aspects of his self-presentation are outside his direct control. Pirandello the author may feel disquiet at having to hand over his stage characters to actors, but that is as nothing when compared to the reactions of the Characters themselves in *Sei personaggi* when they watch the actors 'being' them.

We have seen in Chapter 3 the mechanisms that different social groupings deploy to ensure that their members keep within the definitions of the socially acceptable. Here we return to a much earlier stage in the life-cycle when the unmarked, undifferentiated baby is named in a ritual which, it can usually be safely assumed, will put in place the foundation-stone on which public identity is built. What is fascinating and yet entirely consistent with Pirandello's thinking is the extent to which identity is divorced from biology. It is helpful if biological and legal identity happen to coincide—in other words, to be

---

[2] Paul Ricoeur, *Oneself as Another*, tr. Kathleen Blamey (Chicago and London, University of Chicago Press, 1992), 167.

When it comes to naming, Pirandello uses the full range of possibilities afforded him as author. By withholding the characters' names in *Sei personaggi in cerca d'autore* and referring to them purely in terms of their familial roles, our attention is all the time being drawn back to their relationships with each other. The family becomes archetypal, the transgressive content emphasized by the single name-role (although in practice the family teaches us to occupy different roles in relation to different people—mothers as well as daughters, sisters as well as aunts, and so on). The man identified as the *padre* ('father') is in fact *padrigno* ('stepfather') to the girl whose sexual services he buys in the brothel. In *Enrico IV*, the young aristocrat brought up in Rome early in the twentieth century, and then supported in his delusions by family money, is known to us by no other name, so we can only recognize him by way of the identity that he has adopted. Pirandello's women protagonists, who dominate his theatre in the 1920s, are even less fortunate; lacking both money and privilege, they have not the material possibilities of sharing in and living out fantasies like those of Enrico. The unidentified heroine of *Come tu mi vuoi* (*As You Desire Me*) (1930) who, like Enrico, has lost all memory of the past suffers a very different fate. Referred to throughout the text as L'Ignota (The Unknown), the names attributed to her by the men who lay claim to her, Elma (Greek for water) and Cia, never in the end stick. And it is not only the playwright in Pirandello's work who exercises the right to name and unname, he also shows how the gossiping, interfering circles that gather around these suffering outsiders know the power of the name— that it can, for instance, conceal as well as reveal. ' "Delia Moreno" sarà un soprannome. Chi sa come si chiama? Chi è? di dove viene?' (' "Delia Moreno" must be a stage-name. Who knows what her real name is? Who is she? Where does she come from?') puzzles Diego Cinci in *Ciascuno a suo modo* (*Each in His Own Way*, 1923). In addition to the information the name carries in itself, characters pick up signals about each other from the way they are addressed or referred to by a third party; in *Trovarsi* (*Finding Yourself*, 1932) no matter how irreproachable the mores of the actress Donata Gensi, the nature of her profession (for a woman) allows others to speak of her with an intimacy that violates the codes of conduct between the sexes.

VOLPES. Ah, già, 'la Donata'?
LA MARCHESE BOVENO. Ancora non è discesa.
　[*A Volpes*] Lei che la chiama 'La Donata' . . .
VOLPES. Oh, così per uso . . . tutti.[3]

VOLPES. Oh of course, 'la Donata'?
MARCHIONESS BOVENO. She has not come down yet.
　[*To Volpes*] You who call her 'La Donata' . . .
VOLPES. Oh, it's habit . . . everybody.

In the novel *Suo marito* the proper name is used to even more insidious effect to communicate the contempt felt by the élite of the Roman *letterati* for Silvia Roncella's entrepreneurial husband-manager Giustino. In a society where women are transferred from father to husband, a legal transaction testified to by change of name, to call a man by his wife's name is to attribute the female position to him, with all the insulting connotations that carries of sexual and social inferiority. So when a group of 'giornalisti così detti militanti della Capitale' ('so-called militant journalists of the capital') raise the money to print a hundred visiting cards for Giustino using the formula *Giustino Roncella nato Boggiolo* ('Giustino Roncella born Boggioli'), the reversal of name whereby a husband is identified by his wife's name implies a reversal of roles and is used as an expression of their total contempt for him.[4] Nor are characters always happy with the name that has been given to them by their author, judging by the comments of Dr Fileno in 'La tragedia di un personaggio', where he argues that in his own case the choice of name conferred on him simply shows up the writer's incompetence:

Ma guardi . . . *Fileno* . . . mi ha messo nome *Fileno* . . . Le pare sul serio che io mi possa chiamar Fileno? Imbecille, imbecille! Neppure il nome ha saputo darmi![5]

But look here . . . *Fileno* . . . he called me *Fileno*. Do you seriously think that I can call myself *Fileno*? The fool, an utter fool! He didn't even know how to give me a name!

On the other hand, when it comes to his own activity as writer, Pirandello is careful to note in the meta-tales that when potential characters for future stories present themselves at the door

---

[3] Luigi Pirandello, *Ciascuno a suo modo*, iv. 114.
[4] Pirandello, *Tutti i romanzi*, i. 684.
[5] Pirandello, *Novelle per un anno*, i/1. 821.

to his study and he copies down their personal details, he always begins with their name—'nomi e condizioni di ciascuno'[6] ('each one's name and further particulars')—which they have to provide, he does not impose them. In an early review written in 1895 of *Le vergini delle rocce* (*Virgins of the Rocks*), written by one of his rivals, Gabriele D'Annunzio, Pirandello noted disapprovingly that so indeterminate was the figure of the protagonist that even his name, Claudio Cantelmo, did not belong to him and cropped up elsewhere by mistake (in place of Giorgio Aurispa) in an instalment of *Trionfo della morte* (*The Triumph of Death*).

In *Il fu Mattia Piasca* and *Uno, nessuno e centomila*, the two novels that represent the most protracted crises of identity in Pirandello's entire *opus*, both of the male protagonists have a problematic relationship with their names. The preface to the first work opens with the narrator doing what comes naturally when introducing oneself for the first time—he gives his name—offering it as the one known fact in what is otherwise presented as a life of chronic uncertainties: 'Una delle poche cose, anzi forse la sola ch'io sapessi di certo era questa: che mi chiamavo Mattia Pascal'[7] ('One of the few things I knew for certain, in fact, perhaps the only thing, was this: that my name was Mattia Pascal'). He explains that when friends or acquaintances were foolish enough to come to him for advice, he would reply by telling them his name; when they pointed out that this was something they already knew, he would respond to such casualness with the question: 'E ti par poco?' ('And it doesn't seem much to you?'). At that stage, though, before he personally had experienced the consequences of the separation of person and name, the word and its referent, he admits that he too attributed little significance to such knowledge.

---

[6] Pirandello, *Novelle per un anno*, i/1. 816.

[7] Pirandello, *Tutti i romanzi*, i. 319 (*The Late Mattia Pascal*, tr. Nicoletta Simborowski (London, Dedalus, 1987), 14). There are different views on the choice of name. Théosophile Pascal is the author of two of the books in Paleari's library, while Blaise Pascal is cited as a humorist in *L'umorismo*. Sciascia comes down firmly in favour of Blaise Pascal in *Alfabeto pirandelliano* (Palermo, Sellerio, 1989), 52–4. Finally, and to my mind less convincingly, it has been suggested that Pascal is linked to Pasquale—so connecting the forty days of Lent with the period Pascal spent recuperating from his eye operation. Within the text, Mattia's brother Berto makes the following comment ' "—*Mattia*, l'ho sempre detto io, *Mattia, matto* . . . Matto! matto! matto!"—esclamò Berto' (' "*Mattia*, I always said it myself, *Mattia, mad* . . . Mad! mad! mad!"—exclaimed Berto').

Ma ignoravo allora che cosa volesse dire il non sapere neppur questo, il non poter più rispondere, cioè, come prima, all'occorrenza: —Io mi chiamo Mattia Pascal.[8]

but at that time I didn't realize what it was like not to know even that much, not to be able to reply like that, as I always had done, when the occasion demanded it: 'I'm Mattia Pascal.'

Any notion that the reader may harbour that the protagonist is hinting obliquely at illegitimacy, or other skeletons in the family cupboard, is instantly dispelled by Mattia, who claims that it is not going to be that kind of narrative. He could provide us with a full genealogical tree, but what, he asks, would his readers learn from it? And, following the convention of the literature of the fantastic, he adds: 'Ecco: Il mio caso è assai più strano e diverso; tanto diverso e strano che mi faccio a narrarlo'[9] ('You see, my case is much stranger and more unusual; so strange and unusual that I feel compelled to recount it'). In her deconstructionist reading of the novel, Donatella Stocchi-Perucchio observes that the assumptions contained in the coupling of name with identity, a literary shorthand to give the reader access to the legal line of descent—property, class, social standing—are challenged in the two prefaces that accompany the text:

The first *premessa*, in particular, announces the cognitive problem and, at the same time, renounces a certain epistemological model as inadequate to approach that problem. [. . .] Instead of assuming a symbolic unity between being and name, as a naturalistic writer would do, Mattia's narrative capitalizes precisely on the fracture between the two. His certainty about identity, an unproblematic correspondence between self and name, has been irrevocably shattered. Any attempt to repair this fracture by going back to the origin of his family, the knowledge of which he takes for granted here, seems to be beside the point. The specificity of the vocabulary and the image of the genealogical tree—which incidentally recalls the beginning of *Docteur Pascal* by Zola—clearly indicate that what is being dismissed is the self-confidence of the positivistic epistemology; its way of explaining every human phenomenon in biological, evolutionary, and genealogical terms; its vision of reality as a mechanistic sequence of causes and effects; its notion of the past as the key to an explanation of the present.[10]

---

[8] *Tutti i romanzi*, i. 319 (tr. Simborowski, 14).   [9] Ibid. 320.

[10] Donatella Stocchi-Perucchio, *Pirandello and the Vagaries of Knowledge: A Reading of* Il fu Mattia Pascal (Stanford, Calif., ANMA libri, 1991), 25–6. A number of critics

Mattia's disclaimers stir the reader's curiosity—positivist natu-ralist narrative is denied in the name of something undefined, but which promises far more mystery and excitement. As in the fantastic, the intimation is that his circumstances are so excep-tional that they transcend the usual rules applied by positivist science. (None the less at the very moment that, as readers, our suppositions about the function of naming are undermined, the narrator ensures that his own name is unlikely to slip our mind by reiterating it three times in the first fifteen lines of the *premessa*, so we have a ready means by which we can identify him throughout the narrative. As we shall see in a moment, the point at which he assumes a new name and identity is also emphasized within the text.) A sense of the continuity of a person through time is established from the outset. This is important in the light of Pirandello's fascination with the Pascalian *pensée* that no man differs more from another than he does from himself over time.[11] Seeing his name in print or hearing it spoken might throw Mattia himself into an epistemo-logical crisis, but for the reader it performs its function perfectly satisfactorily.

Early in his life-story, the narrator describes how, on his return journey to the unhappy home and marriage that he had walked out of a few days earlier, now the proud owner of a small fortune that he had won at the gaming tables at the casino in Nice, he learns from the local newspaper of his own suicide—that is to say, he reads a piece on the death by drowning of a man whose corpse has been identified by his wife (with what in his view is indecent haste) as his own. He capitalizes on the favour Fortune has dealt him by deciding to start afresh and create a new life for himself. The unknown victim whose death has been reported in the newspaper is lifeless, but now has a

have discussed the novel's relation to French naturalism and in particular Zola, but Stocchi-Perucchio is alone in seeing a specific parallel between these two texts.

[11] Pirandello refers to Pascal towards the end of *L'umorismo* (*Spsv* 150): 'Non c'è uomo, osservò il Pascal, che differisca più da un altro che da sè stesso nella successione del tempo' ('No man differs from another man, observed Pascal, more than from himself over a period of time'). Lacan in 'Function and Field of Speech and Language' associates Pascal with the 'dawn of the historical era of the "ego", what we would think of as modernity': 'Fonction et champ de la parole et du langage en psychanalyse', *Écrits* (Paris, Seuil, 1966), 111–43 (*Écrits: A Selection*, tr. Alan Sheridan (London, Tavistock, 1977), 71).

name to be buried under; Mattia, on the other hand, at this point has a life but no name, and therefore no identity. Just as a name is conferred on a newborn baby long before the infant can articulate it, Mattia likewise does not invent a name for himself, but adopts the name that is unwittingly presented to him by his fellow travellers: 'Il nome mi fu quasi offerto in treno, partito da poche ore da Alenga per Torino'[12] ('My name was more or less suggested to me in the train, a few hours after I left Alenga for Turin'). An erudite discussion between two travellers sharing the same compartment on the identification of two statues leads to what he refers to as his own 'baptism' as Adriano (the name refers to the claim that the statues are of Emperor Hadrian with the city of Paneade kneeling at his feet) Meis (the same statues are reported on the authority of Camillo de Meis to represent Christ). At the moment of naming the protagonist is making both a metaphysical and a literal journey from being Mattia Pascal to becoming Adriano Meis, where elements of both the secular and the religious are present to contribute to the creation of a new being. But one cannot have a present without a past and Adriano Meis's next task is to set about reinventing himself by creating, retrospectively, his life-story.

Vitangelo Moscarda, the protagonist of *Uno, nessuno e centomila*, has a very different problem with his name. The aptness of his surname, with its root 'mosca' meaning 'fly', for a man whose thoughts buzz round and round with irritating tenacity is noted by him: '*Moscarda*. La mosca, e il dispetto del suo aspro fastidio ronzante'[13] ('*Moscarda*. The housefly, and the shrill infuriating taunt of its tiresome buzzing'), but his concern is not with the connection between his name and the insect. It lies in the irrefutable evidence it provides that he is his father's son. The point is raised only once he is well into his life-story. Not only is he not identified by name in the novel's title, but the title also seems to throw into doubt the very notion of identity and its associations with individuality, replacing it with a sense of fluidity and anonymity. Nameless and numberless, its

---

[12] Ibid. 406. The novel's location is curious; it is situated in Liguria (Alenga is probably a reference to Albenga in the region of Savona) but a Liguria that has all the features of Sicily.

[13] Pirandello, *Tutti i romanzi*, ii. 786.

genericity is complete. In keeping with this impression, in the
first three chapters the narrator is presented to the reader only
by his use of first person singular verbs and pronouns—as illustrated in the title of the first chapter 'Mia moglie ed il mio naso'
('My wife and my nose'). The second person plural used in the
subsequent chapter 'Ed il vostro naso?' ('And your nose?') is
more ambiguous in that it could refer either to the intradiegetic
or the extradiegetic interlocutor or, more likely, both. In other
words, he may be addressing his friends, whose confidence
about their appearance seems to have been undermined by him
to wonderfully absurd effect:

> potrei giurare che per parecchi giorni di fila nella nobile città di
> Richieri io vidi (se non fu proprio tutta mia imaginazione) un numero
> considerevolissimo dei miei concittadini passare da una vetrina di
> bottega all'altra e fermarsi davanti a ciascuna a osservarsi nella faccia
> chi uno zigomo e chi la coda d'un occhio, chi un lobo d'orecchio e chi
> una pinna di naso.[14]

I could swear that, for days in a row, in our worthy town of Richieri,
I saw (unless it was nothing more than my imagination) a very considerable number of my fellow citizens going from one shop-window to
the next and coming to a stop before each of them to scrutinize
themselves, one to study a cheek-bone, another the corner of his
eye, another the lobe of an ear, and another again to investigate his
nostril.

Or he may be addressing us, his empirical readers outside the
text, who are unknown to him. When in chapter 3 of book 1,
'Bel modo d'esser soli!' ('A Fine Way of Being Alone'), our
narrator at last divulges his name, it is provided not in the main
body of the text itself, but in the book's one footnote where he
explains his wife's repetitive recourse to her nickname for him,

---

[14] Pirandello, *Tutti i romanzi*, ii. 744. I shall discuss the relationship between
perception, appearance, and identity in Pirandello's writing in Ch. 8. A similar case
of a wife who uses a nickname for her husband that he feels is a travesty of his true
self occurs with Bernardo Morasco in a short story called 'Coppo' (Earthenware
Jar): 'Nardino. Sua moglie lo chiamava così, *Nardino*. Perdio, ci voleva coraggio! Un
nome come il suo. Bernardo Morasco, divenuto in bocca a sua moglie *Nardino*. Ma,
povera donna, così lo capiva lei . . . *ino* . . . ino . . . ino' ('Nardino. That is what his
wife called him, *Nardino*. Good God you needed courage! With a name like his.
Bernardo Moscarda, became in his wife's mouth *Nardino*. Well, the poor woman,
that is how she understood it . . . *ino* . . . ino . . . ino'). *Novelle per un anno*, i. 609.
Bernardo's indignation at his wife's abuse of his name is similar in tone to Dr
Fileno's reaction to the name his author has conferred on him in 'La tragedia di un
personaggio'.

Gengè: 'Mia moglie, da Vitangelo che purtroppo è il mio nome, aveva tratto questo nomignolo, e mi chiamava così; non senza ragione, come si vedrà'[15] ('My wife had coined this diminutive out of Vitangelo, which unfortunately is my real name, and was used to calling me by it, and not without reason, as will be seen later on').

At this point, he has still not provided us with his full name. He finally mentions it casually towards the end of the next chapter at the moment when it dawns on him that, however terrible the original scenario of a self split into public and private personae may once have seemed to him, it still comes nowhere near the true enormity of his situation:

Ripeto, credevo ancora che fosse uno solo questo estraneo: uno solo per tutti, come uno solo credevo d'esser io per me. Ma presto l'atroce mio dramma si complicò: con la scoperta dei centomila Moscarda ch'io ero non solo per gli altri ma anche per me, tutti con questo solo nome di Moscarda, brutto fino alla crudeltà, tutti dentro questo mio corpo [. . .][16]

I still believed, let me repeat it, that this stranger was a single individual: one person for everybody, just as I believed that I was a single individual for myself. But rapidly my atrocious drama grew more complicated: with the discovery of the hundred thousand Moscardas that I was, not only to others but even to myself, all of them bearing the same name of Moscarda, a name that was ugly to the point of cruelty, all of them lodged within my body [. . .]

To the outside world a surname confers an identity—in Ricoeur's words, it signals 'an unrepeatable, indivisible unity without characterizing it'[17]—but when Vitangelo refers to his, it is in the context of his discovery that the unified self it supposedly refers to is a fiction. Furthermore by using his surname only, without the inclusion of a first name, the son becomes indistinguishable from his father. Nowhere in the text does Vitangelo Moscarda's name appear in its entirety. I shall have more to say shortly about his dislike of his surname, encapsulated in that interesting phrase 'brutto fino alla crudeltà' ('ugly to the point of cruelty') and the presentation of the father–son relationship, but first I want to pursue a little further the curious significance that legal identity enjoys in Pirandello's writing.

---

[15] Ibid. 746.   [16] Ibid. 750–1.   [17] Ricoeur, *Oneself as Another*, 29.

Benedetto Croce, whose long-running polemic with Luigi Pirandello, begun at the turn of the century, had touched mainly on matters of aesthetics, on this occasion attacks the author of *Il fu Mattia Pascal* for giving such prominence in the story to its protagonist's lack of the personal documents needed to own the dog that he yearned to have for companionship.[18] Swept along by his dislike of the writer and his beliefs, what Croce fails to recognize is the point underlying Mattia's predicament—namely that who we are in terms of our biological origins is of little importance what matters is who the state understands us to be. A person is whoever she or he is legally declared to be. In the end it comes down to a question of bureaucracy. Naming is the first and most important moment in a process aimed to confer on us an identity. For most people it takes place within a family context and few writers can claim to have been more exhaustive than Pirandello in their representations of the diversity of practices that come under the umbrella term 'family'. For Pirandello, as for Freud, our problems begin in the home. In the words of Giovanni Macchia 'il nucleo familiare è l'oscuro germe da cui nascono gli infiniti casi pirandelliani'[19] ('the family nucleus is the hidden seed from which the many Pirandellian situations are born'), but one would have to search long and hard to find a family that is what it claims to be. The family is crucial, but for Pirandello it is the legal and not the biological ties that make it what it is. Typical of the confusion that occurs under cover of family life are the activities of Mattia Pascal himself, when in the early pages of the novel, before he embarks on his own odyssey, in a few energetic months he gives one young woman, second wife to his family's corrupt estate manager, the son and heir that they so much

---

[18] Benedetto Croce, *La letteratura della nuova Italia* (Bari, Laterza, 1974), vi. 363. Pirandello ends his essay, *L'umorismo*, with a reference to Chamisso's *Peter Schlemihl*—the man without a shadow. Despite his riches, he is vilified everywhere he goes as soon as it is noticed that he has no shadow. He ends up living the life of a hermit, travelling the length and breadth of the East, but unlike Mattia he can do so because he has a pipe and a dog: 'Instead of my last riches I had a pipe for enjoyment—it took the place of human sympathy—while as an object for my affections, I had a little poodle who loved me and played the watchdog over my cave at Thebes. When I come home, laden with the spoils of my explorations, it sprang eagerly forward to greet me, stirring my heart by its welcome and making me feel I was not quite done in the world.'

[19] Giovanni Macchia, *La stanza della tortura* (Milan, Mondadori, 1981), 107.

desired, while also impregnating the girl he has been assiduously courting on behalf of his best friend.

Sometimes it is simply a question of finding a legal husband who will recognize an unborn child as his, and so conceal a respectable young woman's sexual indiscretion—examples of this are to be found in the two plays, *Il piacere dell'onestà* (*The Pleasure of Honesty*, 1917) and *Pensaci Giacomino* (*Think it Over, Giacomino*, 1916). But a more complicated and intriguing area of sexual irregularity explored by Pirandello is adultery. Unlike many of the great nineteenth-century writers, such as Hawthorne, Tolstoy, Flaubert or Fontane, Pirandello is not so much interested in the figure of the adulteress herself, as in the potential adultery gives him to explore yet another mutation in family life. The gap between Pirandello and other writers can be seen in his own 'novel of adultery', *L'esclusa* (discussed in Chapter 2), where Marta ceases to be seen as an adulteress only after she has finally committed the adultery she unjustly stood accused of, and has been left pregnant. In the days before genetic testing, the novel of adultery was in part a product of men's uncomfortable awareness of the impossibility of ascertaining a biological tie between father and child. Given that inheritance, money, property, and land descended through the paternal line, a wife's sexual fidelity was at a premium, but this was an area of little interest to Pirandello who suggests (quite logically) that there is no problem so long as the husband accepts the heir as being his own. What Pirandello does challenge is the apparently more easily verifiable relationship that exists between mother and child, demonstrating that here too legality takes precedence over biology. In the next section, on the mother's role, I shall look more closely at the representations of sexuality and maternity in Pirandello's work, but here I shall limit myself to the issue of legality.

A remarkable example of legality winning out over biology is provided by a play where, disquieting though they are, the domestic arrangments turn out to be of far less importance that the conclusions that the audience is invited to draw from them. When Livia in *La ragione degli altri* (*Other People's Reason*, 1915) discovers that her husband Leonardo and his mistress, Elena, have a 3-year-old daughter, she insists that if the marriage is to continue she must be allowed to take over the child and rear her as her own (the marriage has produced no children). Her defence for this course of action is as follows: home is where the children are, 'Dove sono i figli è la casa', so her husband must take his child and live either with his legal wife, who is not the child's natural mother, or with his mistress (also his cousin), who is.[20] The implication, which is not as yet spelt out, is that the child's home is where the father is: in other words paternal rights take precedence over the rights of the mother. This is a play in which the word *diritto* ('right') is resorted to and appropriated by each of the characters in turn, but the overall thrust of the play suggests that of the three—mother, wife, and huband—it is the child's 'rightful' mother, her biological mother, who has the least claim to her. Livia wins because she is in a position to confer a legal identity on the child, 'e io sola, io sola potrò dare a lei quello che voi non potrete mai: la luce vera, la ricchezza, il nome di suo padre!'[21] ('and I alone, I alone will be able to give her what you never ever can: the true light, riches, her father's name!'). This extraordinarily hyperbolic outburst can be explained by the power her position as legal wife gives her to confer the name of her husband, which has also through marriage become hers, on a child that is not hers but will, through him, become so. After telling her in no uncertain terms that she is raving, Elena stresses the visceral, physiological basis to the bond between mother and child:

Voi farneticate, signora! Le ho dato la vita, io, il mio sangue, il mio latte le ho dato! Come non pensate a questo! E' uscita dalle mie viscere! E' mia! E' mia! Che crudeltà è la vostra? Venirmi a chiedermi un tale sacrifizio in nome del bene della mia figliuola?[22]

You are raving, Madam. I gave her life, I, it was I who gave her my blood, my milk. How is it that you have not thought of that! Flesh of my flesh! She is mine! Mine! How cruel can you be? To come and ask of me such a sacrifice all for the good of my little daughter?

[20] In *Suo marito* the writer-protagonist Silvia Roncella's second play *Se non così* (*If not like this*), involves a similar triangle, but on this occasion the sterile mother convinces her husband that he must leave her for his lover because they have a child. *Se non così* is also the title of a play Pirandello wrote and had performed by Marco Praga's company on 19 Apr. 1915. The production was not a success and ran for only two nights. Pirandello asked Praga to switch the roles of the two leading actresses. He wrote an interesting preface on the subject, 'Lettera alla protagonista Signora Livia Arciani', which accompanied the text when it was first published by Fratelli Treves, Milan, 1917.

[21] Pirandello, *Maschere nude*, i (1986), 244.   [22] Ibid. 244.

Rarely have the rights of the biological mother been seen to be so explicitly and brutally overruled in the name of the legal and symbolic authority of the father. The implications of the play emerge very clearly in the controversy over its casting. When Pirandello submitted his revised manuscript to Virgilio Talli, Italy's most eminent director at that time, Talli strongly disagreed with the idea that the leading lady, Maria Melato, should take the wife's role and not the mistress's, on grounds that it offended against ideas of motherhood:

Tratta un argomento nobilissimo: *il diritto della maternità.* Ma ne tratta un altro ancora: *il diritto della paternità.* E quest'ultimo mi pare tanto poco ammissibile che non mi meraviglierei se gli spettatori credessero poco al fatto che Leonardo ha quasi abbandonato la moglie perchè non lo ha reso padre e s'è attaccato invece alla cugina perchè gli ha dato subito una figlia,—[. . .] Esaltare la maternità sempre! distaccarsi dalle leggi di natura, cose dette da secoli e, per conseguenza, sapute da tutti.[23]

It is about a very worthy subject: *the rights of maternity.* But it is also about something else: *the rights of paternity.* And this last topic strikes me as being so unacceptable that I would not be surprised if the audience lent little credence to the fact that Leonardo almost abandoned his wife because she did not make him a father and attached himself instead to his cousin because she immediately gave him a daughter.— [. . .] Always exhalt maternity! To distance oneself from the laws of nature, things that have been said over the centuries and, as a result, are known by everybody!

What Talli finds quite unacceptable about the play, and he does not mince his words in the long and very interesting letter he wrote to Pirandello, are the 'veri eccessi di una logica che è la sua, professore, ma che è di una sottigliezza filosofica non certo arrivata a tutte le menti'[24] ('real exaggerations of a train of thought that you, Professor, may be able to achieve, but which

---

[23] Ibid. 152–3. The ideology of motherhood is so engrained that the play continues to be read in this light by some critics today. One synopsis of *La ragione degli altri* reads: 'una donna senza figli può con la forza della volontà e dell'amore considerare sua la figlia del marito e dell'amante di lui' ('a woman without children can by strength of will and love consider as her own the daughter born of her husband and his lover'): see Emanuele Licasto, *Luigi Pirandello dalle novelle alle commedie* (Verona, Fiorini, 1974), 91–2. In the text Livia says she will be 'schiava' ('slave') to the child, but not 'madre' ('mother'). See also Alessandro D'Amico's introduction to the play in *Maschere nude,* i (1986), 139–58.

[24] Ibid. 155.

is of a philosophical subtlety that is certainly not within every-body's reach'). As far as the director is concerned, Livia cannot be played by the lead actress for, by snatching the child from its biological mother, she has forfeited any claim to the audience's sympathy, while the suggestion that her husband, the child's father, could have any interest in the product of a sexual affair is, Talli believes, too implausible to carry conviction. But Pirandello's intention in the play is clear, and it is emphasized by his representation of the very close bonding of mother and child who have, after all, lived together for three years before the drama starts. If Pirandello had left the casting to Talli, by identifying with the suffering of the bereft mother, the audi-ence would have left the theatre emotionally shaken but with their philosophy of life if anything confirmed; as soon as Maria Melato was cast as the wife and not the mistress, the play ceased to be a melodrama and became an unsettling enquiry into the 'rights' of motherhood.

In *La ragione degli altri* Livia wins the child because she has it in her power to confer the name of the father on that child. We have already seen how Croce in his long and acrimonious battle with Pirandello made a serious error of judgement when he dismissed *Il fu Mattia Pascal* as being a novel that might more aptly have been called 'il trionfo dello stato civile' ('the triumph of civil status'). Indeed his total failure to understand the signifi-cance of what he dismisses as merely 'la personalità giuridica' ('the legal person') is vividly illustrated by Sibilla Aleramo in her autobiographical novel *Una donna*, which Pirandello re-viewed very sympathetically (see p. 46 n.). In the following brief extract she describes the consequences of her separation from her husband: 'La legge diceva ch'io non esistevo. Non esistevo se non per essere defraudata di tutto quanto fosse mio, i miei beni, il mio lavoro, mio figlio'[25] ('According to the law I had no existence—except as someone who could be cheated of her rights, of everything she had: her property, her work, her son'). Pirandello never underestimated the role of the symbolic in our construction as individuals.[26] We are who we are legally assumed

---

[25] Sibilla Aleramo, *Una donna* (Milan, Feltrinelli, 1973), 194 (tr. Rosalind Delmar, *A Woman* (London, Virago, 1979), 167).

[26] The conceptualization of the symbolic order as that which structures inter-human reality was introduced by Lévi-Strauss, *Anthropologie structurale* (Paris, 1958),

to be; blood ties do not count unless they are recognized in the eyes of the state. And in a patrilinear society, to assume the father's name is to take a first, important, step in the process of entry into the symbolic.

2. THE MATERNAL ROLE

It's funny about identity. You are because your little dog knows you.

(Gertrude Stein, *Everybody's Autobiography*)

We have seen how crucial the family is in securing for each of its members a name and identity irrespective of biological ties, but this is only the first step in the creation of selfhood. Once the outer carapace has been established, it has to be continuously reaffirmed by others, as Mattia Pascal discovers to his cost in *Il fu Mattia Pascal*, when the elation at having created a new persona and with it a new life for himself as Adriano Meis gradually subsides as he painfully learns that individuality depends on sociality, that he cannot sustain his fictitious self without help from others. Few writers have explored with such persistence and inventiveness the degree to which our sense of selfhood is dependent on the recognition of others. 'I' am not simply 'I' but also a 'You' in the eyes of others—so self, far from being something hived off, is connected and created by others.[27] Indeed, the closer we get to a character in Pirandello's fictions, the more indistinct is our impression, for it is very hard to get any sense of an 'inner self'; what we come up against is, in Lugnani's apt expression, a 'cavernous interiority'.[28] Empty, echoing, drained of content as they are, all we have to decipher them by is external to them. From this comes one of Pirandello's paradoxes: given that our existence depends on

but here I am using it in a Lacanian sense. For Lacan, the Symbolic Order which interacts with the Imaginary, is concerned with the function of symbols and symbolic systems of which the most crucial is of course language (see 'Fonction et champ de la parole et du langage en psychanalyse', in *Écrits*, 111–43).

[27] See Emile Benveniste, 'De la subjectivité dans le langage', *Problèmes de linguistique générale* (Paris, Gallimard, 1966), 248–66.

[28] Lucio Lugnani, 'Nascita, vita-morte e miracoli del personaggio', in S. Milioto (ed.), *Pirandello e il teatro del suo tempo* (Agrigento, Centro Nazionale di Studi Pirandelliani, 1983), 103.

the recognition conferred on us by others, the death of a loved one is also our own death. And this is where in Pirandello's writing women come into their own.

There is precious little love in Pirandello's fictions; marriage itself seems to be marked by an absence of both love and sexual passion, not to mention mutual understanding. There are very occasional moments of tenderness between the sexes, one of the most poignant being found in the doomed relationship between Mattia, now Adriano Meis, and the daughter of the boarding house where he lodges in Rome, but such moments are rare. Where there is however a powerful emotional pull is in a mother's feelings for her child. 'Colloquii coi personaggi', the third and last of Pirandello's meta-tales of creativity discussed in Chapter 2, falls into two parts: the author's encounter with a singularly persistent character who hopes to gain entry into his house of fiction, followed by a conversation with his dead mother. These meetings occur during 'i giorni di torbida agonia' ('days of dark suffering'), in the period leading up to Italy's declaration of war on Austria when the author is entirely preoccupied by the fate of his son, Stefano, who has joined up as a volunteer. The character bursts into his study anxious to hold forth on his own philosophy of life, but as he lives in a dimension of time that is completely cut off from 'real' time as we mortals experience it, what he has to say has no bearing whatsoever on the tragedy then unfolding in Europe. Not un-reasonably, the author, worried sick about the welfare of his son, has no time for the intruder's argument; instead he la-ments his country's ignoble foreign policy—the alliance with Austria that his generation has accepted and lived through for over thirty years and which now has finally reached breaking-point, leaving the generation that should be paying the price of cowardice safe. His is a generation which saw its fathers go to war and now is watching its sons:

E ora che questo freno finalmente accennava a rompersi, ora che il ribrezzo soffocato per trenta e più anni stava per prorompere e avventarsi, ecco, non io, non noi, quanti siamo di questa sciagurata generazione a cui è toccata l'onta della pazienza, l'ignominia di quell'alleanza col nemico irreconciliabile, non noi dovevamo correre alla frontiera, ma i figli nostri, nei quali forse il ribrezzo non fremeva e l'odio non ribolliva come in noi. Prima i nostri padri, e non noi! ora, i nostri figli, e non noi! Dovevo restare a casa, io, e veder partire mio figlio.[29]

And now that the bridle was finally about to snap, now that the disgust that we had suppressed for thirty years was about to break out, just as we were about to give full vent to it, suddenly it wasn't me, it wasn't us, not any of us in this miserable generation who had endured the shame of patience, the ignominy of this alliance with an enemy with whom there could be no reconciliation, it wasn't us who had to hurry to the frontier but our sons who perhaps did not feel that same disgust and who did not have the boiling hatred that we had. First our fathers, and not us! Now our sons, and not us! I had to stay at home and watch my son depart.

It is in this state of mind that he moves to the corner of the room where he finds among the shadows the waiting shade of his dead mother, evoked by him, but present in all her alterity. Drawn back to him by the strength of his anguish, she has come to tell him what distance prevented her from saying before her death. She tells him the history of his family's involvement in the battle for the independence of Italy, their resistance and exile, and she puts his own son's decision in this context. When she tells him not to grieve for her, reminding him that she remains alive in his memory, he interjects with an impassioned paradox:

Io piango perchè tu, Mamma, tu non puoi più dare a me una realtà! [. . .] Ora che tu sei morta, io non dico che non sei più viva per me; tu sei viva, viva com'eri, con la stessa realtà che per tant'anni t'ho data da lontano, pensandoti senza vedere il tuo corpo, e viva sempre sarai finchè io sarò vivo; ma vedi? è questo, è questo, che io, ora, non sono più vivo, e non sarò vivo per te mai più! Perchè tu non puoi più pensarmi com'io ti penso, tu non puoi più sentirmi com'io ti sento! E ben per questo, Mamma, ben per questo quelli che si credono vivi credono anche di piangere i loro morti e piangono invece una loro morte, una loro realtà che non è più nel sentimento di quelli che se ne sono andati.[30]

I cry, because you, Mother, you can no longer confer on me a reality [. . .] Now that you are dead, I'm not saying that you are no longer alive for me; you are alive, as alive as you ever were, with the same

[29] Pirandello, *Novelle per un anno*, iii/2. 1143. The story was first published in the *Giornale di Sicilia* (17 and 18 Aug. 1915).

[30] Ibid. 1152.

reality which for many years I gave you from far away, thinking of you without seeing you, and you will always be alive as long as I live; but do you see? It is this, this, that for you I am now no longer alive and never will be. Because you can no longer think of me as I think of you, you can no longer feel me as I feel you! And it is for this reason, for this very reason, that those who think they are alive think they are crying for their dead and instead they are crying for one of their own deaths, one of their own realities, that is no longer carried by the feelings of those who have gone before us.

While she will always be mother to him, 'io, figlio fui e non sono più' ('I, I was a son and no longer am'). 'Colloquii coi personaggi' is one of Pirandello's most intimate pieces of writing and this may be the reason why he did not include it in the fourteen volumes of *Novelle per un anno* assembled by him between 1922 and 1936. It reveals very clearly the origins in his own life-story of the singularly intense symbiotic relationship between mother and son that one finds in his creative writing.

Pirandello's *mise-en-scène* of maternal self-sacrifice and dedication can perhaps best be understood in the context of his own close relationship with his mother, Caterina Ricci-Gramitto, who also occupied an important role as buffer between father and son.[31] Her political loyalty and commitment to the struggle to throw off the yoke of foreign occupation of Sicily gives her support for her son in the above episode a symbolic as well as a psychological importance. Caterina had met her future husband in 1862, when her brother, who at Aspromonte had fought alongside Garibaldi as his lieutenant, returned home after a period in prison. Caterina came from a family of Sicilian patriots, committed to the separatist cause, who had to go into exile in Malta where her father obtained political asylum, after the anti-Bourbon revolution of 1848 which saw her father a minister in the provisional government established in Palermo. When he died just a few months after reaching Malta, the family

---

[31] In his biography, *Luigi Pirandello* (Turin, UTET, 1963), 17, Gaspare Giudice attributes the author's insecurity to the relationship between father and son: 'Un uomo, questi, tutto diverso, alieno dalle effusioni affettuose, rude e distratto: fisicamente enorme, pieno di violenza e lieto di stare con gli altri 'omaccioni', e fuori, più che dentro casa.' ('He was altogether different this man, he never made any display of affection, and he was gruff and distant. He was a very big man, violent-tempered and he liked to spend his time with other men out-of-doors, away from home.')

were permitted to return to Girgenti where, their possessions confiscated, they lived in poverty off the charitable handouts of an uncle. In the words of Pirandello's son, Caterina 'la gioventù l'aveva data alla Patria'[32] ('had given her youth to her Father-land'). In 'Colloquii', Pirandello has his mother tell the story in her own words, presumably as first he, and then his children, used to hear it related. The episode reveals the importance he gave to his family's, and in particular to his mother's political background. What drew his mother, Caterina, at 28 and no longer expecting to marry, to her future husband, a young man of Ligurian descent who was in Sicily to look after the family's sulphur mines, was his own participation in the struggle for Unification; in her words 'reduce anche lui da Aspromonte, garibaldino anche lui del Sessanta, carabiniere genovese' ('he too was an Aspromonte veteran, a soldier in Garibaldi's army in 1860, a Genoese carabiniere'). Born as he was in the north-western corner of the mainland, his politics were different in that he was committed to the ideal of a united Italy which would include Sicily. But it was not politics that produced a troubled marriage; instead, as is clear from a letter Luigi Pirandello wrote to his daughter in 1931, it was his father's many sexual infideli-ties, which had also resulted in the birth of an illegitimate child. His mother tolerated this along with the other problems in her brave and successful effort to hold the family together.

Pirandello's words to the shade of his mother—'Io piango perchè tu, Mamma, tu non puoi dare a me una realtà! [. . .] Ora che tu sei morta'—are put into practice in reverse in the play *La vita che ti diedi* (*The Life that I Gave You*, 1923) when a living, widowed mother manages through the power of maternal love to bring her dead son back to life. (There is an ambiguity in the title of the play which may well have been intended; depending on who one understands to be the subject of the phrase, it can be taken to refer either to an artistic birth, which sees the author bring a character to life, or to a biological birth in which a mother gives birth to a child, or both.) After living some years away from home, Donn'Anna's son returns to his mother to die, but she, by refusing to accept that the body before her eyes is the son she once bore, keeps him—the son she carried with her

---

[32] Stefano Landi, 'La vita ardente di Luigi Pirandello', *Quadrivio* (13 Dec. 1936).

in her memory through the years of his absence—alive. Indeed, the son who did return to her had, in the years away, changed beyond recognition and, once he is dead, she is free to return to her living memory of him. The otherness, the foreignness of the man who came back to her need no longer disturb the ideal image that she nurtures of him. Donn'Anna tells her shocked sister that her son might have died as far as the life God gave him is concerned, but he is still alive with the life she has imbued in him and he will continue to stay alive for as long as she herself lives. The text also contains the intimation that the son's death is the consequence of his having left home; when he returns, whether alive or dead, he becomes once again a part of her—so much so that her thoughts and writing can, when she wishes, become indistinguishable from his. (Donn'Anna's role was written expressly for Eleanora Duse, who turned down the part, according to Pirandello's son, on religious grounds.)

The play opens with the son already dead and a chorus of voices chanting the litany. The figure of the mother grieving over her dead son in *La vita che ti diedi* echoes the Virgin Mary weeping over another son who was returned to life, the dead Christ. The link between Pirandello's representation of motherhood and the idealization of maternity that developed through the cult of the *Mater Dolorosa* (spread through Europe in the eleventh century, assisted by the Franciscans' stress on her participation in the lives of ordinary people) is acknowledged more explicitly in the description of the Mother in *Sei personaggi in cerca d'autore*. When the six Characters first appear in the play, the stage directions gives to each of them one dominant trait; regret for the Father, scorn for the Stepdaughter, disdain for the Son, and suffering for the Mother who, at this point, is the only Character whose introduction is accompanied by a brief description:

il *dolore* per la Madre con fisse lagrime di cera nel livido delle occhiaje e lungo le gote, come si vedono nelle immagini scolpite e dipinte della *Mater dolorosa* nelle chiese.[33]

Sorrow for the Mother. Her mask should have wax tears in the corners of the eyes and down the cheeks like those you see in paintings or statues of the *Mater dolorosa* in churches.

---

[33] Pirandello, *Maschere nude*, ii (1993), 678 (tr. Linstrum (1985), 75).

The sculptures and paintings referred to by Pirandello usually depict the Virgin as she holds the lifeless body of her son in her arms and gazes down upon his features. The tears she sheds are charged with significance. As Marina Warner points out in her study of the myth of the Virgin Mary, they are the only bodily effusion that is considered to be both pure and purifying: 'Mary's tears do not simply flow in sorrow at the historical events of the Crucifixion, a mother's grief at the death of her child. They course down her cheeks as a symbol of the purifying sacrifice of the Cross, which washes sinners of all stain and gives them new life.'[34] They replace speech. When Pirandello goes on in *Sei personaggi* to describe the style of dress that he feels would best create in the audience an awareness of the Characters' essential otherness in terms of other forms of human life, his instructions that they should be clothed in weighted, stiffened robes recall the ancient, anti-naturalistic theatre of classicism, but they also bring to mind the heavy material that often in the iconography of the *Mater Dolorosa* swathes the body of the Virgin Mary sculpted in byzantine folds to conceal the outline of all but her breasts:

E sia anche il vestiario di stoffa e foggia speciale, senza stravaganza, con pieghe rigide e volume quasi statuario, e insomma di maniera che non dia l'idea che sia fatto d'una stoffa che si possa comperare in una qualsiasi bottega della città e tagliato e cucito in una qualsiasi sartoria.[35]

Her dress should be of a plain material, in stiff folds, looking almost as if it were carved and not of an ordinary material you can buy in a shop and have made up by a dressmaker.

And when he provides further details of each of the Characters in turn, he suggests that the Mother's face, on raising her veil, should appear 'non patito, ma come di cera' ('not suffering, but as if made of wax').

In Western culture, representations of the relationship between mother and child almost invariably show the mother from the point of view of her child, as happens in 'Colloquii'. It is most unusual to have the relationship depicted from the maternal point of view; psychoanalysis for example

---

[34] Marina Warner, *Alone of All Her Sex* (London, Quartet, 1978), 223.
[35] Pirandello, *Maschere nude*, ii (1993), 678 (tr. Linstrum, 76).

speaks extensively on the influence, usually baleful, the mother exercises over the child but remains largely silent on the mother's experiences. Pirandello's own representations of the mother–son relationship retain elements of the child's early phantasy that his mother desires no one else other than him, that she lives for him; a phantasy that is usually overcome, with a struggle, by the entry of a third person into the mother–child dyad. What Pirandello then reserves for the mother is the inevitable sense of personal tragic loss that accompanies her destiny as Mother, which comes about when the children grow up and leave home. Starting out on life as part of her flesh and blood (*La vita che ti diedi* emphasizes the importance of the body in binding mother to child—born of her body, the child continues to feed from her to survive), the journey to adulthood brings physical and emotional separation. Donn'Anna's experiences are echoed in a less dramatic, but still painful way, by her sister who has seen her two children leave home to complete their education and return changed—in the words of the stage directions, 'non solo nel modo di pensare e di sentire, ma anche nel corpo, nel suono della voce, nel modo di gestire, di muoversi, di guardare, di sorridere'[36] ('not only in their way of thinking and feeling, but also in their bodies, the sound of their voices, the way they hold themselves, move, look, smile').

The cast list of *La vita che ti diedi* provides unusual reading in that the only male characters listed are an elderly, celibate gardener, the village priest, and Flavio, one of Donna Fiorina's children, while the women protagonists consist of four mothers, three of whom are widowed while the fourth is carrying her dead lover's child. By making the mothers single, their relationship with their respective children is not diluted by a rival in the shape of husband or lover. In other words, Pirandello presents women whose maternal devotion determines their entire being: a selfless maternal love that in Pirandello's representations of maternity is so all-absorbing that it can only come about in the absence of a man. The separation between maternity and sexuality is more than a question of a child having his mother's undivided attention; it also exhibits itself in an absolute refusal to admit that mothers have a sexuality. Roberto Alonge has

---

[36] Pirandello, *Maschere nude, Opera omnia*, ii (Milan, Mondadori, 1940), 32.

pointed to an important absence running through Pirandello's fictions:

C'è un tabù, una *scena negata* in Pirandello ed è la doppia identità della donna, in quanto femmina, in quanto detentrice di un proprio corpo, per un verso, e in quanto madre per l'altro verso.[37]

There's a taboo, a *censored scene* in Pirandello and it concerns the double identity of woman as female, as owner of her own body on the one hand and as mother on the other.

There are many examples in Pirandello's writings of the denial of a mother's sexuality or conversely of a female lover's maternal desire. In *Il piacere dell'onestà* (*The Pleasure of Honesty*, 1917) the young pregnant heroine for whom a husband has to be found to 'legitimize' the child has to put up both with her mother on the one hand saying 'Agata ora [. . .] non è altro che madre, madre soltanto' ('Agatha now [. . .] is nothing other than a mother, a mother only') and her fiancé on the other telling her 'in voi per forza con la maternità, l'amante doveva morire.—Ecco voi non siete più altro che madre'[38] ('in you inevitably with maternity the lover had to die.—Now you are no longer anything other than a mother'). As if to ensure that there will be few opportunities for a mother to depart from her state of celibacy, Pirandello's mothers are often described as being physically marked by their pregnancy, usually with a brief reference to a 'corpo sformato' ('misshapen body').

Come prima, meglio di prima (*As Before, Better than Before*, 1920) is a play in which the opposition between maternity and sexuality is set out in a particularly uncompromising way. In 1904 Pirandello published a short story called 'La veglia' ('The Watch') in which a dying woman is forgiven by the husband she had deserted some thirteen years previously. When Pirandello used the episode for the first act of *Come prima, meglio di prima*, the 'fallen' woman is resuscitated and, in the guise of her husband's second wife, is brought back to her former home and reunited with the daugher she had deserted; the scene is therefore set for the daughter's misconceived hatred or jealousy of the woman she understands is her stepmother. What is

[37] Roberto Alonge, 'Madri, puttane, schiave sessuali e uomini soli', *Studi pirandelliani: Dal testo al sottotesto*, ed. R. Alonge (Bologna, Pitagora, 1986), 96.
[38] Pirandello, *Maschere nude*, i. 614.

interesting is that in the face of her daughter's unswerving commitment to the memory of her mother who she thinks is dead, Fulvia also loses any instinctual sense of a maternal bond:

Io per lei sono—questa—e non posso essere sua madre! Sono arrivata al punto di crederci io stessa! Mi pare, mi pare veramente figlia di quell'altra . . . e non credo più io stessa, proprio non sento più, che glieli abbia fatti io, quegli occhi, quella bocca, come se veramente ci fosse stata qui un'altra, da cui lei è nata.[39]

For her I am—this—and I cannot be her mother! I have reached the point where I even believe it myself. She seems to me, she really does seem to me the daughter of that other woman . . . and I myself no longer believe, I really do not feel it, that those features of hers come from me, those eyes, that mouth, as if there really had been somebody else here of whom she was born.

Fulvia is finally driven away from the family home after she has revealed to her stepdaughter that she is her biological mother. She is no longer acceptable to her husband once she has made the masquerade public. The topos of the fallen woman who returns home in disguise to see the child she abandoned years before occurs in Oscar Wilde's *Lady Windermere's Fan* (1892) and in the less easily recalled, but in its day sensationally successful novel *East Lynne* by Mrs Henry Wood (1861). This salutary tale was, within months of its publication, turned into a play and repeatedly performed in London and New York. It concerns a woman who takes up a position incognita as governess to her own children. What is markedly different about Pirandello's rendition of this particular family scenario is that where both Oscar Wilde and Mrs Henry Wood show a mother's love remaining steadfast despite absence, the passing of time, and her otherwise low moral standing, the Italian writer adamantly refuses to concede that maternal love in itself enjoys a special status. The strength of the bond derives from the constancy of the mother's devotion to her child—it has to be earned.

Women are divided into two categories in Pirandello's work: the lover or wife who is permitted a sexuality but is, as we shall see in the next chapter, profoundly unhappy, and the asexual mother whose entire selfless being is dedicated to her offspring. As I have tried to show above, particularly in the autobiographi-

---

[39] Pirandello, *Maschere nude*, ii. 568.

cal 'Colloquii coi personaggi', the son's dependence on his mother is commensurate with her dedication to him. Such demands on the mother cannot often be realistically fulfilled, so it is perhaps not surprising that a play which the author saw as light-hearted resolves the maternal versus sexual conundrum by separating conception and gestation from rearing and nurturing. In a letter Pirandello wrote to his son Stefano, he described the play in question, *Liolà* (1916), as arguably his 'liveliest and freshest' ('forse la più fresca e viva') and the work that he held dearest after *Il fu Mattia Pascal*:

> L'ho scritta in 15 giorni, quest' estate; ed è stata la mia villeggiatura. Di fatti si svolge in campagna. [. . .] il protagonista è un contadino poeta, ebbro di sole, e tutta la commedia è piena di canti e di sole. E così gioconda che non pare opera mia.[40]

> I wrote it in a fortnight this summer; and it was when I was away on holiday. In fact the events unfold in the countryside [. . .] the protagonist is a poet-peasant, intoxicated with sun, and the entire play is full of song and sun. It is so cheerful it does not seem like a work of mine.

Written in the dialect of Girgenti that had been the subject of his thesis (Pirandello had wanted to avoid what he referred to as a *dialetto borghese*, 'bourgeois dialect'), the plot is strongly reminiscent of Mattia's own amorous adventures which he describes in Chapter 4 of his novel. The play takes a topos familiar from *commedia* tradition which involves an old, impotent man and a young, virile one, but it does not adopt the traditional finale which would see nature triumph over society and the young man win the girl. On this occasion the protagonist, Liolà, concentrates his energies, when he is not working the land, on his indefatigable sex life, but, in an unusual move, each time one of his lovers conceives and gives birth, he takes the child off her hands and gives it to his mother to rear. The plot focuses on a wealthy and impotent old landowner, Zio Simone, who by the start of the play has been married to a young woman called Mita for some four years but she has not yet borne him a child. Meanwhile Tuzza, a spiteful, opportunistic young woman, claims that the child she has conceived with Liolà is in fact Zio Simone's. He is thrilled at this proof of his virility,

[40] Letter to Stefano written 24 Oct. 1916, repr. *Almanacco Bompiani*, 39–40.

and to stop a scheme to make the baby heir to his fortune, Mita, his wife, agrees to sleep with Liolà. The result is another pregnancy and again Zio Simone is more than happy to recognize the baby as his own flesh and blood—so he now has the 'legitimate' heir he longed for, with the added benefit for Mita that he stops maltreating her because of her supposed infertility. Tuzza's child, whose birth will no longer bring her any material advantage, is handed over to Liola's long-suffering mother to be reared. As a grandmother turned mother to her son's children, she makes possible the dream of motherhood without sexuality. In this utopia, the maternal and the sexual are no longer found together in the same woman, but this play, considered by readers as discerning as Sciascia[41] and Gramsci to be one of Pirandello's greatest works, makes for uncomfortable reading today.

The celebration of maternity reaches its apotheosis in one of Pirandello's late plays *La nuova colonia* (*The New Colony*, 1928). Here the emblematically named La Spera (Hope) is a prostitute redeemed through her love for her child, who together with a group of smugglers travels out to an island that was once a penal colony to create a new society. The Prologue ends with the appearance of La Spera, carrying her child, who announces that her milk has miraculously returned after a period of five months when she was unable to lactate. On the island the men soon begin to quarrel over her, refusing to accept any longer her rebirth as mother, and eventually even her former lover, the father of her child, urged on by the men, tries to separate her from the infant. The play ends with a storm invoked by La Spera in which the island's inhabitants are swept away, while she survives standing on a rock with her child in her arms. The earth and sea have come to her support, the world now no longer springs from man and woman, but mother and son. Maternity is located outside time, outside history, and is returned to the pure realm of nature. *La nuova colonia* proposes in an extreme form the generative symbiosis of mother-earth.[42]

[41] See L. Sciascia, *La corda pazza*, in *Opere 1956–71*, ed. Claude Ambroise (Milan, Bompiani, 1987), 961–1222. He includes an interesting commentary on the play's use of dialect.

[42] For links between Pirandello's representations of maternity and Fascist ideology see Roberto Alonge, *Pirandello tra realismo e mistificazione* (Naples, Guida, 1977), 253–326.

A mother's love is beyond price in Pirandello's work; its sanctification comes about because it is central to the shoring up of the fragile male psyche. Subjectivity for Pirandello is not something inherent to us, but is precariously acquired through relationships with those closest to us and, first and foremost, Pirandello seems to suggest, through the dedicated, self-sacrificing love of mother for son. The examples of motherhood in Pirandello's fictions are many and varied, but the assumptions underlying his representations of maternity remain constant and find their explanation in the revealing and moving encounter between mother and son that we saw enacted in 'Colloquii coi personaggi'. Although in his own life he was sympathetic to women whom he saw as victims of social and legal injustices, women on their own, working women, women in sexual relationships are presented as being a complete mystery (which is why, as we shall see, his representation of childless, solitary women is so interesting). In Pirandello's fictions there are two categories of females: there are women and there are mothers. But the mother's task is never completed. It is handed on from one woman to another because it is the traditional attributes associated with maternity and not maternity itself that makes a mother. As we shall see in Chapter 5, when we turn to the history of Vitangelo Moscarda's crisis in *Uno, nessuno e centomila*, wives can perform the same function for men, but they are less reliable than mothers; the novel is left to trace the crisis that is set in motion when 'maternal' recognition is withdrawn. In a patriarchy men confer a legal identity, but the responsibility for the maintenance of an integrity of selfhood, the belief that the word 'I' is something more than a signifier lacking a signified, devolves on women—mothers and wives.

A fellow Sicilian writer and a great admirer of Pirandello's work, Leonardo Sciascia, has some interesting observations to make about women that indirectly make the same point. The misogyny that lurks at the edges of his novels is much more forthright in his non-fiction. In *La Sicilia come metafora* (*Sicily as Metaphor*) where even emigration is welcomed for the contribution it can make towards what he calls the *desacralizzazione della donna* ('the desanctification of women') Sciascia has a surprisingly straightforward explanation for the island's problems: namely women and, to be more precise, women in their familial

5

Narrative Space and the Multiplying Self: the case of *Uno, nessuno e centomila*

> Or can you think of anything more frightful than that it
> might end with your nature being resolved into a multipli-
> city, that you might really become many, become, like
> those unhappy demioniacs, a legion, and you thus would
> have lost the inmost and holiest thing of all in a man, the
> unifying power of personality?
>
> (Søren Kierkegaard, *Either/Or*, ii)

Pirandello was both a methodical and a fast writer. Often working under financial or personal pressure it was not uncommon
for him to finish a project within a fortnight of starting it, so the
fifteen years it took him to complete *Uno, nessuno e centomila* was,
by his standards, most unusual. He began the novel in 1910 and
published a central section in January 1915 in the journal
Sapientia in commemoration of the earthquake that had struck
Marsica in Sicily that year, but the full work was only finally to
appear, in instalments, between 1925 and 1926.[1] Not long after
he started on the project Pirandello wrote a letter to his fellow-
writer and friend Massimo Bontempelli, dated 26 June 1910, in
which he expressed his confidence that the book would soon be
finished, adding that it was giving him little pleasure: 'Se sapesse
in quale tetraggine io mi sento avviluppato, senza più speranza
di scampo!'[2] ('If you only knew the depths of the gloom enveloping me, with no more hope of escape'). Almost three years

---

[1] It was published in the *Fiera lettararia* (13 Dec. 1925–13 June 1926). Its subtitle
(later dropped), *Considerazioni di Vitangelo Moscarda, generali sulla vita degli uomini e
particolari sulla propria, in otto libri* (*The Reflections of Vitangelo Moscarda, in general on the
Life of Man and in particular on his Own Life in Eight Books*) links it to a literary
tradition that began in England with Laurence Sterne's *The Life and Opinions of
Tristam Shandy, Gentleman*.

[2] See Marziano Guglielminetti, *Il romanzo del Novecento italiano: Strutture e sintassi*
(Rome, Riuniti, 1986), 163.

later in his *Lettera autobiografica* of 1912–13 he wrote that the novel, described here as 'il più amaro di tutti' ('the most bitter of them all') and 'profondamente umoristico, di scomposizione della vita' ('profoundly humouristic, about the breaking up of life'), would be out in *Nuova Antologia* by the end of the year.[3] However, on 20 July 1916, Pirandello mentioned in a letter to his son Stefano that he had resumed work on *Uno, nessuno e centomila* and he intended to complete it by the end of the summer vacation; this was followed a year later almost to the day by another reference to his intention to finish the novel. It is in this last reference that he also mentions his plans for a new novel to be called *Sei personaggi in cerca d'autore*.[4] (In the intervening year his prolific output had included *Liolà* and *Così è (se vi pare)* and the publication of the collection of tales *E domani, lunedì* (*And Tomorrow, Monday*).) In a long preface addressed to his father, published alongside the opening instalment on 13 December 1925, Stefano Pirandello confirmed that the work had put Luigi under great strain, citing the exhaustion and stress that accompanied 'il tuo sotterraneo lavoro al dramma dell'*Uno, nessuno e centomila*[5] ('the hidden work for the drama of *Uno, nessuno e centomila*').

The novel belongs to a tradition of humorous writing that descends from Lawrence Sterne's *Tristam Shandy* and found a response in Italy in such narratives as Ugo Foscolo's *Il sesto tomo dell'io* (*The Sixth Book of Me*, 1790) and Carlo Dossi's *Vita di Alberto Pisani* (*The Life of Alberto Pisani*, 1871)—both these mock autobiographies found an appreciative reader in Pirandello. In *Uno, nessuno e centomila* the humour does not conceal the disturbing nature of the personal odyssey undertaken by its narrator and protagonist, Vitangelo Moscarda, which, coupled with the book's pervasive sense of claustrophobia, makes it an uncomfortable and sometimes oppressive work. Situated in Sicily, the story is enacted in an enclosed world where the self-absorption of the narrator is matched by the inwardness of the community around him. Although the narrative suggests a contemporary setting, no reference is made to the extraordinary events (which

---

[3] Pirandello, *Spsv* 1288.
[4] See *Almanacco Bompiani* (1937), 43.
[5] 'Prefazione all'opera di mio padre' ('Preface to my father's works') in Pirandello, *Tutti i romanzi*, ii. 1057–61.

include the Great War, the Russian Revolution, the rise of Fascism, and the March on Rome) that took place within Italy and beyond during the years of its writing. The present tense dominates in the narrative, but it is a present that is divorced from the possibility of a future. Similarly the location could equally well be an inaccessible island where nobody departs and nobody arrives. In reality the town where Vitangelo Moscarda was born and brought up, referred to in the novel as Richieri, is Girgenti, the town of Pirandello's own childhood years which, a year after the book's publication, was renamed by special decree Agrigento (thus reverting to its ancient Greco-Roman roots). But here it is presented as a place without identity, a townscape of the mind, lacking in topographical features. A sense of time and of place are present in the text only in as much as they exist in the mind of the narrator.[6]

As his determination to finish the manuscript would suggest, *Uno, nessuno e centomila* was held by Pirandello to occupy a particularly important position in his writings. In an interview for the *Messaggero della Domenica* of 23 February 1919, he made its purpose explicit by saying that the novel was intended to be a guide to his work for the stage:

Sto ora ultimando un romanzo che avrebbe dovuto uscire prima di tutte le mie commedie. Si sarebbe forse avuto una visione più esatta del mio teatro. In questo romanzo c'è la sintesi completa di tutto ciò che ho fatto e la sorgente di quello che farò.[7]

I am now finishing a novel which should have come out before any of my plays. That way one perhaps might have had a more exact understanding of my theatre. In this novel there is the complete synthesis of all that I have done until now and the source of what I shall be doing in the future.

The claim he makes for the novel is ambitious: it will encapsulate the preceding works and anticipate everything that is to come. The second is the bigger of the claims, but not even Pirandello could have envisaged in 1919 how much of his theatre, including all the major plays, he was yet to write.

[6] Although less pronounced, the treatment of cityscape in *Il fu Mattia Pascal* is very similar. The Rome glimpsed in the novel is a twilight city, closer to T. S. Eliot's 'unreal city' that opens *The Wasteland* than to the administrative and political capital of Italy in the grip of property speculators.
[7] Guglielminetti, *Il romanzo del Novecento*, 174.

The migration of characters and plots from one piece of writing to another, which is a hallmark of Pirandello's working practices, is not so evident in *Uno, nessuno e centomila*. There is no corollary to the plot elsewhere in Pirandello's fictions, but moments in the protagonist's life-story are to be found in stories written before he began what was to be to be his last novel. For example, from 'Quando ero matto' ('When I was Mad', 1902) comes the belief that by refusing to take one's part in the world and its fictions one can, through an act of will, reach a state of mystical union with the universe, while the protagonist of 'Stefano Giogli, uno e due' ('Stefano Giogli, One and Two', 1909) discovers more mundanely three months after his wedding that his wife has dispossessed him of his personality and created an altogether different persona who occupies the role of her husband; a literal enactment of the idea that one 'loses oneself' on falling in love. From the evidence we have available to us, which includes a friend's recollection of hearing him read aloud the opening chapters to the novel (quoted at the beginning of this study), it is clear that Pirandello's relationship with his protagonist was far from being that of the dispassionate, impartial 'observer' lauded by naturalism. Long before his wife manifested the first disturbing symptoms of her chronic illness, Pirandello had been aware of the fragility of the psyche; as a young man he had written movingly on how he believed that he was losing his sanity.

Pirandello had to find a way to reconcile the two potentially contradictory features of his novel. It is written entirely from the perspective of a man thought by his community to be going mad, and at one stage judged to be dangerous, yet there is a need at the same time for the readership to lend credence to his protagonist's philosophical speculations. To ensure that his readers take Vitangelo's views seriously, he marshalls all the requisites necessary for the presentation of an argument that is designed to persuade: logic, rationality, and clarity. It is the speculative content of the text, whose importance is reflected in its author's stated intention that the novel should be seen as the key to his theatre, that contributes to its distinctly essayistic aura; the critic Debenedetti described it as being more of a treatise than a novel.[8] Notwithstanding the pressure to read the work as

[8] Giacomo Debenedetti, *Il romanzo del Novecento* (Milan, Garzanti, 1971), 270.

a novel of ideas, this chapter in keeping with what has preceded it will concentrate on the story or, to be more exact, the material and psychological determinants that shape Vitangelo's life and determine the direction his intellectual and philosophical quest will take. First, however, a word is needed about the hybridity of the text, in particular its essayistic qualities.

In an interesting study of the development of what he terms 'essayism', Thomas Harrison examines the relationship between essay and fiction in turn-of-the-century writers, selecting Robert Musil, Joseph Conrad, and Luigi Pirandello for close study (although others, most notably Marcel Proust, immediately spring to mind), suggesting that they are trying to work towards a new morality, a 'conscious bearing towards reality' which draws on a harmony between thought, emotion, and action and which finds in fiction the medium best suited to this purpose. Their work presents a particular kind of open-ended and obsessively speculative fiction drawing on those features of the essay which link it to its origins in the verb 'assay'—to try out or to test: 'not only does the essay give shape to a process preceding conviction, or perhaps deferring it forever. More important, it records the hermeneutical situation in which such decisions arise. For this reason the essay ultimately requires novelistic form, which can portray the living conditions in which thought is entangled.'[9]

For Pirandello it is the superfluity ('il superfluo'), the critical, self-questioning dimension, of existence that leads to the essayism whose presence is so marked in *Uno, nessuno e centomila*. The literary properties Harrison identifies with the essay—fracture, interrogation, taking apart, trying out, the triumph of disunity over unity, discordance over harmony—are the hallmarks of Vitangelo's discursive style with regard both to his disjointed language and its fragmented presentation. It is the 'essayistic' qualities of Pirandello's writings that led Benedetto Croce, who held firmly to the conviction that reflection is

---

[9] Thomas Harrison, *Essayism: Conrad, Musil and Pirandello* (Baltimore and London, The Johns Hopkins Press, 1992), 4. See also T. W. Adorno, 'The Essay as Form', *New German Critique*, 32 (1984), 151–71: a translation of an essay written between 1954 and 1958 where he discusses the 'childlike freedom of the essay', its organization of experience and its recognition in its very structures of fragmentation and open-endedness, that 'control of the totality' is unrealizable. Ibid. 162: 'It thinks in fragments just as reality is fragmented and gains its unity only by moving through the fissures, rather than by smoothing them over.'

harmful to the spontaneity of creative intuition, to condemn Pirandello's writings as being:

taluni spunti artistici, soffocati o sfigurati da un convulso includente filosofare. Né arte schietta, dunque, né filosofia: impedita da un vizio d'origine a svolgersi secondo l'una o l'altra delle due.[10]

some artistic bursts, suffocated or disfigured by a fitful and inconclusive philosophizing. Neither clear-cut art nor philosophy, then: writing impeded by an originary vice from unfolding according to one or the other.

As we have seen in Chapter 1, the erasure of the stylistic divisions separating the essay from the novel is not reserved for Pirandello's fictions alone, but is present in equal measure in his essays where he eschews the abstract, and replaces it wherever possible with figurative language and the anecdote, modes of narration also associated with storytelling. I have chosen an example (see also Chapter 1) in which Pirandello's technique illustrates the very point that he wishes to make. In a critique of contemporary rhetorical writing which he includes in his article 'Soggettivismo e oggettivismo nell'arte narrativa', Rhetoric is presented in the guise of a series of pots or cruets that Time in the persona of the kiln-owner (*fornaciajo*) shapes. But at times of dissatisfaction with his craft, or even moments of mental aberration, the craftsman turns out such peculiarly shaped vessels that people are at a complete loss to know what to do with them, and so the pots remain empty. Thoughts and feelings that should have been poured into them lie around like so much spilt liquid. Just in case his readers have not understood the reason behind this digression into the art of pot-making, Pirandello does not leave the story there, but goes on to explain that what he has described is the effect that much contemporary writing has on him when adjectives, adverbs, and turns of phrase that should have been carried by the force of the rhetorical expression, instead lie around uselessly in the text because nobody can understand what their purpose is.[11]

The pleasure Pirandello takes in elaborating, adding to, or repeating tales marks him out first and foremost as a storyteller. But if we turn to a classic among philosophical works, it soon

---

[10] Benedetto Croce, 'Pirandello', in *La letteratura della nuova Italia*, 362.
[11] 'Soggettivismo e oggettivismo nell'arte narrative', *Spsv* 185.

becomes clear that the discipline itself is not as immune to contamination from other narrative practices as Croce would have us believe. To illustrate the point I shall take Descartes's *Meditations*, a work which stands at the opposite philosphical pole to Pirandello's *Uno, nessuno e centomila*, to suggest, very briefly, that although considered a pure work of philosophy which was not intended for a fiction-reading public, it draws on similar rhetorical devices to win the consent of its readers. Descartes rejects the idea that madness could have a part to play in the pursuit of truth so adamantly that he cannot even allow it to be present as just one among many instruments of doubt because, he claims, thinking and madness are mutually exclusive ('I who am thinking cannot be mad'). Pirandello's narrator-protagonist only really begins to meditate seriously once he has delivered 'il mio primo riso da matto'[12] ('my first madman's laugh'). Both texts, however, give shape to speculation by presenting it within the context of the conditions that gave rise to it. Drawing on techniques commonly associated with storytelling, both describe in the first person a venture or quest pursued with a conviction and with reserves of courage and determination that most of us, the implication is, could not begin to emulate. Their respective narrators present themselves as uncompromising individuals whose lonely journey has taken them in pursuit of their radical insight into the illusory nature of what human beings will usually be content to accept unquestioningly as the truth. The French philosopher sets out in his first Meditation the personal qualities such an arduous intellectual journey demands. Under a heading that Vitangelo Moscarda would have appreciated, 'Of the things as to which we may doubt', Descartes establishes the enormity of the undertaking (such as to 'cause [him] to delay'), and attributes the quest to a personal need to find his way back to the roots of understanding:

It is now some years since I detected how many were the false beliefs that I had from my earliest youth admitted as true, and how doubtful was everything I had since constructed on this basis; and from that time I was convinced that I must once for all seriously undertake to rid myself of all the opinions which I had formerly accepted [. . .][13]

---

[12] Pirandello, *Tutti i romanzi*, ii. 758.
[13] René Descartes, *The Philosophical Works of Descartes*, tr. Elizabeth S. Haldane (Cambridge, CUP, 1968), i. 144.

The opening lines stimulate the reader's curiosity, a desire to know more, that is then confirmed and indeed reinforced by the subsequent statement which sees Descartes, like Moscarda, go on to make his radical epistemological uncertainty the basis for a revolutionary experiment: 'I realized that for once I had to raze everything in my life, down again to the very bottom, so as to begin again from the first foundations, if I wanted to establish anything firm and lasting in the sciences.'[14] Where the two books sharply diverge is that the narrator of *Meditations* only comments about himself in the context of the moment at which he is writing (he is seated, in his dressing gown, by the fireside) and he remains silent on the subject of his personal history, while Vitangelo clearly believes that by providing the reader with the details of his family background, the information not only helps explain who he is, or, as he would see it, who he is not, but also goes some way to making the exact nature of his quest comprehensible to the outsider.

I have referred earlier to the methodological difficulty of getting a readership to listen to the message when the messenger is presented as potentially 'unsound'. But there is a further interesting point of tension within the work which concerns on this occasion the relationship between message and genre. An autobiographical narrative involves a process of remembering, but also of selection, sifting through the events of a life to identify those instances that the autobiographer finds relevant to her or his purpose—otherwise he or she will reach the impasse experienced by Tristam Shandy. (Of all the narrative devices at work in Lawrence Sterne's novel, it is the art of digression that Pirandello was to exploit to greatest effect in Vitangelo Moscarda's story.) Recollection is not a total return to the past, a reliving moment by moment, second by second; it is the past as it presents itself in the present, as it presents itself now. The writing is performative as well as interpretative in that it does not mirror so much as construct an identity. This creates an interesting tension within Vitangelo's narrative. On the one hand we see him engaged in a process of dismantling himself so that he is effectively freed to live purely in and for the present; to do this he has to work towards a position where he

---

[14] René Descartes, *The Philosophical Works of Descartes*, tr. Elizabeth S. Haldane (Cambridge, CUP, 1968), i. 145.

has lost all self-awareness, that consciousness of self, the *superfluo* ('superfluous'), that blights human life. Yet as a performative act, the narrative is constructing an identity and the narrator has to draw continuously on reserves of self-consciousness to achieve his goal. In Locke's words: 'Nothing but consciousness can unite remote existences into the same person [. . .] as far as [. . .] consciousness can be extended backwards to any past action or thought, so far reaches the identity of that person.'[15]

Actions taken by Vitangelo that at the time were construed as wilful, childish, or simply irresponsible, he now reclaims, organizes, and interprets in the light of the philosophy that gave rise to them. His narrative reproduces the sequence of events leading up to the trial and court-scene at the end of the book when Anna Rosa, a mutual family friend, stands accused of attempting to shoot Vitangelo in response to what she interpreted as a sexual advance on his part. Episodic and discontinuous though the narrative is, each incident contributes another layer to the reader's understanding of what has taken place, while never allowing us a full understanding of the sequence of events. Yet there is a contradiction inherent to a project which sees the narrator and protagonist divest himself of all identity and write a narrative account of it once he has successfully realized this aim, for this spiritual quest entails the undermining of that very dimension of self-awareness that is so necessary to autobiography. Although he is writing after he has shed all identity or identities, the very success of the experiment should preclude the ability to write such a narrative. Given that he has moved beyond the narcissism which allows one to sustain an awareness of one's individuality and that is so essential to the autobiographical project, and in the light of his final words ('muojo ogni attimo, io, e rinasco nuovo e senza ricordi: vivo e intero, non più in me, ma in ogni cosa fuori'[16] ('I am dying every instant, and being born anew and without memories: alive and whole, no longer in myself, but in everything outside'), it is a mystery as to how he manages to construct a narrative at all. The

---

[15] John Locke, *An Essay concerning Human Understanding* (New York, Dover, 1959), i. 458.

[16] Pirandello, *Tutti i romanzi*, ii. 902 (tr. Samuel Putnam, *One, None, and a Hundred-Thousand* (New York, Howard Fertig, 1983), 268.)

mystery is left unresolved because, unlike Mattia Pascal who introduces his story with a description of his present situation at the time of writing, Vitangelo communicates only those details that have a direct bearing on the philosophy his experiences have given rise to: his is an experiment in autobiography purged of selfhood.

Both Mattia in *Il fu Mattia Pascal* and Vitangelo in *Uno, nessuno e centomila* conduct a radical experiment with their respective identities. On the surface Mattia's appears the more far-reaching of the two in that he changes his name, habitation, family background and history, and, with surgery, his appearance, but despite all this, in and of himself he remains the same man. He is somebody else for others but not for himself. So it falls to Vitangelo to conduct the most devastating experiment in selfhood of all Pirandello's heroes; his efforts go entirely into losing every one of his identities, so making his legally recognized identity about as helpful as a label detached from a medicine bottle. By staying in the community he was born into, grew up in, and married in, he remains in their eyes the same person, the only difference is that where he was once sane he is now mad, but for himself he has in a very radical way become a different being. As somebody who manages to slough off all the social selves that had accrued to him over the years. Vitangelo's life, as we shall see shortly, presents the reader with an inversion of the traditional tale of success: from starting out, albeit in a modest way as a 'somebody' he becomes a 'nobody', just as at the beginning of the narrative he has the trappings of, if not exactly a hero, at least a protagonist. As the reader turns the pages, so Vitangelo sheds the layers until at the end of his tale he is reduced to pure textual presence. What does writing the events down achieve for either Mattia Pascal or Vitangelo Moscarda? Neither man loses the capacity to think of himself as a unitary subject—the same person over time and place—and how far this is purely the product of the act of narration itself is hard to gauge. Narration does inevitably give continuity and, through continuity, unity to the fractured self. It gives content and meaning to actions. A narrative creates a tapestry whereby each single act, however discontinuous, will be incorporated through the act of reading into a pattern whose sense is conferred retrospectively on completion of the book. It is what an author can confer on a character, when that character is not himself. As a secular thinker Pirandello would have been aware that life affords no similar privilege—we will never see our lives in their completed or finished form and once dead we are no longer in a position to make sense of our lives, although others who knew us may be.

Uno, nessuno e centomila opens on what is in itself an insignificant incident that occurred on an ordinary day in Vitangelo's life when his wife, who is standing behind him as he studies his reflection in the mirror, makes a comment about his crooked nose. As if that were not enough for a man who had hitherto considered his nose 'se non proprio bello, almeno molto decente'[17] ('if not altogether handsome, at least a very respectable nose') she goes on to list his other physical defects. After subjecting himself to a careful self-scrutiny he has to acknowledge that although he has been living with his body much longer than she, her description is the more accurate of the two. Friends and acquaintances approached by him do nothing to restore to him his former sense of well-being that came from knowing that the person he took himself to be and the person others took him to be were one and the same:

L'idea che gli altri vedevano in me uno che non ero io quale mi conoscevo; uno che essi soltanto potevano conoscere guardandomi da fuori con occhi che non erano i miei e che mi davano un aspetto destinato a restarmi sempre estraneo, pur essendo in me, pur essendo il mio per loro (un 'mio' dunque che non era per me!); una vita nella quale, pur essendo la mia per loro, io non potevo penetrare, quest'idea non mi diede più requie.[18]

The idea that others saw in me one that was not the I whom I knew, one whom they alone could know, as they looked at me from without, with eyes that were not my own, eyes that conferred upon me an aspect destined to remain always foreign to me, although it was one that was in me, one that was my own to them (a 'mine' that is to say, that was not for me!)—a life into which, although it was my own, I had no power to penetrate—this idea gave me no rest.

In common with all of Pirandello's characters, Vitangelo knows that a condition of living is that we cannot watch

---

[17] Ibid. 39 (tr. Putnam, 13).
[18] Ibid. 752 (tr. Putnam, 31–2).

ourselves doing it, self-recognition is always routed through the eyes of others, a process that begins with the mother, so that his wife's failure to reflect back the identity he thought was his has devastating consequences. It is a conundrum that another famous theorist of the non-essentialist self comes up against soon after beginning his own experiment in autobiography. In *Roland Barthes par Roland Barthes* the author reconstructs his childhood in a series of photographs of family, friends, and places: opposite two photographs taken twenty-eight years apart stands the following text.

Mais je n'ai jamais ressemblé à cela?
—Comment le savez-vous? Que'est-ce que ce 'vous' auquel vous ressembleriez ou ne ressembleriez pas? Où le prendre? A quel étalon morphologique ou expressif? Où est votre corps de vérité? Vous êtes le seul à ne pouvoir jamais vous voir qu'en image, vous ne voyez jamais vos yeux, sinon abêtis par le regard qu'ils posent sur le miroir ou sur l'objectif (il m'intéressait seulement de voir mes yeux quand ils te regardent): même et surtout pour votre corps, vous êtes condamné à l'imaginaire.[19]

'But I never looked like that!'—How do you know? What is the 'you' you might or might not have looked like? Where do you find it—by which morphological or expressive calibration? Where is your authentic body? You are the only one who can never see yourself except as an image: you never see your eyes unless they are dulled by the gaze they rest upon the mirror or the lens (I am interested in seeing my eyes only when they look at you): even and especially for your body, you are condemned to the repertoire of images.

The use of the second person plural in French, *vous*, intensifies the ambiguities of the occasion. By its presence, the text creates the space for an empirical reader to recognize and appropriate the experience as her own, while at the same time it emphasizes the split between the two Roland Barthes: the one who functions as subject of the gaze and the other who is object of the gaze, and who also looks back. *Vous*, whether intended to be understood as a plural 'you' or as formal address, augments the uncanniness of the encounter. For his part, Vitangelo will have to wait until he is alone in the house before he can study his own mirror image.

---

[19] *Roland Barthes par Roland Barthes* (Paris, Seuil, 1975), 40 (tr. Richard Howard (London, Macmillan, 1977), 36).

His madness, as he calls it, is still in its infancy—'nella vispa infanzia della mia follia'[20] ('the sprightly infancy of my folly')— and what at this stage is its principal manifestation, an obsessional need to track down all his mirror images, has until now been inhibited by the need to keep a lookout for his wife in case she notices his extraordinary behaviour. When shortly before the end of book 1, his wife, who has remained at his side like a shadow, leaves the house to visit a sick friend, her absence frees him to stand, without her mediation, in front of the mirror and reflect upon the image that he sees before him. In this, the most intimate and solitary of moments, he realizes that he is not alone. It is a crucial moment for it will represent his definitive break with a subjective and coherent identity, registered in the chilling words that conclude the episode: 'E guardai nello specchio il mio primo riso da matto' ('And I studied in the mirror my first madman's laugh'). It is now that Vitangelo, like Mattia before him, discovers that the home, far from being in Pirandello's words a 'rifugio' ('refuge') or 'nido' ('nest') away from the public eye, is the place where masculine selfhood first breaks down. The house often has negative connotations in Pirandello's work. Both Silvia Roncella in the novel *Suo marito* and Stefano Giogli in the story 'Stefano Giogli, uno e due' undergo the profoundly alienating experience of finding themselves living lives which, in ways both visible (the décor of the houses they live in for instance) and invisible (preferences and traits attributed to them by husband or wife), have no bearing on their own knowledge of themselves, their interests, or choices. In other words all that they have taken to be part of themselves is denied recognition by the other. The home Silvia's husband has set up for her 'non le pareva sua, ma estranea, fatta non per viverci come finora ella aveva vissuto, ma per rappresentarvi d'ora in poi, sempre e per forza una commedia; anche davanti a se stessa'[21] ('seemed not hers, but something outside of her, made not to live in as she had lived up to now but to put on a play, henceforth forever more, of necessity, even in front of herself'). Stefano Giogli similarly after three months of marriage returns to his former, less enraptured self to find himself living in a neat little detached house

---

[20] Pirandello, *Tutti i romanzi*, ii. 751 (tr. Putnam, 30).
[21] Pirandello, *Tutti i romanzi*, i. 646.

that is quite antithetical to his own tastes. Even his visitors are amazed. The house, like the city, is part of that world of artifice that stands in opposition to the countryside and it is not by accident that in his first emblematic gesture of liberation, Vitangelo cries 'Lasciamo le case, lasciamo la città' ('Let us leave the houses, let us leave the town'). When, early in the novel, Vitangelo makes his momentous discovery that there are as many Moscardas around as there are people to meet them, his actions are confined to the privacy of the home where his movements are determined by his urge to try to catch sight of his mirror image without forewarning. The question, however, remains as to what provokes that first bout of mad laughter.

A highly persuasive explanation for what has happened, or in the event has failed to happen on this occasion, is provided by Lacan in his well-known paper on the mirror stage, whose relevance to Vitangelo's condition is immediately apparent from its full title; 'Le stade du miroir comme formateur de la fonction du Je'[22] ('The Mirror Stage as Formative of the Function of the I'). According to Lacan, at about six months the child catches sight of himself in the mirror and, for the first time, experiences himself as a unified being. Although the identification with his specular image is based on the mistaken belief that the reflected image is the self, when what is taking place is really a *méconnaissance* or a misrecognition in which the mirror image which seems so self-affirming and reassuring is in fact an illusion, a trap, none the less our ability to distinguish self from other, inner from outer, subject from object, is conditional upon it. To the baby it brings an entirely illusory sense of control and mastery over its own body, which is seen for the first time as an entirety. It opens the way for the formation of the ego. Although Lacan is referring here to a specific developmental stage, one which marks out the difference between humans and animals, the term *le stade du miroir* not only carries a temporal dimension, but also encompasses what Malcolm Bowie has described as 'a stadium in which the battle of the human subject is permanently being waged'.[23] In Vitangelo's case his first laugh

---

[22] Jacques Lacan, *Écrits* (Paris, Seuil, 1966), 89–97 (tr. Alan Sheridan, *Écrits: A Selection* (London, Tavistock, 1977), 1–7). The paper was delivered at the 16th International Congress of Psychoanalysis, Zürich, 17 July 1949.

[23] Malcolm Bowie, *Lacan* (London, Fontana, 1991), 23.

as madman is a recognition of his failure to identify himself in the mirror image. He should be able to respond by saying 'That's me'. Instead he finds himself looking at: 'Un povero corpo mortificato, in attesa che qualcuno se lo prendesse.— *Moscarda*— . . . mormorai, dopo un lungo silenzio. Non si mosse; rimase a guardarmi attonito.'[24] ('A poor, mortified body, waiting for someone to take it. "*Moscarda*," I murmured, after a long silence. It did not move, but stood gazing at me in astonishment.') The moment registers Vitangelo's inability to identify himself in another being and, with it, his rejection of other people's projections of him. The experience of physical and psychical unity through which a continuous sense of selfhood is acquired is not achieved in this episode, and with the identificatory mechanism having failed, Vitangelo is in no position to be able to assimilate or recognize himself in other people's reflections of him. Just as the mirror stage is a spatial phenomenon, the body image is formed at a distance, through the eye of an imagined other. In Pirandello's representation of the attainment of selfhood, the visual image, the gaze, is crucial. The relationship between identity and image and the influence Pirandello's insight has on his theatre (and I am thinking in particular of his representations of women protagonists in the plays of the 1920s) will be examined in Chapter 8.[25]

By rejecting his mirror image, Vitangelo has taken his first step in shedding all those aspects of life that contain, fix, freeze, and define each and every one of us. In this respect the

---

[24] Pirandello, *Tutti i romanzi*, ii. 756 (tr. Putnam, 37).

[25] In an interview with Adriano Tilgher in 1921, Pirandello had given the philosopher permission to define his theatre as 'teatro dello specchio' ('theatre of the mirror'). This is how Pirandello presents the concept: 'Quando uno vive, vive e non si vede. Orbene, fate che si veda, nell'atto di vivere, in preda alle sue passioni, ponendogli uno specchio davanti: o resta attonito e sbalordito del suo stesso aspetto, o torce gli occhi per non vedersi, o sdegnato tira uno sputo alla sua immagine, o irato avventa un pugno per infrangerla; e se piangeva, non può più piangere; e se rideva, non può più ridere, e che so io. Insomma, nasce un guaio per forza. Questo guaio è il mio teatro.' ('When you live, you live and you do not see yourself. Well, just imagine that by placing a mirror in front of you, you see yourself in the act of living, in the grip of your emotions: either you are left astonished and stunned by your own image, or you look the other way to avoid seeing yourself, or in scorn, you spit on your own image, or in anger you raise a fist to smash it; and if you were crying, you can no longer cry; and if you were laughing, you can no longer laugh, and so on. In short, there is always a problem. That problem is my theatre.') An important difference between text, be it narrative or play, and performance is that the reader, unlike the theatre-goer, cannot return the gaze.

language Lacan uses to describe the mirror image is revealing in the way it too emphasizes fixity:

C'est que la forme totale du corps par quoi le sujet devance dans un mirage la maturation de sa puissance, ne lui est donnée que comme *Gestalt*, c'est à dire dans une extériorité où certes cette forme est-elle plus constituante que constituée mais où surtout elle lui apparaît dans un relief de stature qui la fige et sous une symétrie qui l'inverse, en opposition à la turbulence de mouvements dont il s'éprouve l'animer. Ainsi cette *Gestalt* dont la prégnance doit etre considérée comme liée à l'espèce, bien que son style moteur soit encore méconnaissable—par ces deux aspects de son apparition symbolise la permanence mentale du *je* en même temps qu'elle préfigure sa destination aliénante; elle est grosse encore des correspondances qui unissent le *je* à la statue où l'homme se projette comme aux fantômes qui le dominent, à l'automate enfin où dans un rapport ambigu tend à s'achever le monde de sa fabrication.[26]

The fact is that the total form of the body by which the subject anticipates in a mirage the maturation of his power is given to him only as *Gestalt*, that is to say, in an exteriority in which this form is certainly more constituent than constituted, but in which it appears to him above all in a contrasting size (*un relief de stature*) that fixes it and in a symmetry that inverts it, in contrast with the turbulent movements that the subject feels are animating him. Thus, this *Gestalt*—whose pregnancy should be regarded as bound up with the species, though its motor style remains scarcely recognizable—by these two aspects of its appearance, symbolizes the mental permanence of the *I*, at the same time as it prefigures its alienating destination; it is still pregnant with the correspondences that unite the *I* with the statue in which man projects himself, with the phantoms that dominate him, or with the automaton in which, in an ambiguous relation, the world of his own making tends to find completion.

In the word-play which is so important to Lacan's expository technique, the mirror (*miroir*) in the first line becomes *mirage*—i.e. an illusion by which one appears to see something that is not actually there—reflecting a *Gestalt*, namely a totalized, complete external image of the subject. The fixity and exteriority of the *imago* is reaffirmed by the use of such words as 'statue', 'phantom' and 'automaton' which are 'in contrast with the turbulent movements that the subject feels are animating him'. Malcolm

[26] Lacan, *Écrits*, 91 (tr. Sheridan, 2–3).

Bowie describes how in the process the 'alienating destination' of the 'I' is such that the individual is permanently in discord with himself: 'the "I" is tirelessly intent upon freezing a subjective process that cannot be frozen introducing stagnation into the mobile field of human desire'.[27] Lacan's *Gestalt* that passes itself off as, and is accepted as being, the self, differs little from the myriad forms that give an identity to the Pirandellian protagonist. In what remains a very valuable, albeit reductive and schematic analysis of Pirandello's work, Adriano Tilgher discusses the fundamental dichotomy of life (what Pirandello calls 'il movimento vitale') and form, which he argues informs all Pirandello's writing, in terms of what he describes as 'a basic dualism': 'On the one hand, blind, dumb Life will keep darkly flowing in eternal restlessness through each moment's renewals. On the other hand, a world of crystallized Forms, a system of constructions, that will strive to dam up and compress that everflowing turmoil.'[28]

The imagery has changed, the terms in which it is couched are different, but the problem is the same: if the mechanism fails by which one accepts that the 'form' (in Pirandellian terms), the *Gestalt* (in Lacanian imagery), is oneself, how does one function? For both Lacan and Pirandello the joke is that identity pivots on a fiction; what makes the joke bitter is that we cannot live our lives without that fiction. Vitangelo Moscarda, it is true, succeeds, but he does not succeed as Vitangelo Moscarda; he succeeds because he has managed to stop being Vitangelo Moscarda, he is no longer 'himself'. His withdrawal from society is registered by a loss of name. Without a name he has no history or biography for he no longer has a continuity of identity through past, present, and future that can be construed as such. Existence is now coterminous with the present, the moment of being. In the following passage he suggests that names are appropriate for the dead, who, now that life is over, can be fixed by a name:

Nessun nome. Nessun ricordo oggi del nome di ieri; del nome d'oggi, domani. Se il nome è la cosa; se un nome è in noi il concetto d'ogni

---

[27] Bowie, *Lacan*, 25.

[28] Adriano Tilgher, 'Life versus Form', in Glauco Cambon (ed.), *Pirandello: A Collection of Critical Essays* (Englewood Cliffs, NJ, Prentice-Hall, 1967), 21.

cosa posta fuori di noi; e senza nome non si ha il concetto, e la cosa resta in noi come cieca, non distinta e non definita; ebbene, questo che portai tra gli uomini ciascuno lo incida, epigrafe funeraria, sulla fronte di quella immagine con cui gli apparvi, e la lasci in pace e non ne parli più. Non è altro che questo, epigrafe funeraria, un nome. Conviene ai morti. A chi ha concluso. Io sono vivo e non concludo. La vita non conclude. E non sa di nomi, la vita.[29]

No name. No memory of yesterday's name today: of today's name tomorrow. If the name is the thing, if a name in us is the concept of everything that is situated within us, if without a name there is no concept, and the thing remains blindly indistinct and undefined within us, very well, then, let men take that name which I once bore and engrave it as an epitaph on the brow of that pictured me that they beheld; let them leave it there in peace, and let them not speak of it again. For a name is no more than that, an epitaph. Something befitting the dead. One who has reached a conclusion. I am alive and I reach no conclusion. Life reaches no conclusion. Nor does it know anything of names.

With these words Vitangelo speaks as a man who has come through; he speaks on behalf of the many Pirandellian heroes who were never able to reach this point, but remain trapped in the reflecting mirrors created by family, friends, colleagues, and even complete strangers. But to do so he has divested himself of everything that was once part of him, including his wife, his home, and his business, and even the name, 'Moscarda', has finally been emptied of content. With no external self to look back at him, he stops checking in the mirror. The psychological distance that he has travelled between the beginning and the end of his narrative becomes apparent when, in the closing pages, he describes his appearance in court where the defendant, Anna Rosa, stands accused of attempting to kill him. He attributes her acquittal to the general hilarity provoked by his appearance among those present (he is kitted out in a beret, clogs, and a workman's blue overshirt provided by the hostel). The courtroom is popular in theatre and cinema as well as narrative because of its dramatic potential, but also because of its specularity; the different parties are called upon to perform before judge and jury. What might have brought a sense of shame, social embarrassment, and a 'loss of face' leaves

---

[29] Pirandello, *Tutti i romanzi*, i. 901 (tr. Putnam, 266–7).

Vitangelo untouched because the 'audience' can no longer reflect a self, an *imago*, back to him. His indifference to the effect his appearance has on others demonstrates that he has moved beyond the rules binding his community. Not only is he now immune to the reactions of others, but he has also eradicated the presence of the other in himself—in other words he has ceased to internalize the codes and prescriptions of his society.

It is impossible to determine the degree of alienation experienced by Vitangelo. There is however a marked difference depending on whether one understands Moscarda to be addressing his multiplying selves, in which case the narrative acquires an hallucinatory, disassociated quality, or takes the 'you' to refer to his audience, in which case the narrative assumes a more monologic and, indeed, at times didactic tone. On reaching the end of the book, it is not at all clear to the empirical reader when or how Vitangelo wrote his story or, therefore, for whom. Renato Barilli in his analysis of the text refers to Vitangelo as the 'avvocato della nuova morale' ('advocate for the new morality') engaged in a long debate with his readers trying to persuade us to see reason, in other words urging us to adopt his perspective. Barilli has caught the narrative tone perfectly in the following passage:

Il tono generale è quello di un dibattito che il protagonista, avvocato della nuova morale, tiene in prima persona al pubblico dei lettori, con il solito, ben noto spirito causidico. Non si parla quindi di monologo interiore, se in tale dizione l'oggettivo porta inevitabilmente a pensare ad un'esibizione di interiorità e di introspezionismo, qui inesistenti (giacchè i motivi anche più privati vengono sbandierati alla luce del sole, addirittura declamati); e tanto meno di 'corrente di coscienza', in quanto non c'è proprio nessun proposito di trascrizione diretta, asintattica delle associazioni psichiche: le regole della sintassi sono più che rispettate, come si conviene a chi ha scelto di muoversi a livello di mezzi rettorici.[30]

The overall tone is that of a speech given by the protagonist, the advocate of the new morality in his own person to the reading public in the customary well-known courtroom spirit. We cannot therefore talk of interior monologue, if by this term we are inevitably led to a display of inwardness and introspection which here do not exist

---

[30] Renato Barilli, *Pirandello: Una rivoluzione culturale* (Milan, Mursia, 1986), 131.

(because even the most private topics are flagged up in broad daylight); still less can we speak of 'stream of consciousness', in that there is absolutely no suggestion of direct unstructured transcription of psychological associations: the rules of syntax are fully obeyed, as is fitting for someone who has chosen to operate at a level that engages with rhetorical devices.

But Barilli has taken it for granted that the audience is made up entirely of extradiegetic readers. By assuming that Vitangelo is addressing a reader outside the text, the implication is that the journey he undertook has, despite far-reaching changes of lifestyle and philosphy, left him in himself more or less as he was, just purged of the inauthentic selves that had accrued in him over the years. According to my reading, the consequences of our protagonist's insight are more radical than that: modernist terminology such as 'interior monologue' and 'stream of consciousness' deployed in the above quotation still suggest a unitary personality, and there is an important distinction to be made between the subtle descriptions of the fine shifts of personality that we undergo according to the people and circumstances we meet (such as we find in modernist writers like Proust, Svevo, Woolf, or Joyce) and the solitary road that Pirandello takes us down. I would suggest that Vitangelo has moved beyond that stage to an awareness of the multiplicity of selves that each of us potentially contains. So that while he could be addressing an extradiegetic reader, he could equally well be addressing himself—the self that his wife at the outset of the account had denied him. The choice of an alter ego as addressee has a long history in Pirandello's writings which can be traced back to a letter he wrote to his future wife Antonietta dated 7 January 1894 and is then developed in the early short story 'Dialoghi tra il Gran Me e il piccolo me'[31] ('Dialogues between the Big Me and the little me'). The first three sections were written over two years between 1895 and 1897, and the fourth and final section was added in 1906. It was included in the appendix to *Novelle per un anno,* along with other stories omitted by Pirandello when he originally prepared the collection and although this can only be speculation, it is possible that he did not consider the work to be a story at all. The four

[31] See Gaspare Giudice, *Luigi Pirandello* (Turin, UTET, 1963), 172–3.

episodes are each prefaced by a brief paragraph which sets the scene much in the style of his stage directions, while the narratives themselves are dialogues that the protagonist's two squabbling selves conduct with each other. Where in the first three sections the text is made up only of speech, in the final episode the speakers are identified by name, but at no point do the 'Big Me' and the 'little me' unite to form a unitary voice and self.

While the catalyst that gave rise to a course of action that will eventually take Vitangelo Moscarda to the hospice outside town was the moment in front of the mirror when his wife failed to confirm his mirror image, the crucial determinant had been in place long before that and it is to be found in the relationship between father and son.[32] In the section on naming in the previous chapter, I linked Vitangelo's aversion to his name to the barely suppressed hostility he feels for his father; now is the moment to look more closely at how Vitangelo experiences his relationship with a dead father in whose shadow he continues to live. Looked at through the eyes of the community who always think of him in terms of his father, he is both financially and sexually a failure. Even the house he lived in, built by his father after his wife, Vitangelo's mother, had died, stands as a visual reminder of who he is and how he has failed to carry his father's authority. Left unfinished, as it was at the time of his father's death, once Vitangelo became proprietor the courtyard has gradually been taken over by a group of down-and-outs—an invasion of personal space that would never have occurred in his father's day. But it is when he starts attacking the source of the family's wealth carefully built up by his father, by meddling in the affairs of the family bank from which he derives his wealth but within whose organization he has no role, that he gets the measure of just how powerless he is. The first time we

---

[32] Pirandello presented his own relationship with his father as difficult and added that it was an important aspect of his own artistic development, Gindice, *Pirandello*, 31: 'Piccino mi tornava difficile [comunicare] persino con mia madre; e con mio padre m'appariva impossibile non già mentre mi ci preparavo, ma all'atto della prova, che il più delle volte finiva miserabilmente. Molto debbo a lui, come artista, per le angosce spasimose di quei momenti.' ('As a child I found it difficult [to communicate] even with my mother; and with my father it seemed impossible not so much while I was getting myself ready to do so, but in the moment when I tried, and most of the time it was a miserable failure. As an artist, I owe a great deal to him for the spasms of anguish that I experienced on those occasions.')

see Vitangelo in action (other than walking his wife's dog) is when he sets in motion plans to evict his father's eccentric tenant, Marco di Dio. To do so he finds himself having to steal the documents that he thought were by rights his. An earlier challenge over Marco's future from Firbo, one of his father's two right-hand men, who behind the façade of deference are actually responsible for running the bank, elicits from Vitangelo the response: 'T'avverto, caro mio, che non sono mio padre'[33] ('I must warn you, dear Sir, that I am not my father'). A statement whose truth becomes apparent even to Vitangelo himself on a subsequent meeting with Firbo when he discovers that it is one thing to have a name, another to be master of that name. Although the bank bears his name, both he and it are his father's creatures:

—Oh guarda un po'! Non sono padrone del mio nome? del nome di mio padre?
—No, perchè è negli atti di costituzione della banca, quel nome; è il nome della banca: creatura di tuo padre, tal quale come te! E ne porta il nome con lo stesso stessissimo tuo diritto![34]

'Stop and think a minute! Am I not the proprietor of my own name? Of my father's name?'

'No, because that name is part of the bank's charter; it is the name of the bank, which is your father's creature as much as you are! And it bears his name by the very same right!'

But it is not only the two men who have replaced his father in the management of the bank who remind him of this; in a wonderful piece of street theatre the onlookers who gather to observe Marco di Dio's eviction comment among themselves, 'Più schifoso del padre!' ('Even more digusting than the father!'), but when the lawyer announces that the tenant is being given another property to replace the shack, the crowd's attitude switches from belligerence to bewilderment.[35] This gesture, which is so out of character precisely because it is not consistent with his father's behaviour, earns him for the first time the label 'pazzo'. Mad because, as he says in the conclusion to the chapter, his behaviour is at odds with what people thought of him. Living within the structures and lifestyle estab-

---

[33] Pirandello, *Uno, nessuno e centomila*, ii. 828 (tr. Putnam, 193).
[34] Ibid. 856.   [35] Ibid. 832.

lished for him by his father (his wife was also chosen by his father),[36] he endures a double humiliation that comes both from the ill-concealed scorn of fellow-citizens for a son who lives off his father and his own newly acquired realization that his father in his day was viewed with contempt, seen not as a banker (*banchiere*), but as a moneylender (*usurajo*).

If one were to return to the Lacanian reading begun earlier, Vitangelo's rebellion suggests a failure or refusal on his part to enter the symbolic. The mirror stage anticipates the subject's assumption of the signifying position of 'I' within language. With the acquisition of an identity comes access to the signifying systems and codes of the social worlds. But this is associated with the authority of paternal logocentric law which guarantees identity and orders experience. We are back with Vitangelo's problematic relationship with his father and paternal authority:

C'est dans le *nom du père* qu'il nous faut reconnaître le support de la fonction symbolique qui, depuis l'orée des temps historiques, identifie sa personne à la figure de la loi.[37]

It is in *the name of the father* that we must recognize the support of the symbolic function which from the dawn of history, has identified the person with the figure of the law.

It could be argued that what Vitangelo aspires to is a return to the imaginary where the self is undifferentiated from the world. The difficulty for a writer is that it is a pre-verbal order, which again raises the question of how, if Vitangelo has indeed successfully re-entered this state by the end of the book, he has written the narrative we have just read. The symbolic grants a conditional identity and with it entry into language, the imaginary does not.

Vitangelo Moscarda himself theorizes throughout his narrative; events are presented not in relationship to the light they throw on his own psyche but in terms of the succession of

---

[36] Just as Vitangelo's relationship to his father is structured around power and possession, so is his wife's relationship to him. She has created in her Gengé an ideal husband—docile, malleable, controllable—exactly what she wanted in light of the other attribute he brought with him to the marriage, his father's wealth. It is an arranged marriage, arranged for him by his father. The only disappointment is in an area where his father cannot intervene: the failure to produce a child.

[37] Lacan, *Écrits*, 157–8 (tr. Sheridan, 67).

revelations or insights that accompany them. He steers well clear of psychological speculation. Simmel's description of Goethe as a man for whom 'everything factual is already theory' could well be used of Moscarda. Although Vitangelo includes enough information in his narrative to allow us to see that his life is inextricably bound up with his father, his own interpretation of events presents an ontological quest for authenticity without drawing attention to the deeply problematic father–son relationship that gave rise to it. His journey takes him along a route which carries him further and further away from his father's influence until he sets off down the one path where he can finally shake himself free altogether: the road to madness. The desire for authenticity, to be 'himself', is inextricably caught up with his need to have nothing of his father in him— but even his idleness, the only characteristic that he considers to be truly his, owes something to his father because it is his father's money that permits it. At the very end of his narrative Vitangelo takes refuge in a newly built hospice in the country-side beyond the reach of the city; it has been built with the money from the sale of his father's bank, but the irony cuts both ways in that he has brought his father's business to a close, but his new life has been paid for by his father's estate. There is a moment in the narrative when Vitangelo acknowleges the influence exercised by his father, but he tries to limit it to the importance that his family has in the eyes of others:

La storia della mia famiglia! La storia della mia famiglia nel mio paese: non ci pensavo, ma era in me, questa storia, per gli altri; io ero uno, l'ultimo di questa famiglia; e ne avevo in me, nel corpo, lo stampo e chi sa in quante abitudini d'atti e di pensieri, a cui non avevo mai riflettuto, ma che gli altri riconoscevano chiaramente in me, nel mio modo di camminare, di ridere, di salutare.[38]

My family history! My family's history in the province. I had never given it a thought; yet that history, for others, was in me; I was an individual, the last of that family; I bore the mark of it in me, in my body, and who could say in how many habitual thoughts and actions, on which I had never reflected, but which it was obvious that others already recognized in me, in my way of walking, of smiling, of exchanging a greeting.

---

[38] Pirandello, *Uno, nessuno e centomila*, ii. 789 (tr. Putnam, 92).

Once he has begun to see the extent to which his father continues beyond the grave to exercise control over his own life, all his effort goes into undoing his father's work. Starting out as a man of substance, his place assured in the community by virtue of his being the only son of a successful businessman, Vitangelo Moscarda's chosen path through life will lead him to a 'nameless' mendicant existence in a hospice outside town. The hospice is built with his father's money; erected by the son, it is a symbol of everything the father stood against.

Despite the singularity of Vitangelo's story, the figure he cuts of the 'hopeless' or 'useless' son is one he shares with a 'number of other late nineteenth-, early twentieth-century literary protagonists who do not fit the Napoleonic mode. Earlier nineteenth-century realist fiction had offered the reader many examples of the self-made hero: young men such as Rastignac in *La Comédie humaine* and Sorel in *Le Rouge et le noir* who rise rapidly in the world from inauspicious beginnings. Moscarda in *Uno, nessuno e centomila* takes a road that leads in the opposite direction. From riches to rags, from being a somebody (in that telling phrase, the traditional hero sets out to 'make a name for himself') to becoming a nobody or the hundred thousand of the title. Far from being seen as a sign of failure, this is in Vitangelo's terms symptomatic of a success all the more precious because it is without materialist associations. Both Vitangelo and Mattia in *Il fu Mattia Pascal* belong to a literary generation that has reacted against the entrepreneurial political or social ambitions associated with post-Napoleonic heroes. They are, though, anti-heroes of a very specific type: defined in Italian cultural history as the *inetti*, the term is used to describe the main attribute of the anti-hero who, while alienated from the society he is part of, none the less does not follow a course of open rebellion. Detached from his own life, he feels equally dissociated from the world of politics and the ideals of the Risorgimento. The son rebels, as Barilli has put it:

non con forza e violenza, perchè questo significherebbe uccidere il padre per sostituirsi a lui, per ereditarne le più tipiche funzioni e prerogative, ma al contrario con docilità e apparente acquiescenza[39]

---

[39] Barilli, *Pirandello*, 131. He continues: 'Il figlio infatti, in regime psicanalitico, può sperare di condurre a termine una vera rivolta solo volendosi diverso dal padre,

not by force and with violence, because that would mean killing the father so as to take his place, to inherit from him his most obvious duties and prerogatives, but on the contrary meekly and with apparent acquiescence.

In terms of background he is likely to be the son of a businessman who has been successful in an all-male world of commerce and who now, probably unconsciously, connives to keep his son financially dependent on him. Despite the differences that growing up in a Jewish environment in Trieste and a Catholic background in Richieri bring with them, there are interesting similarities in the case histories of Vitangelo Moscarda and Zeno Cosini, narrator and protagonist of Italo Svevo's *La coscienza di Zeno*, two novels that were published within three years of each other. The protagonists' respective fathers have ensured that the running of the family business is transferred upon their death to trusted managers, while at the same time arranging that a substantial part of the revenue is received by their son, who is free to pass the time dabbling in relatively harmless pursuits. So the son is left well provided for, but remains financially dependent on his father. He is expected to procreate to ensure the continuation of the family name and in this area Zeno is successful, while Vitangelo is signally unsuccessful. (One inevitable consequence of these arrangements is the amount of empty time available to the protagonists to devote to self-absorption. Moscarda at 28 has no work, no family responsibilities, and a wife to ensure the smooth running of domestic life.)

The presence of the *inetto* is neither restricted to a Catholic culture, as the reference to *La coscienza di Zeno* has made clear, nor is he only to be found within Italy. The most poignant representation of the figure of the ineffectual son comes with Franz Kafka's self-portrait in his 'Letter to My Father'. Written

uscendo fuori dalla logica del dominio che si incentra nell'istanza parentale: egli dunque 'farà finta' di seguire i buoni precetti del genitore volti a ricavarne un 'dritto', un lottatore nella vita, ma in realtà procurerà di volersi inetto, incapace di scegliere'. ('From a psychoanalytic point of view the son can only hope to bring his rebellion to a successful conclusion by wishing himself to be different from his father and escaping from the logic of domination that is focused on the demand represented by the parent. So he will "pretend" to follow his father's good advice which is meant to make him "upright", a fighter in life, but actually he will try to make himself inept, someone who cannot choose, someone for whom choice is impossible.')

in November 1919, it was never delivered to the person to whom it was addressed. If anyone had ever considered the *inetto* to be purely a literary stereotype, here is the evidence to the contrary. The letter-writer lists his father's attributes as including 'strength, health, appetite, loudness of voice, eloquence, self-satisfaction, worldly dominance, endurance, presence of mind', while of himself he writes that even if he had been brought up away from his father 'I should probably still have become a weakly, timid, hesitant, restless person'. Nor are the distinctions between father and son limited to character; physically too the son lacks his father's masculinity: 'There was I, skinny, weakly, slight, you strong, tall, broad.'[40]

As Kafka's letter makes clear, it is the father who provides the yardstick by which his son is found wanting, but what is the mother's role in the formation of her 'inadequate' son? Here it seems to be a question of her presence rather than what she actually does to her offspring that is important. In both *Uno, nessuno e centomila* and *La coscienza di Zeno* the mother seems more akin to an older sister than an autonomous adult figure, an impression that is accentuated, in both cases, by her early death. In *Il fu Mattia Pascal* she long outlives her husband, but here too she never really grows up and remains, to her sister-in-law's despair, the helpless young girl that she was at the time of her marriage. Adored by her son (we have seen how, throughout Pirandello's fictions, the maternal mother who devotes herself to her children with selfless disregard for her own welfare and health is revered), she remains completely unworldly, innocent, and trusting, attributes which permit the estate manager to cheat the family with impunity of most of what they possess. The same word, *inetta*, is also used to refer to Mattia's mother's disastrous failure to look after the family inheritance, but it is rare to see it used of a woman. When at the end of his tale Mattia returns to his birthplace, he moves into his aunt Scolastica's house, where he sleeps 'nello stesso letto in cui morì la povera mamma mia'[41] ('in the same bed as the one my poor mother died in'). Both Zeno's and Vitangelo's mothers die when they are still young, so any description of them is nostalgic

[40] Franz Kafka, 'Letter to my Father', in *Wedding Preparations in the Country and Other Stories* (Harmondsworth, Penguin, 1982), 30–76.
[41] Pirandello, *Tutti i romanzi*, i. 577.

and their sons remain wedded to their memory; Zeno even manages in effect to 'marry' his mother. At an early stage in his self-analysis he recalls an occasion when his mother shielded him as he lay on the sofa with her from his father's anger about a cigar that had gone missing (the child was at this stage taking and smoking his father's cigarette and cigar butts). It is her smile that his memory dwells on—a smile which he will experience again, years later, on the lips of his wife.

Vitangelo's circumstances are a little different; not only did his mother die when he was very young, but his father chose to escape the memories of her by having a new house built for himself and his son, and it is to this house that Vitangelo's wife comes to live. It would appear that the memories he holds of his father are different in intensity from the memories his father held of his mother:

Io abitavo con mia moglie la casa che mio padre s'era fatta costruire dopo la morte immatura di mia madre, per levarsi da quella dov'era vissuta con lei, piena di cocentissimi ricordi.[42]

I was living with my wife in the house that my father had had built after my mother's premature death, because he wished to move out of the one in which he had lived with her, which was full of harrowing memories.

Not only would it be hard to disagree with Zeno's analyst in *La coscienza di Zeno*, who tells his patient that he is suffering from an Oedipus complex, even allowing for the twists and turns of this most duplicitous of narratives, but the very characteristics that give rise to the diagnosis are markedly present in both Mattia and Vitangelo. Whereas neither Vitangelo nor Zeno have to renounce their incestuous desire for their mother because she dies when they are very young, Mattia need never experience rivalry with his father, who died when he was 4 and was largely absent from his life before then. In a letter Freud wrote to Fliess on 15 October 1897, he refers to the Oedipal complex as 'a universal event in early childhood'. It is none the less interesting that so often in the writing of Umbertine Italy one encounters this particular configuration of 'unsuccessful' masculinity that is encapsulated in the figure of the *inetto*. In Mattia Pascal's case, the critic Renato Barilli has identified a

[42] Pirandello, *Tutti i romanzi*, ii. 762.

new, psychoanalytic form of *inettitudine* which has been grafted on to an older, sociologically oriented manifestation of the condition, which he links in turn to a prevalently Sicilian topos whereby 'Mattia rientrerebbe nell'ambito dei possidenti terrieri destinati per incuria a dilapidare il patrimonio (nel senso letterale dei beni ereditati dal padre)'[43] ('Mattia is one of those landowners destined through neglect to squander their patrimony (in the literal sense of belongings inherited from the father)').

What Pirandello sets out to do with Mattia Pascal and Vitangelo Moscarda is to salvage them as figures of failed masculinity so that by the end of their respective stories, they have earned for themselves the right to join a select group of male protagonists in Pirandello's fictions who, in terms of the authority with which they speak and the tangential social position they hold, enjoy a special status. The Pirandellian hero is a character who in some sense has come through and has created for himself a life which, whether lived within the community he grew up in or not, is detached from the collective set of beliefs that works as that society's social glue. He finds himself at a remove from his former world: Mattia in a deconsecrated church turned library that nobody visits, Vitangelo in a hospice for the destitute that lies beyond the city.

---

[43] Barilli, *Pirandello*, 111.

6

Pirandello's Philosophers

> Chi ha capito il giuoco, non riesce più a ingannarsi: ma chi non riesce più a ingannarsi non può più prendere nè gusto nè piacere alla vita. Così è.
>
> (He who has understood the game can no longer deceive himself: but he who is no longer able to deceive himself can neither have an appetite for, nor take pleasure in life. That's how it is.)
>
> (Luigi Pirandello, *Lettera autobiografica*)

In all, Pirandello wrote three first person novels where a male narrator charts the circumstances of a life made exemplary by the insights he has gained from his experiences. The previous two chapters followed closely Mattia Pascal's and Vitangelo Moscarda's careers through their respective narratives. The third of the male protagonists is a cameraman who once worked in the nascent film industry in Rome and whose memoirs appear in the form of seven notebooks collectively called *Quaderni di Serafino Gubbio, operatore* (*The Notebooks of Serafino Gubbio, Cameraman*).[1] Looked at collectively, it is striking how removed these 'authors' are from the traditional preoccupations of fictional autobiography: the three protagonists have each undergone an experience which may appear to be quite without significance, but which has brought in its wake an unflinching clarity of vision such as to ensure that they cannot resume their former lives. While the act of writing postdates the crisis, taking place after their withdrawal from society and their previous existences, they each begin their respective narratives

---

[1] *Quaderni di Serafino Gubbio* was first published in instalments in *Nuova Antologia* between 1 June and 16 Aug. 1915 with the title *Si gira* . . . Each of the 'notebooks' was described as a *fascicolo* ('file'). It retained the title *Si gira* . . . when it was published as one volume the following year. The title was changed when the 3rd rev. edn. was published by Bemporad in Florence in 1925.

with the events leading up to the watershed. Of the three narratives, Vitangelo's comes closest to a sustained monologue: it is written mainly in the present tense, but it is impossible for the reader to identify the moment of writing or indeed to know whether it emanates from a particular period in the narrator's life or, like a *journal intime*, is part of a continuing practice of writing.

All three protagonists live and write in a place which, as we have seen in the previous chapter, is both geographically and socially at a remove from their previous lives; they remain within its sphere, but only on the margins. This is at its most apparent in the case of Mattia Pascal who makes the journey back to the community in which he grew up and married, but with no intention of resuming, even were it possible, his former life. Quite the contrary, not only does he fail to cancel his name from the register of deaths, he even goes so far as to tend his own gravestone, and when the custodian of the library, Don Eligio, observes that one cannot live on the outside of society, he retorts 'che non sono affatto rientrato nè nella legge, nè nelle mie particolarità'[2] ('that I haven't stepped back within the law nor the framework of my life'). Vitangelo, as we have seen, retreats to a hospice he has had built with his own money (that is to say, his father's money) in the countryside just beyond his home town of Richieri. Serafino Gubbio's profession as cameraman in *Quaderni di Serafino Gubbio, operatore* has to some extent ensured that he has always lived on the outside watching others, both at work in the film-studio and also, as is clear from his opening words, in daily life ('Studio la gente nelle sue più ordinarie occupazioni',[3] 'I study people in their most ordinary occupations'). After impassively filming the dying moments of an actor who has been mauled by a tiger, Serafino retreats into a silence that is not the result of post-traumatic shock, but deliberately self-imposed; 'Io mi salvo, io solo, nel mio silenzio'[4] ('I have found my salvation, I alone, in my silence'). The episode has brought home to him the alienating nature of his voyeuristic relationship to the world about him.

Before we put to one side Pirandello's first person novels, I

[2] Pirandello, *Tutti i romanzi*, i. 578.
[3] Pirandello, *Tutti i romanzi*, ii. 520.
[4] Ibid. 734.

wish to introduce one other individual who makes a brief appearance in the first 'notebook' of *Quaderni di Serafino Gubbio operatore* and who, in many ways, can be seen as a precursor to Vitangelo Moscarda (the novel was written and published in the middle of the protracted period Pirandello spent working on *Uno, nessuno e centomila*). An old friend of Serafino's from Sassari, Simone Pau, 'uomo di costumi singolarissimi e spregiudicati'[5] ('a man of singular and uninhibited behaviour') escorts him on his arrival in Rome to what he refers to as his *albergo* ('hotel') but which turns out to be an *ospizio di mendicità* ('hospice for beggars') where Simone sleeps for six nights of the week—the seventh, in conformity with the rules of the institution, is spent sleeping rough on the streets. Serafino describes with care their journey to the hospice; how they set out, first leaving behind them Imperial Rome, and then Vatican Rome, before entering into an unfamiliar, disconcerting no man's land where there is only the 'vuoto orrore delle vie deserte piene di strane ombre vacillanti'[6] ('the empty horror of the deserted streets full of strange, wavering phantoms'). He goes on to explain the procedures for admittance to the establishment which include, for those thought to require it, a ritualistic cleansing in which the men have to strip naked and step into a large water tank where they are hosed down, before they are permitted to proceed to the communal dormitory. Although the occasions themselves could not be more different, the underlying symbolism of the procedure described here is analogous to the episode on the train in *Il fu Mattia Pascal* when Mattia, having just learnt of his suicide from the newspaper, decides to begin again as a different man with a new identity. In both episodes the transitional moment is presented as a *rite de passage* in which the protagonist undergoes a ritualistic 'baptism' before beginning his new life. 'Ciascuno qua si leva le proprie vergogne d'addosso, e si presenta nudo al battesimo'[7] ('Everyone here strips himself of his shame, and presents himself naked to the baptism') is how Simone Pau interprets the scene to Serafino, while Mattia similarly concludes his

[5] Pirandello, *Tutti i romanzi*, ii. 525 (*The Notebooks of Serafino Gubbio*, tr. C. K. Scott Moncrieff (London, Dedalus, 1990), 12).

[6] Ibid. 528 (tr. Scott Moncrieff, 17).

[7] Ibid. 531 (tr. Scott Moncrieff, 21).

Living with a retinue of servants in a country house in the Umbrian countryside not far from Rome, visitors to his villa step into a palace at Goslar, and a moment in history that had occurred some eight hundred years earlier when the Emperor Henry IV of Germany clashed with his rival, Pope Gregory VII. Like Sleeping Beauty's bewitched castle, the country villa inhabited by Henry and his court is frozen at a literal point in time, but unlike the fairy tale, he is not completely cut off from contemporary life. He can be visited, although only on condition that when his visitors enter his country house, they divest themselves of all signs of the present day and assume roles from the history of the Emperor Henry IV. The moment of transition from one epoch to another is visibly identified to the audience when his visitors have to get out of their everyday clothes on stage and disguise themselves in the costumes of the period. What makes Enrico's position interesting and confers on him the special status of the marginal is that, unbeknown to his peers, he is perfectly well aware that he is not Emperor Henry IV of Germany and that his guests are not who they claim to be. He sees through the masquerade, his eye penetrates his guests' historical dress and identifies the other personae that lie beyond it, and yet he is still capable of playing his role with consummate skill. His guests on the other hand believe what they see and what they have been told—that they have before them a man who thinks he is Emperor Henry IV of Germany. Unknown to them, the post-traumatic amnesia incurred by a fall from his horse during a historical cavalcade had lifted some twelve years before the visit that marks the start of the play. But Henry had decided to continue playing the same role, fully aware all the while of the intrinsic absurdity of what he was doing. He knows that in real time he is middle-aged and growing older by the minute, but in his historical set piece he remains the young Henry IV. He also knows that outside the masquerade, beyond the walls of the villa, he is powerless. The men acting as his servants are in practice his gaolers, and although he is treated with respect to his face, the doors that are opened so deferentially before him are hastily locked as soon as his back is turned. For most of the play he is a voluntary prisoner who has chosen to stay with a role that he had long before learnt was a fiction. However after he kills a rival of old called

Belcredi, he is left with no choice but to remain imprisoned in the villa and 'insanity' for life. Excluded forever from contemporary life, he can no longer occupy the marginal position he once held. He is locked out for the rest of his years.

An exploration of a similar pattern of withdrawal from the body social can be found in the work of a contemporary of Pirandello's, the Belgian ethnographer Arnold van Gennep. He first developed in 1908 in *The Rites of Passage*[13] a concept which is pertinent to the condition of Pirandello's outsiders. He demonstrates in his study how a significant number of rituals, most notably initiation rites, involve a process of withdrawal from society which divides into three stages: separation, margin or limen, and reaggregation, or what he refers to as 'preliminal', 'liminal', and 'postliminal'. What interests him in particular in his study of liminality is the relationship between change in status and spatial movement. In Pirandello's fictions characters such as Mattia, Vitangelo, or Serafino, burdened with a knowledge that most of us neither have attained nor would want to (so great are the penalties in terms of human happiness), have passed through the period of withdrawal, but in their case the revelation it gives rise to has precluded the possibility of reintegration.

For his own part, however, Luigi Pirandello appears from his writings to have turned not to ethnography but to nineteenth-century spiritualism for his model. One does not have to look far for the source of his interest. When he took up residence in Rome, shortly after the two and half years spent studying in Bonn, he became interested in his friend Luigi Capuana's wide-ranging study of psychic and metaphysical phenomena *Spiritismo?* which was published in 1884. Capuana's *La scienza della letteratura* (1902) also includes an account of the analogies that can be drawn between communication with spirits and the process of artistic creation. In Chapter 10 of *Il fu Mattia Pascal*, the protagonist moves to Rome where he finds lodgings with a landlord, Anselmo Paleari, who has a small but select theosophical library. An enthusiastic proselytizer, Anselmo lends him books and discusses their contents with him. Despite his initial scepticism, Mattia is none the less quick to seize upon the

[13] Arnold van Gennep, *The Rites of Passage* (repr. London, Routledge and Kegan Paul, 1960), 42.

similarities between the fate ascribed to some of the dead, including the suicides, by Leadbeater and his own 'suicide' and 'afterlife'.

Mi trovavo coi libri d'Anselmo Paleari tra le mani, e questi libri m'insegnavano che i morti, quelli veri, si trovavano nella mia identica condizione, nei 'gusci' del Kâmaloka, specialmente i suicidi, che il signor Leadbeater, autore del *Plan Astral* (premier degré du monde invisible, d'après la théosophie), raffigura come eccitati da ogni sorte d'appetiti umani, a cui non possono soddisfare, sprovvisti come sono del corpo carnale, ch'essi però ignorano d'aver perduto.[14]

Reading Anselmo Paleari's books now, I learned that genuinely dead people were exactly like me, going about in the 'shells' of the *Kamaloca*. I was especially like the suicides, which Leadbeater, the author of the *Plan Astral* (premier degré du monde invisible, d'après la théosophie) portrays as tormented by all kinds of human appetites which they are unable to satisfy, since they have no carnal form but are unaware that they have lost their bodies.

It was widely believed in late nineteenth-century spiritualist circles that when we die we proceed to another stage of existence, except for the few for whom attachment to their previous existence on earth is so strong that their souls cannot break the ties holding them back and they remain trapped within the ambit of their previous lives. *Limen* appears in its literal sense of 'threshold' in a one-act spiritualist play Pirandello wrote during the the First World War called *All'uscita* (*At the Exit*, written in 1916 but only performed in 1922), where the title refers to the gateway at the back of the cemetery that the spirits pass through on their way to the next world, having left their bodies behind in the graveyard. The cast includes a child with a half-eaten pomegranate, a woman murdered by her lover, a philosopher still attached to the land he used to cultivate—characters who have been ejected violently or abruptly from life and yet who retain strong attachments to it. It is the character who is simply described as 'Il Filosofo' ('The Philosopher') who, trapped at this point of transition and fearing that he will never pass through the gates to the world beyond, will be the founding father of Pirandello's succession of stage *raisonneurs*. The short play ends on his words: 'Ho paura ch'io solo resterò sempre qua

---

[14] Pirandello, *Tutti i romanzi*, i. 439 (tr. Simborowski, 121).

seguitando a ragionare'[15] ('I fear that I alone will be left here still caught up in thought'). Victor Turner, whose own work has drawn extensively on van Gennep's concept of liminality, describes in an anthropological context the state that the Philosopher in *All' uscita* experienced:

The attributes of liminality or of liminal *personae* ('threshold people') are necessarily ambiguous, since this condition and these persons elude or slip through the network of classifications that normally locate states and positions in cultural space. Liminal entities are neither here nor there; they are betwixt and between the positions assigned and arranged by law, custom, convention, and ceremonial. As such, their ambiguous and indeterminate attributes are expressed by a rich variety of symbols in the many societies that ritualize social and cultural transitions.[16]

Where Pirandello's heroes differ from the subjects of ritual is that in their case liminality is not a stage in preparation for re-entry into society, but will remain a permanent state of what Turner calls 'outsiderhood',[17] a term which he uses to refer 'to the condition of being either permanently and by ascription set outside the structural arrangements of a given social system, or voluntarily setting oneself apart from the behaviour of status-occupying, role-playing members of that system'.[18] By divesting themselves of the outer attributes of their social position—property, wealth, rank, and office, what Simone Pau in *Quaderni di Serafino Gubbio* refers to as 'il superfluo'—Pirandello's protagonists enter into *communitas,* a timeless condition where in the absence of all structure they are freed to exist in an eternal present (the principle, writes Turner, is simple: 'Cease to have and you are').[19] In Pirandello's writing *communitas* is to be found in the hospice, but it finds its fullest expression in his last play *I giganti della montagna* (*The Mountain*

---

[15] Pirandello, *Maschere nude,* i. 254.

[16] Victor Turner, *The Ritual Process, Structure and Anti-Structure* (New York, Aldine, 1969), 95.

[17] Victor Turner, *Dramas, Fields and Metaphors: Symbolic Action in Human Society* (Ithaca, NY, and London, Cornell University Press, 1990). See in particular Ch. 6, 'Passages, Margins and Poverty: Religious Symbols of Communitas', 231–71. Turner is interested in groups rather than individuals. As examples of 'outsiderhood' he includes mediums, shamans, hoboes, and gypsies. These are to be distinguished from 'marginals' who are simultaneously members of two or more groups.

[18] Ibid. 233.   [19] Ibid. 266.

Giants, 1938) where Pirandello chooses as his setting a villa, 'la Scalogna', which is not fully in or of this world. It has been abandoned by its owners who were driven away by the 'Spirits' who haunt it and it occupies a liminal position—in the words of the stage directions: 'Tempo e luogo, indeterminati: al limite, fra la favola e la realtà'[20] ('Time and place, indeterminate: on the borderland between fantasy and reality')—a place of illusions and hallucinations where a group of misfits live under the 'directorship' or 'leadership' of one Cotrone, arch-illusionist and magician. In the Villa of the Scalognati authority, hierarchy, and structure have been replaced by spontaneity, disorganization, and creativity. Turner describes 'marginals' as usually 'highly conscious and self-conscious people' who may produce from their ranks 'a disproportionately high number of writers, artists and philosophers'.[21] When, in an essay on 'Dewey, Dilthey and Drama', he writes: 'Liminality can perhaps be best described as a fructile chaos, a storehouse of possibilities, not a random assemblage but a striving after new forms and structures',[22] he could be describing life for *gli scalognati*. The 'storehouse of possibilities' is provided by the protagonist of Pirandello's last play—the master-illusionist and wizard Cotrone.

In *I giganti della montagna* which, although it was begun in 1928–9, remained unfinished (the final act missing) at the time of Pirandello's death in 1936, spiritualism and theatre are brought together. An actress, Ilse, accompanied by an exhausted and depleted company of travelling actors arrives at a villa situated on the margins of life. They have been travelling the world driven by her need to perform a play written by her dead lover. The villa is under the control of Cotrone, who, although described as a magician, also has some of the characteristics of both theatre-director and author. He is sorcerer and artist (the attributes cannot be separated from each other) and he and the *scalognati* live as exiles, having removed themselves from society. Under his orchestration dead men come to life

---

[20] Luigi Pirandello, *I giganti della montagna* (Milan, Mondadori, 1986), 142 (tr. Felicity Firth, *The Yearbook of the British Pirandello Society,* 10 (1990), 1–129).

[21] Turner, *Dramas*, 233.

[22] Victor W. Turner and Edward M. Bruner (ed.), *The Anthropology of Experience* (Urbana and Chicago, University of Illinois, 1986), 42.

and puppets speak. It is pure theatre issuing directly from the creative mind. There is no text, no truth. When Ilse says he is inventing the truth, Cotrone agrees:

Non ho fatto altro in vita mia! Senza volerlo, Contessa. Tutte quelle verità che la coscienza rifiuta. Le faccio venir fuori dal segreto dei sensi, o a seconda, le più spaventose, dalle caverne dell'istinto. Ne inventai tante al paese, che me ne dovetti scappare, perseguitato dagli scandali. Mi provo ora qua a dissolverle in fantasmi, in evanescenze. Ombre che passano.[23]

I have done it all my life. Without meaning to, Contessa. All the truths which the conscious mind rejects. I draw them out from where they lurk among the senses, or perhaps, some of the more appalling ones, from the caverns of instinct itself. I invented so many when I lived down in the village that I had to leave, pursued by scandal. My efforts here are aimed at dispersing these truths in the form of evanescent phantoms.

Cotrone points out that where actors lend their bodies to phantasms so they may live, at the villa they do the opposite: they make phantasms of their bodies. They inhabit an unreal world where it is enough to think something for it to come into being, but to reach this stage Cotrone had first to renounce everything held to be of worth in life—a list that he opens by citing dignity, decorum, honour, and then proceeds with it no further. He is a *dimissionario* who lives beyond the confines of reality. On the mountains beyond live the giants who will be the audience for Ilse's play. In the unwritten final act of this extraordinarily bleak play, the giants who wanted entertainment—a song-and-dance routine would have been welcomed by them—respond to Ilse's performance when she fails to address their demands, by invading the stage, attacking her, and dismembering her.

The inhabitants of the Villa of the Scalognati, Henry IV, Mattia, Vitangelo, and Serafino are all outsiders who have moved beyond the reach of the social structures that hold their readers or audiences in place. They look back and can speak with an authority that only experience can confer. We are being asked by them to follow a line of reasoning that leads to conclusions that are not just at odds with the way we live our lives, but are so intransigent that if translated into practice would make

---

[23] Pirandello, *I giganti della montagna*, 635 (tr. Firth, 65).

those lives untenable. What his privileged few reveal by their lifestyles is that the only way to achieve unity of thought and life is by occupying a space which is often literally a physical space contiguous with, but detached from, their former existence.

There are, however, other socially marginalized characters in Pirandello's work who choose to remain within the social order; men who have not allowed their awareness of life's inherent absurdity to determine their lifestyles, but who are continuously negotiating between living and thinking. As figures who, while not fully integrated, none the less continue to interact with their peers, they are ideally suited to theatre where they can function as mediators between events unfolding on stage and the audience. Included in this category are Laudisi in *Così è* (*se vi pare*, 1917), forerunner to Baldovino of *Il piacere dell'onestà* (*The Pleasure of Honesty*, 1917), and Leone Gala in *Il giuoco delle parti* (*The Rules of the Game*, 1918) who shares some of the same characteristics. (As the dates show, the three plays in question were written within two years of each other during the First World War.) In the last play, Leone Gala is separated from his wife Silia, but under the terms of the separation he has retained the right, which he exercises, to visit her every evening for exactly half-an-hour. In an attempt to free herself of him, Silia manipulates a chance occurrence so that Leone has to fight a duel with a young man who had insulted his honour by mistaking her for a prostitute. But Leone does not play according to the rules of the game. (Already in Pirandello's day this particular practice, the duel, was outmoded.) On the morning of the duel, having agreed to the arrangements up to that point, he refuses to honour the challenge, leaving Guido who is Silia's lover and his second, to stand in for him. Guido dies as a result of the wound he sustains in the duel. Contrary to what the word may suggest, being a *raisonneur* does not in itself imply passivity or pure cerebrality; on the contrary, both Leone Gala and Henry IV are men driven by passion and both are killers. The one cold-bloodedly negotiates the death of another man, the other kills in the heat of the moment. Neither experiences remorse.

While Baldovino and Leone Gala are *actants* who stand both inside and outside their roles, Laudisi's only theatrical function in *Così è (se vi pare)* is to comment on his peers. He is on stage for most of the play, his presence a visible reminder to the audience of the absurdity inherent in the community's search for the truth. At the end of Act III, after the veiled lady has withdrawn, it is Laudisi who has the last word and he directs it both at his fellow citizens on stage and at the audience:

LAUDISI. Ed ecco, o signori, come parla la verità!
[*Volgerà attorno uno sguardo di sfida derisoria*] Siete contenti?
[*Scoppierà a ridere*] Ah! ah! ah! ah!
Tela[24]

LAUDISI. Well, ladies and gentlemen, you've heard the voice of truth!
[*Looking around the company in mocking defiance*] Are you happy?
[*He bursts out laughing*] Ha! ha! ha! ha!
Curtain

Laudisi, Baldovino, and Gala are observers from within their given societies and their mark of difference lies in their non-conformity. Like the figure of the joker or court clown, Pirandello's *raisonneurs* enjoy the privilege of being able to say certain things in a certain way with impunity. Even Vitangelo Moscarda only becomes a threatening figure within his community when he starts undermining social structures by giving his wealth away—a gesture that is made socially acceptable at the end of book by the channelling of his wealth into a philanthropic enterprise, the construction of a hospice for the dispossessed. Having failed to internalize the prescriptions of their group, Pirandello's thinkers can observe and denounce, but they cannot effect change. His universe cannot accommodate the idea of change stemming from the individual, much less the group. In his bleakly pessimistic view of life, it is always external forces, often of an arbitrary and impersonal nature, that act upon the subject. With no social or political role for the individual, beyond that of negotiating his or her own life, one ends up with a dangerously dehistoricized universe where the only room for manœuvre left to the individual is either to quit, like Vitangelo, or to comment from the side-lines, like Laudisi.

According to Arnold van Gennep and Victor Turner, liminality occupies a unique position within religious ritual (the pilgrimage in Turner's work for example). In Pirandello's case, although he borrows from the rituals of the Church to mark the

---

[24] Pirandello, *Maschere nude*, i. 509.

protagonist's rebirth, the particular vision of life held by his *raisonneurs* and philosophers is a product of their unflinching secularity. One recalls in this context how Mattia Pascal started writing by the light 'che mi viene dalla lanterna lassù, della cupola' ('that comes from the lamp that hangs above me in the dome') in a 'chiesetta sconsacrata' ('deconsecrated church').[25] Religion has given way to learning, a church to a library, but it is by no means assured that learning provides a path to knowledge. In the library where Mattia works not only are the books and manuscripts unclassified, but having come from here and there, they are now kept in a state of indescribable confusion which is exacerbated by the damp that has glued together for all eternity the most incompatible of texts. Far from knowledge having replaced belief, the chaos of this 'vera babilonia di libri'[26] ('this absolute Babylon of books') can be seen as a symbol of the intellectual confusion of the age described so feelingly by Pirandello in his very early essays.

Two years of personal freedom in Germany, combined with direct access to a German philosophical culture, had exploded any residual belief the young Pirandello may have had in the existence of a given, ordered reality whose characteristics could be commonly agreed upon. But coming from Sicily with its highly codified, authoritarian structures, where Church, family, and society practised an effective and rapidly internalized social and moral control that went unchallenged, Nietzschean relativism held out no heady promises to Pirandello. Quite the contrary; in those early essays we see all the signs of what Robert Brustein has diagnosed as 'Cartesian anxiety', namely 'that dread of madness and chaos where nothing is fixed, where we can neither touch bottom, nor support ourselves on the surface'.[27] In 'Arte e coscienza d'oggi', an article written in 1893 where he analyses the problems born of the clash between science and faith,[28] Pirandello paints a bleak picture of the crisis

---

[25] Pirandello, *Tutti i romanzi*, i. 321.   [26] Ibid. 321.

[27] Robert Brustein, *Beyond Objectivism and Relativism* (Oxford, Blackwell, 1983), 18.

[28] 'Arte e coscienza d'oggi' in *Spsv* 899. The article reappears in *L'esclusa* in the guise of a lecture given by Gregorio Alvignani, Marta's lover. 'Dall'esame della coscienza intendeva passare all'esame delle varie manifestazioni della vita, e principalmente di quella artistica—"Arte e coscienza d'oggi"—ecco il titolo della conferenza' ('He intended to turn from the examination of consciousness to an

that has hit modern consciousness, exacerbated by the intellectual and scientific pusillanimity of his age which has sent the older generations scuttling back to the consolations of religion, while the younger, trapped in the crossfire of conflicting philosophies, sinks ever deeper into the quagmires of neurosis. In his early writings he frequently presents thought as an abyss, descent into which induces vertigo and terror with no light of day to come:

la meditazione è l'abisso nero, popolato dai foschi fantasmi, custodito dallo sconforto disperato. Un raggio di sole non vi penetra mai, e il desiderio di averlo ti sprofonda sempre nelle tenebre dense [. . .]. È una sete inestinguibile, un furore ostinato; ma il nero t'abbevera, la immensità silenziosa t'agghiaccia.[29]

Meditation is a black abyss, inhabited by gloomy phantasms, guarded by a despairing disquiet. No ray of sun ever penetrates, and the desire to see it only sinks you still further into the deep shadows [. . .] It is an unquenchable thirst, a persistent rage; but blackness engulfs you, the silent immensity makes your blood run cold.

Here one finds a fear edging into despair, sparked by the absence of all certainties about the self, the world, and the relationship between the two, and without the consolations of religion.

In *Il fu Mattia Pascal*, the problems the protagonist experiences in getting his story under way leads to the inclusion of not one but two prefaces, of which the 'Premessa seconda (filosofica) a mo' di scusa' ('Second foreword (philosophical) by way of an excuse') offers an explanation for his procrastination and doubt. Mattia tells his mentor, the librarian Don Eligio, that it is an unpropitious time to embark on a book because the very tenet underpinning the narrative enterprise, namely that human beings are important enough to have stories made up about them, is utterly fallacious. It is our very insignificance that makes realism untenable as an aesthetics.[30]

examination of the different manifestations of life, and in particular artistic life—"Art and consciousness today"—that was to be the title of the paper'). *Tutti i romanzi*, i. 150.

[29] Luigi Pirandello, *Lettere ai familiari*, ed. Sandro D'Amico, in *Terzo programma*, 3 (1961).

[30] In a third addendum, an afterword called 'Avvertenza sugli scrupoli della fantasia' ('A Warning on the Scruples of the Imagination') which was first published

Some critics have taken Mattia's commentary as a point of departure for their own reading of the novel, so that Leone de Castris, for example, calls *Il fu Mattia Pascal* Pirandello's 'Copernican revolution in the novel' where nineteenth-century narrative practices are jettisoned in favour of a new decentred consciousness of crisis.[31] I would argue, however, that one of the interests this novel holds for the reader is that, rather than representing a break with tradition, it is constantly negotiating between past practices and present needs. Responsibility for the end of traditional narrative, like so much else in Pirandello's writing, is placed firmly on the shoulders of Copernicus. On the day he carried to his fellow creatures the news that the sun does not revolve around the earth, and therefore we are not the centre of the universe, he brought with it our ruin:

Siamo o non siamo su un'invisibile trottolina, cui fa da ferza un fil di sole, su un granellino di sabbia impazzito che gira e gira e gira, senza saper perchè, senza pervenir mai a destino, come se ci provasse gusto a girar così, per farci sentire ora un po' più di caldo, ora un po' più di freddo, e per farci morire—spesso con la coscienza d'aver commesso una sequela di piccole sciocchezze—dopo cinquanta o sessanta giri? Copernico, Copernico, don Eligio mio, ha rovinato l'umanità, irrimediabilmente. Ormai noi tutti ci siamo a poco a poco adattati alla nuova concezione dell'infinita nostra piccolezza, a considerarci anzi men che niente nell'universo, con tutte le nostre belle scoperte e invenzioni; e che valore dunque volete che abbiano le notizie, non dico delle nostre miserie particolari, ma anche delle generali calamità? Storie di vermucci ormai, le nostre.[32]

Are we or are we not on an invisible spinning-top, whipped by a ray of sunlight, on a grain of crazed sand which turns and turns without ever knowing why, without ever reaching a destination, as if it enjoyed turning like that, to make us feel a little colder or warmer, and make us die (often making us feel that we have merely carried out a series of meaningless gestures) after fifty or sixty turns? Copernicus, Copernicus, my dear Don Eligio, was the ruin of mankind, quite

in *L'Idea nazionale* (22 June 1922) and then added to the 3rd edn. of *Il fu Mattia Pascal*, realism is under attack from another direction. Pirandello argues against mimesis on grounds that fictions have to appear credible while life simply is not. Life has the rare privilege of being able to ignore credibility.

[31] Arcangelo Leone de Castris, *Il decadentismo italiano* (Bari, De Donato, 1974), see 'Del rigore di Pirandello', 155–207.

[32] Pirandello, *Tutti i romanzi*, i. 324 (tr. Simborowski, 18).

irredeemably. By now we have all gradually adapted to the new idea of our own infinite puniness, to considering ourselves less than nothing in the universe, in spite of all our discoveries and inventions. What value then, can you expect any detail to have, not only regarding our individual problems but even regarding general calamities? They are just accounts of the lives of worms.

The comparison with the spinning-top to describe the earth in motion echoes Pirandello's reference to 'una trottoletta volgarissima' ('a vulgar little spinning-top') in 'Arte e coscienza d'oggi', which in turn is an image Pirandello uses in an early story of 1895 called 'Pallottoline' ('Little Balls'); a story whose location in a meteorological observatory that is above what was once a monastery and is now a hotel prefigures Mattia's deconsecrated church turned library.[33] As daughter Didina huddles together with her mother in the kitchen in search of warmth, her astronomer father holds forth on the insignificance of their lives in face of the immensity of the universe. It is a philosophy that is put seriously to the test when the professor suffers a chronic toothache that causes him acute pain, but by fixing his mind on the enormity of the universe he gradually manages to shrink his awareness of his physical pain to the point at which it disappears from his consciousness. (Experience no doubt played a part here, for Pirandello uses toothache elsewhere in his fictions as trigger for its victim's existential crisis. In the story 'L'avemaria di Bobbio' the protagonist's bouts of agonizing toothache lead to loss of religious belief and a crisis of identity.) Pirandello's own description of our planet in *Il fu Mattia Pascal* as a 'granellino di sabbia' circling the universe is taken from Leopardi's version of the Copernicus story which appears in the *Operette morali*.[34] Here it is the Sun

---

[33] The friars have been 'chased away'; their modest cells transformed into hotel bedrooms for summer visitors. See 'Pallottoline', *Novelle per un anno*, iii/i. 186.

[34] Written in 1827, it was included for the first time in Leopardi's *Operette morali* in 1834. In Leopardi's version, once the Sun has decided on its future course of action, it decides to summon a philosopher from earth to take instructions on future arrangements and then carry the bad news back to his fellow men. The idea that philosophers are the source of our dissatisfaction and unhappiness comes in this *operetta*. Here the Sun explains his choice of mediator to First Hour who is then dispatched to earth to fetch one (*Works*, 163): 'I fear that a poet would not be listened to by the Earth, any more than by me, or that, if he were, he would not seem impressive. So we had better turn to a philosopher; for although philosophers are not usually fit, and still less inclined, to incite others to work, yet it may be that, in

who having summoned First Hour informs him that he has decided to stop 'quella sciocchissima fatica di correre alla disperata, così grande e grosso come io sono, intorno a un granellino di sabbia'[35] 'this absurd task of racing about like a madman, in spite of my great size, around a little grain of sand'.

It is interesting to see how in a completely different context, but with the same underlying intention, Freud, a few years later, claimed that the two major blows to human vanity that had been delivered by Copernicus and Darwin had now been joined by modern psychology:

In the course of centuries the *naive* self-love of men has had to submit to two major blows at the hands of science. The first was when they learnt that our earth was not the centre of the universe but only a tiny fragment of a cosmic system of scarcely imaginable vastness. This is associated in our minds with the name of Copernicus, though something similar had been asserted by Alexandrian science. The second blow fell when biological research destroyed man's supposedly privileged place in creation and proved his descent from the animal kingdom and his ineradicable animal nature. This revaluation had been accomplished in our days by Darwin, Wallace and their predecessors, though not without the most violent contemporary opposition. But human megalomania will have suffered its third and most wounding blow from the psychological research of the present time which seeks to prove to the ego that it is not even master in its own house, but must content itself with scanty information of what is going on unconsciously in its mind.[36]

Pirandello displayed scant interest in Freud's work; indeed if his claim that he only encountered Freud's writing in 1926 is accurate, his writing was unimpeded by any knowledge of the analyst's systematization of the psyche. But he would have con-

so extreme a case as this, they will go against their usual habit.' Copernicus who is scanning the skies with a rolled-up sheet of paper (the telescope has not yet been invented) is the first to be spotted, with the outcome we all know.

[35] Giacomo Leopardi, 'Il Copernico', in *Operette morali*, ed. Mario Fubini (Turin, Loescher, 1970), 252.

[36] Sigmund Freud, *Introductory Lectures on Psychoanalysis (1916–17 [1915–17]). Part III. General Theory of the Neuroses (1917 [1916–17])* in *Sigmud Freud 1: Introductory Lectures on Psychoanalysis* (Harmondsworth, Penguin, 1975), 325–6. Freud again refers to three blows dealt to humankind—psychological, cosmological, and biological—in vol. xv. *Historical and Expository Works on Psychoanalysis* (Harmondsworth, Penguin, 1986), 72–3.

curred in the view expressed above, down to the very image used of the 'ego', that 'is not master in his own house'.

L'umorismo was published four years after *Il fu Mattia Pascal*; the first edition even carried a dedication on the part of the author 'alla buon'anima—di Mattia Pascal—bibliotecario' ('to the good soul—of Mattia Pascal—librarian'). It is towards the end of the essay that Copernicus puts in an appearance as one of the great humorists (albeit unwittingly) of all time and Pirandello recommends to his readers' attention the dialogue by Leopardi.[37] What Copernicus's presence among a pantheon of humorists that includes Manzoni, Sterne, and Dostoevsky, illustrates is how central the disproportionate gap between our insignificance in the face of the cosmos and the importance we attribute to ourselves is to Pirandello's concept of *umorismo*. Being a humorist is no joke; in the absence of God, in the absence of any certainties, of any significance, his *umoristi* have seen through all those concepts we hold dear. Concepts such as 'normality' or 'individuality' or 'identity' depend on the barriers and limits that we ourselves have imposed on our individual and collective consciousness. We structure life, we order it, we impose time, coherence, and meaning—and they are all delusions. The humorist's materials are those structures that we hold in place to protect ourselves from the abyss that we spend our lives tiptoeing around and pretending not to see. In the same way that 'l'umorismo potrebbe dirsi un fenomeno di sdoppiamento nell'atto della concezione'[38] ('one could call humour a phenomenon of doubling in the act of conception'), so to be a humorist 'è una speciale fisionomia psichica, a cui è

---

[37] The reference comes towards the end of the essay (*Spsv* 156): 'Uno dei più grandi umoristi, senza saperlo, fu Copernico, che smontò non propriamente la macchina dell'universo, ma l'orgogliosa immagine che ce n'eravamo fatta. Si legga quel dialogo del Leopardi che s'intitola appunto dal canonico polacco.' ('Copernicus was, without being aware of it, one of the great humorists. He took apart not exactly the mechanisms of the universe, but the proud image of them that we had made for ourselves. Read Leopardi's dialogue which has as its title the name of the Polish canon.') Here I am concerned with the figure of the *umorista* rather than the concept of *umorismo* as such. For a discussion of the essay and its sources see Olga Ragusa, *Pirandello: An Approach to his Theatre* (Edinburgh, Edinburgh University Press, 1980), 30–42; Giacomo Debenedetti, 'L'umorismo di Luigi Pirandello', *IL romanzo del Novecento* (Milan, Garzanti, 1971), 390–414, and Franco Zangrilli, 'L'umorismo: poetica morale', *Rivista di studi pirandelliani*, 3/6 (Centro nazionale di studi pirandelliani, Agrigento, June–Sept. 1980).

[38] Pirandello, *Spsv* 142.

7

The Author as Director:
Characters and Actors

The theatre cannot die. It is a form of life itself and we are
all actors in it.

(Luigi Pirandello, presidential address at the Volta
Conference on Dramatic Theatre, 1934)

In the light of Pirandello's claim that *Uno, nessuno e centomila* was
to be the book that held the key to his theatre, I shall begin this
chapter with a brief survey of what the author as playwright, and
then as director, was doing during the sixteen years it took him
to complete his manuscript. The year that marked the start of
work on the novel also saw the seeds of his interest in Sicilian
dialect theatre come to fruition with a group of what were
mainly one-act plays (often originating in one or more of his
short stories). His commitment to the idea of bringing Sicilian
theatre to mainland audiences whose knowledge of the island
was limited or misinformed[1] led to a close collaboration from
1910 to 1917 between Pirandello, the Sicilian actor and director
Angelo Musco, and the dramatist and director Nino Martoglio.
But by 1919, the year he made the statement linking the novel
and the plays, his involvement with theatre had, at every level,
intensified, even though, as is clear from the essay of 1918
called 'Teatro e letteratura' ('Theatre and Literature'), he still
thought of theatre as the translation of a pre-existing text to the
stage, a process in which the written work will inevitably lose
out. Despite such reservations about theatre as a performing

[1] Pirandello published an essay on Sicilian theatre called 'Teatro siciliano?' in
1909 where he calls into question the feasibility of exporting Sicilian, or indeed any
other regional culture (see *Spsv* 1205–8). However after moving away from regional
theatre he published a further article in 1921 called 'Dialettalità' (ibid. 1209–11) in
which he champions regional and dialect literature, claiming that Italy should stop
pretending to be France and start looking to where its true cultural heritage lies.

art, he did emphatically reject the view that drama itself was a lesser or inferior literary genre.[2] As writer for the stage, his move away from dialect was accompanied by the beginnings of a theatre which responded positively to the possibilities perform-ance and spectatorship afforded the playwright. The evolution can be traced back to 1917, a troubled year in personal terms, but rich creatively with *Così è (se vi pare)*, followed over the next four years by plays of the stature of *Sei personaggi in cerca d'autore* and *Enrico IV*. All of this helped bring Pirandello the interna-tional fame that in 1923 allowed him to travel abroad to see, among other things, Pitoëff's celebrated Paris production of *Sei personaggi* and two years later, just before the completion of *Uno, nessuno e centomila*, his emergence as director of his own theatre company.

Writing for the stage is of a very different order from writing novels. The private one-to-one relationship imposed by the novel is in marked contrast with the more collaborative nature of theatre. When writing a play Pirandello usually had a director in mind, and a venue, and he had identified who the leading actors were to be. He also knew what kind of audience to expect. Indeed, according to Rina Franchetti, one of the com-pany's actresses who is quoted in Claudio Vicentini's fascinating study of Pirandello's theatre, the most unnerving experience for the playwright and company came, not with the vociferous and predictable reception given by audiences in major cities such as Rome and Berlin, but with the complete lack of re-sponse from a largely peasant audience who had been coerced by local landowners into attending a performance of *Sei personaggi in cerca d'autore* at Canicattì, a small town about thirty kilometres outside the playwright's native Agrigento. Where the bourgeois audiences the company played to were familiar with the conventions of theatre and even a hostile response meant that they had, none the less, entered into some kind of dialogue with the performance, the peasants who attended a production of *Sei personaggi* in December 1927 stayed put in their seats, silent and still, at the end of the performance and when eventu-

---

[2] See 'Teatro e letteratura' of 1918 (ibid. 1018–24) which is an entirely consistent successor to the much earlier essays 'Azione parlata' (ibid. 1015–18) and 'Illustratori, attori e traduttori' (ibid. 207–24) where he continues to see perform-ance as a translation-travesty of the written text.

ally the actors returned to the stage as 'themselves' to tell the audience that it was all over and they could go home, this too was taken to be a part of the performance and nobody stirred. It was only very, very gradually, when they realized that nothing further was going to happen, that silently and cautiously they left the theatre. It was a vivid illustration of how defiance of convention can only function where the rules are understood and agreed in the first place; on this occasion so unsettling was the experience that there was a real fear among members of the company that the absolute uncomprehending silence on the audience's part might turn into physical violence.[3]

We have seen how the protagonists of Pirandello's first person narratives are able to dominate the other characters to a degree that might well be the envy of the protagonists of his plays. But there is a further distinction to be made between the condition of a character in a play that is read as text, and that of a character in a play seen in performance. The staging of a play introduces the potential for two further constraints on the autonomy or power of the character; the one comes in the shape of the actor who assumes the role of the character and the other in the figure of the director who has overall artistic responsibility for the presentation of the work. In Chapter 6 we saw how, in the case of Pirandello's chosen few, character and author can merge to speak with one voice, with the result that when it comes to the performance of a play the author and character may find themselves united in battle against actor and director. So the struggle for dominance between our author and his characters seen in the earlier part of the study may in his theatrical works extend to other participants who are involved, not in the play's conception, but in its realization.

This chapter will take as its focus characters who from their inception are destined for the stage and who are associated with the period in Pirandello's creative career when he had stopped thinking of himself primarily as a writer of short stories and novels. Unlike the protagonists who have appeared in earlier chapters in this book, who are held by familial and social networks which may oppress them but which also identify them, these are solitary creatures who make and unmake themselves

---

[3] See Claudio Vicentini, *Il disagio del teatro* (Venice, Marsilio, 1993), 191–2.

in and through performance. Once Pirandello decided to commit himself to the theatre, he thought through the medium he
had chosen, manipulating it both in an exploration of its own
potential and for the possibilities it created for him to turn his
fascination with character into the subject of his theatre. We
have seen how Pirandello both experienced and presented writing as character-led, but what, if any, difference did writing for
performance make to his output? To understand the processes
at work here, we shall start out by looking at his increasing
involvement in live theatre, and the brief but eventful history of
his own theatre company.

When Pirandello travelled abroad in 1923, more than thirty
years had gone by since he had last left Italy. His children had
left home, while his marriage had ended in all but name after
Antonietta was permanently hospitalized in 1919. When in
April 1923 he travelled to Paris for the French première of *Sei
personaggi in cerca d'autore*, a production which was to exercise
such an informative influence on the revisions he made for the
1925 edition, it was as a playwright of international repute, and
no longer a reluctant teacher dogged by the persistent financial
worries of his early career. While in Paris he met with three
leading French playwrights, Maurice Maeterlinck, Roger Vitrac,
and Rolland Romains. At the end of 1923, a two-month visit to
New York gave him the opportunity both to meet the director
who, at George Bernard Shaw's instigation, was preparing a
season of his plays, and to become acquainted with a number of
new productions from a repertoire which was new to him and
which included works by Lord Dunsany and Evreinov—two
playwrights whose work he was later to stage in Rome. It was on
his return to Italy, ten years after the start of his career as
dramatist, that Pirandello began to think seriously about estab-
lishing his own theatre company. This decision marked an important change of heart on the question of the value of having
theatre companies with their own fixed residence. In a written
answer to a referendum held on the subject in the summer of
1906, he had argued that permanent (as opposed to travelling)
theatre companies were not suited to an Italian context in
which a fickle and heterogeneous public would always choose
the entertaining and accessible over the more demanding repertoire that a resident company would wish to provide. The

effort that would have to go into making the company a success, he concluded, would induce either exhaustion or satiety.[4] The Italian public was simply not up to such an enterprise. But the intervening years, which had seen Pirandello establish himself as dramatist, also witnessed the rise of what the actor Lamberto Picasso in his own proposal for an arts theatre (which was then superseded by the company Pirandello helped found and which Picasso joined as both actor and co-producer) called 'special theatres'—that is to say, 'permanent theatres for permanent companies'. The most innovative, but not very influential of these in Italy was Anton Giulio Bragaglia's experimental company, Teatro degli Indipendenti, which was founded in Rome in 1922 and had staged some thirty-seven plays by the time that it closed in 1926; it was the only one still in existence when, in 1925, Pirandello's company, the Teatro d'Arte, began its own short life.

On 20 May 1924, Pirandello announced from a stage in Milan, his plan to open a theatre company to be known as the 'Teatro dei Dodici' ('Theatre of the Twelve', the number of subscribers and associates; there was some doubt over whether it was to be the 'Teatro degli Undici' or 'dei Dodici' or even drop down to ten). The company would be modelled in both aim and structure on George Bernard Shaw's Stage Society in London. The intention was to produce twelve plays a year (eight of which were to be Italian), to favour new work over an established repertoire, and to make a name for itself as a non-commercial theatre. All this required money, and in his search for sympathetic benefactors, Benito Mussolini, Prime Minister since 30 October 1922, seemed an obvious candidate. He was powerful and Pirandello liked his politics. The company, which finally came into existence on 2 April 1925, was helped on its way by the active support Pirandello had given to the Fascist regime on his visit to America the previous winter, a tour which had been partly arranged to provide an opportunity for him to extol the virtues of Fascism. On his return, the playwright met with Mussolini to brief him on his own impressions of the country and its attitude to Italy. Four months after declaring his

[4] The interview was given to *Il Tirso* (22 July 1906). It is quoted in A. D'Amico and A. Tinterri, *Pirandello capocomico: La Compagnia del Teatro d'Arte di Roma 1925–28* (Palermo, Sellerio, 1987), 5

intention to establish a new theatre company, on 12 September 1924, Pirandello joined the Fascist Party and, a week later, in a carefully stage-managed gesture of support, he gave an interview on the subject to the editor of the Fascist paper *L'Impero*. The date is highly significant for it comes after the murder in June that year of the socialist deputy, Giacomo Matteotti, a leading anti-Fascist politician in the Chamber of Deputies, a crime which had left the Fascist Party looking for a time exposed and vulnerable. If one then puts Pirandello's statement of allegiance to the regime in context, it becomes apparent that his was no innocent or idle choice. Between May 1924 and April 1925, when the company held its première in the presence of the Duce and the royal family, Matteotti had been murdered and the Aventine secession in January 1925 had seen opposition deputies abandon the Chamber of Deputies in protest at the assassination. Mussolini had responded by closing down Parliament, assuming full personal responsibility for the murder of the Socialist deputy, and embarking on a widescale suppression of the opposition. It marked the transition from consensus to coercion politics. Nobody could harbour any further illusions about the nature of Fascism. So in effect the writer made his public declaration of support in the very period when the violent and anti-democratic face of Fascism was unmasking itself.

Pirandello's active involvement with Mussolini was motivated first by financial concerns and secondly by his hope that a national theatre company would be established under his director, but in the event both hopes were left unfulfilled. Shortly after Pirandello's first meeting with Mussolini, his son, Stefano Landi, and a group of associates, realizing that the company needed subsidies to survive, made their own visit to Mussolini to appeal for funds to assist them in their restructuring of the Teatro Odescalchi in Rome. They were promised 250,000 lire (most of it did not materialize), 50,000 of which Mussolini took from his wallet and handed over to them on the spot. Four of those involved in the theatre project resigned soon afterwards; two of them, both anti-Fascists, for political reasons—Leo Ferrero, a talented, young writer who was to die in Mexico in 1933, and Corrado Alvaro, an established author and journalist. Alvaro explained in his letter of resignation that he felt unhappy with the request that he should refrain in his writing from making any political allusions that might displease the Fascists.

It was also quite clear from Pirandello's own public statements that he anticipated that his theatre company would, with the help of the Fascist Party, develop into Italy's first national theatre company, a *teatro di stato*. In a letter inviting Mussolini to the inaugural ceremony on the 29 March 1925, he emphasizes the political role of the company in promoting Fascism abroad. He also lists the theatre companies outside Italy that had offered them contracts and refers to 'the active work of national propaganda' that they would conduct when they were on tour. Indeed he goes further than that and links their projected foreign tours directly to the propaganda that he personally would make on behalf of the regime:

Riceviamo inviti da ogni paese; tutte le maggiori imprese teatrali ci fanno proposte di contratti: nell'America del Sud, in Ispagna, nel Belgio, in Francia, in Germania. Queste offerte sono da ma prese in viva considerazione poichè mi propongo di seguire la Compagnia all'estero, dove, con conferenze e pubbliche interviste sulla vita contemporanea italiana, intendo svolgere un'attiva opera di propaganda nazionale come ho già fatto l'anno scorso nell'America del Nord. Questo è il vero modo con cui io posso svolgere una diretta azione politica, non del tutto infeconda, e lo spendermi per un tale scopo non è soltanto per me fonte di viva soddisfazione morale, ma anche l'adempimento di una missione che io mi sento spiritualmente commessa da V.E.[5]

We are being invited by all countries; all the major theatrical bodies are offering us contracts: in South America, in Spain, in Belgium, in France and in Germany. I have given serious consideration to these offers since I propose to accompany the Company abroad where, through conferences and public interviews on contemporary Italian life, I propose to undertake a propaganda exercise for the State, as I did last year in North America. This is the real way in which I can have a direct political impact that is not entirely wasted, and putting my efforts into such an undertaking is not only a source of lively moral satisfaction, it is also the fulfilment of a mission that I feel I have been appointed by Your Excellency to undertake.

[5] Alberto Cesare Alberti, *Il teatro nel fascismo: Pirandello e Bragaglia* (Rome, Bulzoni, 1974), 131 (tr. S. Bassnett and J. Lorch, *Luigi Pirandello in the Theatre* (Reading, Harwood Academic Publishers, 1993), 99).

He did indeed put all this into practice while on tour by appearing on stage during the interval, or at the end of a performance, to address the audience with explanations both of the play and of the new political situation in Italy. So seriously did he take his duties as a roving cultural spokesman for Fascism that one account describes a two-hour argument with an anti-Fascist reporter during the interval of a performance in Chicago. It is difficult to weigh up how far Pirandello's allegiance to the regime was motivated by the benefits he hoped it would bring to his own company in particular and Italian theatre in general. If such was his intention, he was to be disappointed; most of the money promised them never materialized, and the company never managed to balance its books, which meant that in June 1925, just two months after opening at the specially refurbished Teatro Odescalchi in Rome, they had to relinquish the lease and revert to being a travelling company. The conversion of the building had fallen further and further behind schedule and the costs had continued to spiral. Industry declined to contribute, the banks not only failed to donate but refused to extend credit, while only part of the sum promised by Mussolini had been forthcoming, so the company was simply unable to make good its losses. Again in spring 1927 the company took a three-month lease on another Roman theatre, the Teatro Argentina, in the hope that talk of the government founding a national theatre company would translate into action, but their hopes were ill-founded and they had to seek a remedy for the financial disaster they had incurred with an extended tour in South America which took them to Brazil, Uruguay, and Argentina.

Evidence seems to suggest that in the 1930s the relationship between Mussolini and Pirandello became more strained, after that earlier period when both parties had found it was in their mutual interest to be accommodating. Some years after the closure of the Teatro d'Arte, one of Pirandello's own plays, *Il figlio cambiato* (*The Changeling*) was banned. Mussolini had attended the opening night on 8 June 1934 and was seen applauding enthusiastically at the end of the first act, but when the curtain rose on a second act located in a brothel, Mussolini was described as entering into a state of fury and openly inciting the audience to rebel.[6] Furthermore a report of 5 May 1933, prepared for the Ministry of the Interior, claimed that Pirandello had been heard to pass unflattering comments on the Duce. Acccording to the report's author:

Ero stato informato della facilità come [sic] l'Accademico parlasse del DUCE, permettendosi sul palcoscenico e avanti a comici ed altri, di dire delle cose poco belle nei riguardi del Regime e di come il DUCE conduce le cose che riguardano la politica interna e quella esterna.[7]

I had been informed of the ease how [sic] the Academician spoke about the DUCE, making free on stage and in front of actors and others to say things that were not at all friendly in respect of the Regime and how the DUCE conducts those affairs that bear upon internal and external politics.

Pirandello was awarded the Nobel prize for literature in the same year. Although his candidature received the support of the regime, it is clear from the following extract from a further report for the same Ministry that the view in some quarters was that his work (not unexpectedly) did not best represent the spirit of Fascism:

La attribuizione del premio Nobel a Pirandello suscita una giusta considerazione da parte dei competenti, tutti si dicono se proprio il Pirandello sia un esatto esponente della realtà corporativa, egli così analitico e anatomizzatore, contrario ad ogni sintesi, e che nella essenza della sua arte è quanto di meno corporativa si possa pensare. Si giudica che coloro che gli hanno assegnato il premio Nobel abbiano voluto fare una dimostrazione arguta e pacata ma ferma di anticorporativismo.[8]

The awarding of the Nobel prize to Pirandello gave rise to an entirely proper discussion on the part of qualified persons, who all queried among themselves whether Pirandello was a clear exponent of corporate reality, he who is so analytical and so keen to dissect, hostile to any synthesis, and who in the essence of his art is the least corporative that one could imagine. One assumes that those who have awarded him the

---

[6] Ibid. 216.
[7] Ibid. 210. The author of the report goes on to note: 'Pirandello racconta della sua permanenza a Parigi con entusiasmo rimarcabilissimo' ('Pirandello described his stay in Paris with a very remarkable degree of enthusiasm').
[8] Ibid. 217.

Nobel prize had wanted to make a peaceful, pointed, but strong statement against corporativism.

The Sicilian writer, Leonardo Sciascia, puzzling over the question of how far Pirandello's espousal of Fascism can be attributed to an ideological affinity and how far to personal expediency, argued that if one were to judge by his work alone the 'vein of antiparliamentarism' that runs through it is not sufficient to explain his adherence to Fascism, particularly after the murder of Matteotti.[9] The assessment seems unduly generous; Pirandello's political views were inescapably authoritarian and anti-democratic, revealing something more that just a 'vein of antiparliamentarism'. This can be seen in the following extract from his early novel, *Il fu Mattia Pascal*, which comes when Mattia, now Adriano Meis, encounters a drunk late at night in a deserted Roman street who gives him a homily on democracy. The passage, which is uncharacteristic only in that it is so forthright, claims that the real cause of Italy's evils lies in democracy because it is 'a tyranny masked as liberty':

'Ma la causa vera di tutti i nostri mali, di questa tristezza nostra, sai qual è? La democrazia, mio caro, la democrazia, cioè il governo della maggioranza. Perchè, quando il potere è in mano d'uno solo, quest'uno sa d'esser uno e di dover contentare molti; ma quando i molti governano, pensano soltanto a contentar se stessi, e si ha allora la tirannia più balorda e più odiosa: la tirannia mascherata da libertà.

---

[9] 'Chi nulla sapendo della vita di Pirandello e conoscendone l'opera riuscirebbe a immaginare un'adesione al fascismo che sembra addirittura entusiastica? [. . .] C'è, sì, una vena di antiparlamentarismo che corre nell'opera: ma non è sufficiente a spiegare l'adesione al fascismo, specialmente dopo il delitto Matteotti.' ('Who, knowing nothing about the life of Pirandello and knowing his work, could manage to imagine an adherence to Fascism that gives the appearance of actually being enthusiastic? [. . .] Yes, there is an anti-parliamentary vein running through his works: but it is not enough to explain his adherence to Fascism, particularly after the Matteotti crime.') From a speech given by Leonardo Sciascia at the University of Unamuno in Salamanca and quoted in Maria Luisa Aguirre D'Amico, *Album Pirandello* (Milan, Mondadori, 1992), 215. This biography written by a granddaughter of Pirandello's, also a writer, suggests that his espousal of Fascism was intended to further the fortunes of his theatre company, and that, for its part, Fascism remained deeply suspicious of Pirandello and his writing. She quotes (pp. 218–19) from official police archives that described Pirandello as 'fascista di coloro che portano il distintivo all'occhiello, ma non nel cuore, ambizioso, maldicente, ciarlatano, facile a cambiare idee e padrone a seconda del tornaconto' ('the sort of Fascist who wears a badge in his lapel, but not in his heart, ambitious, malicious, a charlatan, quick to change ideas and boss according to where his interests lie').

Ma sicuramente! Oh perchè credi che soffra io? Io soffro appunto per questa tirannia mascherata da libertà . . . Torniamo a casa!'[10]

'But the real cause of all our evils, our sorrow, if you but knew it, is democracy, dear chap, democracy, government by the majority. Because, when power is in the hands of a single man, he knows he is alone and must satisfy the majority; but when the majority has power, each only thinks about satisfying himself and so the most distorted and hateful tyranny is created: tyranny disguised as freedom. This is the truth! Why do you think I suffer so? Because of precisely this tyranny disguised as freedom . . . Let's go home!'

As this is a novel written nearly two decades before Mussolini came to power, it illustrates how Pirandello's support for the regime did not represent so much a change of ideology as a realization of a political position that was not alien to his thinking. In view of this, it is perhaps not surprising that the events in Italy had little impact on his writings. Indeed at the very time he was making himself a spokesman for the regime, the status he enjoyed in his own country allowed him to travel abroad, meet writers and directors, see productions, and generally come into contact with European culture, and above all German and French theatre. Where a tension does then develop is in the fact that while Italian culture under Fascism drew in on itself, becoming provincial and hostile to the impact of modernism, Pirandello's theatre in the same years lost more and more of its indigenous origins and became increasingly Europeanized.

Pirandello usually maintained a clear distinction in his speeches and writings between aesthetics and politics (his most overtly political work was his historical novel *I vecchi e i giovani* (*The Old and the Young*, 1908) which was located in the Sicily of the late nineteenth century) and in the 1920s his Fascist sympathies did not infiltrate his public comments on the artistic choices that confronted his new theatre company, Il Teatro d'Arte di Roma. He concentrated instead on the ways in which the company would be different from other experimental companies, singling out the attention that would be paid to the technical and artistic aspects of staging ('tutto dovrà concorrere a rendere perfetto il quadro scenico e compiuta la realizzazione dell'opera d'arte', 'everything should contribute towards

---

[10] Pirandello, *Tutti i romanzi*, i. 448–9 (tr. 128).

perfecting the scenic picure and the realization of the work of art'), the seriousness that would be given to casting ('io avrò, per esempio, quattro prime attrici, tre primi attori e via discorrendo in modo da poter scegliere gli individui più adatti ad interpretare i vari lavori', 'for example I will have four first actresses, three first actors and so on so that I will be able to choose the individuals who are best suited to interpret the different works'), the importance that would be given to rehearsals and, in keeping with this, the expectation that the actor would actually learn the lines, and so remove the need for a prompter to speak the lines throughout the performance.[11] In the contract issued to the actors who became members of the theatre company, a clause was added where they had to agree to act without a prompter—a radical move at a time when in Italian theatre the prompter still spoke the whole play in a voice that was clearly audible to the audience.[12] Pirandello foresaw a repertoire of some twenty to twenty-five plays in the first season, all of them new to the Italian stage ('Molti giovani italiani, qualche espressionista tedesco, Vildrac e Romains tra i francesi, uno e due ungheresi, uno o due russi postbolschevichi',[13] 'Many of the young Italians, a few German Expressionists, Vitrac and Romains from among the French, one or two Hungarians, one or two post-Bolshevik Russians'). Although the reality was to be more limited, none the less, alongside some of the most interesting works of the European avant-garde (including Jarry, Strindberg, Apollinaire, Schnitzler, and Brecht), the company staged contemporary Italian plays, most of them new to the Italian public, by among others, Rosso di San Secondo, Marinetti, Bontempelli, De Stefani, and Savarese.

The project itself was attracting considerable interest in the press. Pirandello's idea was that the Teatro Odescalchi, redesigned by the Futurist architect and stage designer Virgilio Marchi, should be a centre for all the performance arts—afternoon concerts, dance, and mime as well as theatre—and along

---

[11] D'Amico and Tinterri, *Pirandello capocomico*, 15.

[12] A concluding comment in a review in *The Times* (25 June 1925) of a production of *Vestire gli ignudi* that the Teatro d'Arte brought to London in 1925 noted the audibility of the prompter: 'And, as usual with these Italian companies, the prompter kept up a kind of hissing commentary on the play throughout the evening'. Bassnett and Lorch, *Pirandello in the Theatre*, 117.

[13] D'Amico and Tinterri, *Pirandello capocomico*, 15–16.

with the thirteen actors and actresses, he included a Russian choreographer and co-ordinator and his wife, the dancer Raissa Lork, who was later to marry Giorgio de Chirico, one of the five set-designers. He himself was artistic director, a role he shared with three others—his son Stefano Landi, Oriano Vergani, and Lamberto Picasso. Among the actors that were signed up came one complete surprise. From Milan came news of a new production of Chekhov's *The Seagull* with a stunning performance by a very young actress called Marta Abba, who was appearing in her first professional role. Pirandello dispatched Guido Salvini to Milan to see her perform and sign her up if she was good. In the event he was so excited by her that they even agreed to the unusually high fees that she demanded—she entered the company as one of its most inexperienced members, but also the best paid.

The Teatro d'Arte was finally launched on 2 April 1925 with two short, visually spectacular plays; Pirandello's *Sagra del Signore della Nave* (*The Festival of Our Lord of the Ship*) and Lord Dunsany's *The Mountain Gods* (*Gli dèi della montagna*). Marta Abba's début with the company came on 22 April 1925 in Bontempelli's *Nostra Dea* (*Our Goddess*) for which she received excellent reviews. The first season, which ended in June that year, was generally held to have been a great artistic success; among the few dissenting voices was that of Adriano Tilgher,[14] who criticized it for failing to be an avant-garde theatre and for presenting works that could have been staged at any other theatre. Financially, though, the season was a disaster and the company had to take the first steps towards becoming exactly what Pirandello had intended it should not be, a travelling theatre.

What importance should we give to the period 1925 to 1928 when Pirandello was director of his own company? Did it lead to significant changes to his work as playwright? One must distinguish between what Pirandello the dramatist writes on the question of the *mise-en-scène* and what he, as director, practised. Let

---

[14] The relationship between Pirandello and Adriano Tilgher, one of his most energetic supporters, had become strained for political reasons. After *Il Tempo*, the newspaper where Tilgher published his theatre reviews, was closed down by Mussolini, Tilgher, an anti-Fascist, had joined *Il Mondo* a newspaper under the editorship of the courageous anti-Fascist leader Giorgio Amendola.

us turn first to his activities as theatre director. In this field he was more conservative than the texts of his theatre would lead us to believe, with the result that when he took his company on tour to Germany in the autumn of 1925, audiences were surprised at how conventional his presentation of his plays was when compared with what they were accustomed to. While the plays themselves, and in particular the trilogy, seemed to be written to fit with the vogue in 1920s Germany for the kind of directors' theatre practised by Appia, Piscator, and Reinhardt, his own productions of these works seemed by contrast oddly dated.

To understand the gap between what Pirandello created as director and what Pirandello wrote as playwright, one has take into account the state of Italian theatre at that time. In contrast to the director-led theatre found abroad, when Pirandello turned to directing he joined a long-established Italian tradition of playwright-directors reaching back to the Renaissance and including Carlo Goldoni. (This is not to suggest that the *commedia dell'arte* exercised a negative influence on then current theatre practices; on the contrary many of the innovations on stage introduced by Pirandello, and more radically by the Italian Futurists, had their origins in *commedia* theatre. For example, by trying to work against the division between auditorium and stage they were returning theatre to earlier practices, although Pirandello never, as in Goldoni's day, seated spectators on stage. Closer to Pirandello's interest in performance was the *commedia dell'arte*'s emphasis on the skills of the actor over and above the written text.) Indeed the concept of the professional director who was neither author of the work nor a member of the cast was so unfamiliar in Italy that, according to the philologist Bruno Migliorini, the word for director (*regista*), did not appear in the language until 1931.[15] The word used by Pirandello to refer to the role of the director in *Sei personaggi in cerca d'autore* is *capocomico* (the *Nota bene* and cast-list preceding Act I refer to the *Direttore-Capocomico*), which translates as 'actor-manager' or 'stage-director'. It was also the term used to describe Pirandello's function within the Teatro d'Arte. The first written reference in Italy to the figure of the theatre-director

---

[15] Bassnett and Lorch, *Pirandello in the Theatre*, 147.

appeared in an article on an Italian tour by the French director Pitoëff whose production of *Sei personaggi in cerca d'autore* had exercised such a powerful influence over Pirandello. Written by the influential theatre historian and close friend of Pirandello, Silvio D'Amico, the title speaks for itself: 'L'avvento di un despota nuovo sulla scena del teatro drammatico'[16] ('The Advent of a New Despot on the Theatrical Stage'). Pirandello took a similar position when, late in his career, he was asked to comment on the awkwardly expressed assertion: 'La diminuzione dei nostri grandi attori dipende dalla supremazia del regista?' ('Does the diminishing of our great actors stem from the supremacy of the director?') and in his reply suggested that the director's presence disrupts the creative process by which the actor internalizes the character he or she is to play:

Essi continuano a parlare secondo il testo stabilito, ma è come se lo creassero essi spontaneamente e si ha la precisa impressione che una battuta improvvisata non li metterebbe in imbarazzo, che essi potrebbero seguitare [. . .] a parlare spontaneamente senza tradire la loro 'parte' [. . .]. In questo momento privilegiato, ogni intromissione del regista, soprattutto quello moderno, diventa inutile, incongruente. L'attore 'rigetta' letteralmente il *metteur-en-scène* [. . .]. Ed io mi domando se la diminuzione dei nostri grandi attori non dipenda appunto dalla supremazia data al regista.[17]

They continue to speak according to the established text, but it is as if they had created it spontaneously themselves, and one has the very clear impression that an improvised riposte would not cause them any embarrassment, that they could continue [. . .] speaking spontaneously without betraying their 'part' [. . .]. In this privileged moment, any intervention by the director, and above all a modern director, would be useless, incongruous. The actor literally 'rejects' the *metteur-en-scene* [. . .]. And I ask myself if the diminishing of our great actors does not stem, precisely, from the supremacy of the director.

The above statement is entirely consistent with Pirandello's presentation of the figure of the director in *Questa sera si recita a soggetto* (*Tonight We Improvise*, 1929), the third in the trilogy of meta-plays. Where *Sei personaggi* dramatized the struggle

---

[16] Silvio D'Amico, *Comoedia*, 8/8 (15 Apr. 1926), 11–14.
[17] Franca Angelini, 'Dall'arrazzo alla scena: Pirandello e la messinscena', in AAVV, *Testo e messinscena in Pirandello* (Urbino, La Nuova Italia Scientifica, 1986), 17. The interview was given to *L'Illustrazione del popolo* in 1935.

between actors and characters, and *Ciascuno a suo modo* that between actors and audience, *Questa sera si recita a soggetto* presents the issue of director-led theatre in terms of a power struggle between director and actors—on this occasion the author is knocked out in the first round. Dr Hinkfuss, referred to as *direttore*, compensates for his absurdly diminuitive stature— 'un omarino non più alto di un ditino' ('a tiny little man no taller than a little finger')—with dictatorial posturing; he is a *supremo* who resists all challenges to his authority from audience and actors alike. The decision to improvise the play is motivated purely by his wish, in his words, to eliminate the author. The play was unfavourably received at its première in Königsberg where the caricatured director was interpreted as being a thinly veiled attack on Max Reinhardt—an assumption that was probably incorrect given that Pirandello owed much of his success in Germany to its leading director, a debt which he acknowledged in a dedication he wrote in the copy of *Questa sera* that he gave to him ('A Max Reinhardt, la cui incomparabile forza creatrice ha dato magica vita sulla scena tedesca a *Sei personaggi*, io dedico con profonda riconoscenza', 'To Max Reinhardt, whose incomparable creative force has given to *Sei personaggi* a magical life on the German stage, I dedicate this with profound gratitude'). The play was much more consonant with attitudes expressed in Italian circles where, as we have seen, hostility to the concept of a director continued to be voiced.

There were other significant differences between theatre practices in Italy and elsewhere in Europe, among which arguably the most fundamental was the antiquated structure of the touring company itself—something that Pirandello had to contend with in his work as dramatist and which he tried to resolve in his period as director. In his last play, *I giganti della montagna*, he includes in its cast just such a traditional company whose actors travel great distances, often on foot, carrying all their props, sets, and costumes with them. It was a practice that, as we saw, Pirandello had wished at all costs to avoid with his own company. The travelling company frequently had a repertoire of as many as thirty plays and with very few rehearsals, staging a different play every night, actors were not expected to know their parts perfectly. Small wonder that the prompter would speak the roles with the actors.

However, as Pirandello saw it, not all the problems were explained by the difficult conditions under which actors had to work; for instance it is clear from *Sei personaggi* that the use of a crude, basic set was simply the result of sloppy, unprofessional practice. At the beginning of the play, Pirandello has the prompter read aloud his stage directions for Act II of *Il giuoco delle parti*, the play the company has assembled to rehearse (and which some of the audience may have seen performed). In this way he draws the audience's attention to the gap between the detailed stage directions provided by the dramatist in the written text and their casual interpretation by the *capocomico* on stage. What is intended by the playwright to make an impact on the audience, namely, the eccentric impression communicated by a set that crosses a dining-room with a study, 'una strana sala da pranzo e da studio'[18] ('a peculiar room, both dining-room and study'), is brushed aside by the *capocomico* who orders instead the standard scenery for a drawing-room. Later in the play, another standard set representing 'the small drawing-room' is used for Madama Pace's dress-shop and brothel. The Stepdaughter's protest that the sofa used in the seduction scene was yellow and not green: 'Era giallo, fiorato, di "peluche", molto grande! Comodissimo'[19] ('It was yellow, yellow velvet with flowers on it: it was enormous! And so comfortable!') is dismissed with the comment 'Ma non importa! metta quello che c'è' ('It doesn't matter! Give me whatever there is'). Such a cavalier approach to stage scenery, which both ignores the playwright's instructions and runs counter to the meticulous attention to detail that was a mark of late nineteenth-century realism, is later shown much more sympathetically in *I giganti della montagna* (and, as we shall see, experience may have played a part here) to be the result of financial hardship and the nomadic existence of companies, but in *Sei personaggi* it is a manifestation of the director's indifference to theatre as an art-form. At the same time elsewhere in Europe, helped again by the arrival of the professional director who, given his independence from both the writer and the leading actor, would have been driven by a desire to leave his own imprint on the production, a new interest in and exploration of the semiotic function of the

---

[18] Pirandello, *Maschere nude*, ii. 675.   [19] Ibid. 708.

stage-set was under way. From Edward Gordon Craig's 'stage-visions', where the sets carry their own semiotics of meaning that the actors with their programmed function as *Über-marionette* endorse, through to the thirty-second play by Samuel Beckett, *Breath*, where only the set appears and the human agent is dispensed with altogether, one finds in twentieth-century avant-garde theatre a developing exploration of the signifying capacity of the set beyond its being a mere backdrop. It was not to be so during this period in Italy. Pirandello for his part never sought to make the set the subject of a play, but he does insist that costume and stage should be metonymic accessories to his characters. And nowhere is this illustrated more succinctly than in the literal turn given to the evocation of character through ambience in *Sei personaggi*, with the materialization of the dressmaker cum brothel-keeper Madama Pace who, as the Father suggests, is drawn from the back of the auditorium to the stage by the fixtures and fittings of her profession: 'Ecco, signore: forse, preparandole meglio la scena, attratta dagli oggetti stessi del suo commercio, chi sa che non venga tra noi'[20] ('Yes, of course: perhaps, if we dress the set better, she will be drawn by the articles of her trade and, who knows, she may even come to join us').

These aspects of stagecraft are secondary, however, to Pirandello's main theoretical and practical concern with the actor and acting. If, after a struggle, author and character can merge in a unity of expression and purpose, can the same be said of actor and character? While Pirandello both directed his own and other playwrights' work, and in so doing frequently demonstrated to his actors how a role was to be performed, he never acted professionally, so he always had to entrust his characters to others. The rest of this book will focus on the different issues raised by the relationship Pirandello establishes in his work between actor and acting. For much of the playwright's adult life, Italian theatre remained burdened with the remnants of the convention of the *mattatore* or star who dominated every show, a practice which descends from an acting tradition associated with the stereotyped roles of *commedia dell'arte*. A widely used term, *mattatore* referred to the lead role. It has a comic

---

[20] Pirandello, *Maschere nude*, ii. 717.

origin, a pun on 'matadore' or killer of bulls; in theatre it was used to refer to the killer of roles. Until the beginning of the 1920s the power exercised by the *mattatori* was so absolute that they could change the lines to their advantage, dictate how the play was to be performed, and in every conceivable way ensure that their own performance took precedence over the script. Such displays of *protagonismo* were inevitably to the detriment of the integrity of the artistic work. Acting in Italy continued well into the twentieth century to be more of a science than an art, with actors learning their techniques from early nineteenth-century acting-manuals,[21] although many of them also learnt their trade on the job by being born into actors' families. The trilogy presents many of the shortcomings and abuses of then current acting practices: to identify just one, the satire on the company of stock character-actors in *Sei personaggi*, referred to purely in terms of their position within the hierarchy of the company ('first actress', etc.) who show themselves to be as inflexible as the stage-sets that they have to perform against. Before we go on to the final play in the trilogy, I want to return to a play which we looked at briefly Chapter 6 and which though one of his most frequently performed, is not often discussed in terms of a commentary on acting.

One of only two extant plays by Pirandello to be labelled 'a tragedy'—the other is *La vita che ti diedi* (*The Life That I Gave You*)—*Enrico IV* is not commonly read as meta-theatre[22] and yet there are interesting points of comparison with its immediate predecessor, *Sei personaggi in cerca d'autore*. Both are plays within plays, but in *Enrico IV* there is no frame to help distinguish the different levels of reality. Where in the one the audience arrives in an auditorium with a bare stage which has not been prepared for a performance, in the other the curtain rises on a set which is 'rigidamente parato' ('carefully prepared') to represent as accurately as possible the throne-room of Henry IV. Even the costumes, an entire wardobe of them, are all authentic, we learn, 'eseguiti a perfezione, su modelli antichi' ('perfectly

---

[21] Manuals such as Antonio Marrochesi, *Lezioni di declamazione e d'arte teatrale*, or Alamanno Morelli's *Prontuario delle pose sceniche* (a handbook of stage poses). See William Weaver, *Duse: A Biography* (London, Thames and Hudson, 1984).

[22] See Franca Angelini, in *Il Novecento*, i (Bari, Laterza, 1976), 418–20, and Lucio Lugnani, 'Intorno a *Enrico IV*', in *Testo e messa in scena di Pirandello*, 36.

made to period designs'). And yet it too opens in confusion for it is not clear if what is being presented is a play or, in the light of its predecessor, a rehearsal for a play. Its claim to be a historical costume drama is undermined by the stage-set which includes in the midst of the antique furnishings two full-length contemporary portraits executed in oils. This is a play which from the outset emphasizes its theatricality. The costumes, though, as we have seen, are perfect—no expense has been spared. It falls to one of the courtiers, Landolfo, to speak with pride on several occasions about the costumes, for they are his special responsibility. Not only, he claims, would they make, 'una bellissima comparsa in una rappresentazione storica, a uso di quelle che piacciono tanto oggi nei teatri'[23] ('And these costumes would look tremendous in a history play . . . history plays are all the rage these days'), but there is also such a wealth of cloth that they could provide for several such historical dramas.

The audience's attention, however, is held by something other than the extravagance of the wardrobe itself as they watch the group of visitors to Henry's court at Goslar dress up in their historical costumes on stage. In the case of Belcredi, who disguises himself as a harmless Cluniac monk, the costume fails to conceal his identity as Henry's former rival in love and on meeting him Henry will insist that he is his arch-enemy Pietro Damiani. But for the timorous, colourless Frida, stepping into the Marchioness Matilde Spina's magnificent ballgown means she acquires another persona, as is revealed in her newfound imperious hauteur. (Such careful attention to dress contrasts with the shocked reaction of the actor Ruggero Ruggeri when he heard that he was to wear a new costume especially designed for the role of Henry in his performance at the Teatro d'Arte in the summer of 1925, instead of his customary 'costume nero', which he claimed had always brought him both luck and success.) Dress alone though does not make the part, as the ever perspicacious Landolfo points out, for the courtiers exist in a vacuum. Unlike their historical counterparts who were unaware that they were playing a part, they know they are performing and yet at the same time they have no 'content' or script: 'Come

---

[23] Pirandello, *Maschere nude*, ii. 785 (tr. J. Mitchell, in *Three Plays* (London, Methuen, 1985), 141).

sei pupazzi appesi al muro, che aspettanto qualcuno che li prenda e che li muova così e cosii e faccia dir loro qualche parola'[24] ('We're like six puppets hanging on the wall, waiting for someone to take us down and move us about and give us something to say'). What becomes clear soon after the play opens is that one of the 'courtiers' is in an even worse situation: thinking that he was preparing for a role in the story of the more familiar historical figure of King Henry IV of France, he has learnt the wrong part altogether. It sets the scene for a play which continuously returns to questions of identity, particularly, of course, in relation to Henry IV himself. On this occasion, instead of considering him in terms of the fiction within which he has chosen to live, I shall look at Henry's performance as a commentary on acting.

Where in *Sei personaggi in cerca d'autore* a rehearsal is disrupted by the arrival of a group of people who come from outside the theatre, in *Enrico IV* the carefully recreated court of the eleventh-century Holy Roman Emperor is invaded by a group of wealthy outsiders dressed in a style consonant with their own reality; they belong to Roman high society of the 1920s. (In Pirandello's day it meant that they were part of a reality that the audience shared; produced today, a director has to decide whether to introduce a second level of historicity or make them the audience's contemporaries.) They invade a set where the eponymous protagonist functions both as *primo attore* and *capocomico*, enjoying a power over his sham court comparable to that exercised by the *mattatore* over his company. Only the text comes from elsewhere but even that is appropriated by Enrico for his purposes, as Franca Angelini points out:

L'*Enrico IV* è anche e principalmente un apologo dell'attore. Un attore protagonista [. . .], un attore dittatoriale, che piega ai suoi piani e obbliga alla recitazione tutti coloro che si mettono nella sua strada; che guida la recitazione degli altri usandoli senza esserne usata. Un attore che dunque è anche regista, perchè impone l'ordine della scena, le entrate, le presenze e che impone i ruoli assegnando i nomi secondo il suo capriccio. [. . .]

Il testo che Enrico 1V usa per la sua vendetta è, con molta ironia, nientemeno che la storia.[25]

[24] Ibid. 786 (tr. J. Mitchell, 141).
[25] Angelini, *Il Novecento*, i. 67–8.

Henry IV is also and principally an apologist for the actor. An actor-protagonist [. . .], a dictatorial actor who subordinates others to his designs and demands a performance from all those who come his way, who directs the performance of others and uses them without being used by them. So an actor who is also a director, because he imposes the way the scene will go, the entrances, the presences and who imposes the roles distributing names according to his whims.

The text used by Henry IV for his revenge is, with great irony, nothing less than history itself.

When the audience watch him on stage, he is a man who knows that he is playing a role, the script has been given to him by history, and he enacts it over and over again with consummate skill. We learn from the visitors, who are of course unaware of the dimension of self-awareness in his performance that their friend had over a period of twelve years, acted out the part of Henry IV, without distinguishing between himself and the historical figure whose persona he had adopted. He had initially taken on the part when, as a young man, he had participated in a cavalcade devised by his circle of friends to idle away the time, but while the others 'recitava ognuno per burla la sua parte'[26] ('acted out our parts for fun'), he identified completely with the persona. In a letter Pirandello wrote to Ruggero Ruggeri giving an outline of the projected play, he includes in his account of the *antefatto* (the events leading up to the story enacted on stage), the following description of the protagonist:

Uno di questi signori s'era scelto il personaggio di Enrico IV; e per rappresentarlo il meglio possibile s'era dato la pena e il tormento d'uno studio intensissimo, minuzioso e preciso, che lo aveva quasi per circa un mese ossessionato.

One of these gentlemen had chosen for himself the part of Henry IV; and to perform it to the best of his ability, he had given himself the anguish and torment of a very intensive analysis, very detailed and precise, which had obsessed him for about a month.

After falling from his horse, he continues, the bang to his head left him in such a state of cerebral confusion that he came to believe that he was the Emperor:

Non ci fu verso di rimuoverlo più da quella fissazione, di fargli lasciare quel costume in cui s'era mascherato; *la maschera*, con tanta ossessione

---

[26] Pirandello, *Maschere nude*, ii. 803 (tr. as Pirandello, *Three Plays*, 154).

studiata fino allo scrupolo dei minimi particolari, diventò in lui *la persona* del grande e tragico Imperatore.[27]

There was no way to remove that fixation from his head, to get him to abandon the dress which masked him; *the mask* studied with such scrupulosity in every one of its smallest details, became in him *the persona* of the great and tragic Emperor.)

As one of the visitors to his court says, the result is that 'è diventato, con la pazzia, un attore magnifico e terribile!'[28] ('he became, with the madness, a magnificient and terrifying actor'). Where before the start of the play he was a 'madman' who believed himself to be the part he was playing, by the time we see him on stage, he plays the role in full consciousness of what he is doing. A public is essential to turn him into the consummate actor that he is and although accustomed to perform in front of his court, he now has the added incentive provided by his visitors. When in Act II he reveals that he is 'cured' (the verb 'curare' can mean both 'to treat' and 'to cure' in Italian), he acknowledges that he knows that he is not Henry IV by abandoning both the script and the role, but far from feeling liberated, the courtiers are terrorized, no longer knowing what to do with themselves, and so he resumes the fiction with a tyrannical gesture and orders them to bow before him touching the ground three times with their foreheads. They obey.[29]

The play can be seen as heralding the way to a different and more frightening representation of the actor who transmogrifies into the role, losing him or herself in the process. The risks are appalling, as we shall shortly see confirmed in *Questa sera si recita a soggetto*, the last in the experimental trilogy. *Enrico IV* marks an important moment in the evolution of Pirandello's thinking about acting. It is an unusual play in the author's career not only because he called it a 'tragedy', but also because it is one of the few that have no links with his narrative. It is not a translation from page to stage, but is conceived of entirely in terms of performance, in which theatricality operates as metaphor for life off-stage. Pirandello makes the metaphor explicit in one of the last public statements he was to deliver on theatre

---

[27] Letter written to Ruggeri, 21 Sept. 1921. See *Maschere nude*, ii. 761.
[28] Ibid. 802.   [29] Ibid. 844.

before his death. It comes in his presidential address at the Volta Conference on Dramatic Theatre of 1934 already quoted from in the epigraph to this chapter:

Il Teatro non può morire.
    Forma della vita stessa, tutti ne siamo attori, e aboliti o abbandonati i teatri, il teatro seguiterebbe nella vita, insopprimibile; e sarebbe sempre spettacolo la natura stessa delle cose.[30]

The theatre cannot die.
    It is a form of life itself and we are all actors in it. If theatres were abandoned and left to rot, then theatre would continue in life, it could not be suppressed, and the very nature of things would always be spectacle.

It underlines the evolution in his thinking which took him from a concept of theatre conceived of primarily in terms of the written word where the text had precedence over performance, to theatre understood not only as performance art but as 'a form of life itself'.

    To appreciate the extent to which Pirandello's ideas on theatre changed one need only look back to his essay 'Illustratori, attori e traduttori' ('Illustrators, Actors, Translators') of 1908, where his argument is built on the unquestioned primacy of the written text. Here he saw the actor much in the same way as he would later look upon the director—as an unfortunate, but inevitable element in the stage-production of a play. The only way, he suggested, that a performance could avoid being a travesty of the written text would be if the characters were to leap, miraculously, from the page and come to life before the audience's eyes, like the figures who step down from the tapestries that line the walls of the Castle of Blaye in Heinrich Heine's poem.[31] As it is, the actor has to translate into performance what is inscribed on the page and in the process will inevitably create a character who will be markedly different from how either author or reader had imagined. The terms in which he presents the discussion are in themselves revealing. Just as an illustration to a piece of text (here he refers to the then recent practice in France of using photographs to accompany realist narratives with the idea of heightening their aura of

---

[30] Pirandello, *Spsv* 1037 (tr. Bassett and Lorch, *Pirandello in the Theatre*, 173).
[31] See Ch. 1, p. 13.

reality) conflicts with the visual picture created by the reader in the reading-process, so the actor conceives the character from her or his own viewpoint. The influence exercised by *verismo* in Pirandello's literary formation can be adduced from his unquestioning adoption of its hermeneutics of reading whereby primacy is given to a visual rather than a literary aesthetics. In a section of Barthes's *S/Z*, called 'Le modèle de la peinture' ('Painting as a model'), Barthes notes that:

Toute description littéraire est une *vue*. On dirait que l'énonciateur, avant de décrire, se poste à la fenetre, non tellement pour bien voir, mais pour fonder ce qu'il voit par son cadre même: l'embrasure fait le spectacle.

Every literary description is a *view*. It could be said that the speaker, before describing, stands at the window, not so much to see, but to establish what he sees by its very frame: the window frame creates the scene.[32]

He goes on to claim that in copying the real the writer is in practice copying a copy of the real. Barthes is interested in the reality-effect, the illusion of reality that is thus created for us. Pirandello is interested in how reading as a medium allows us each to develop a hermeneutics based on sight in which, within the guidelines provided by the text, we are free to picture each in our own way. What concerns him is the presence of a go-between, be it actor or director, who provides their version of the written portrait. It is an argument that is reiterated by the theatre director, Dr Hinkfuss, in *Questa sera si recita a soggetto* when he notes that one cannot know the written text by watching it performed on stage:

L'unica sarebbe se l'opera potesse rappresentarsi da sè, non più con gli attori, ma coi suoi stessi personaggi che, per prodigio, assumessero corpo e voce. In tal caso sì, direttamente potrebbe essere giudicata a teatro.[33]

The only way it could be done would be if the work could perform itself, no longer with actors, but with its very own characters who, by some miracle, acquired a body and a voice. In such circumstances, yes, one could make a judgement on the production.

---

[32] Roland Barthes, *S/Z* (Paris, Éditions du Seuil, 1970), 61 (tr. Richard Miller (Oxford, Blackwell, 1974), 54).
[33] Pirandello, *Maschere nude, Opera omnia*, i (Milan, Mondadori, 1948), 205.

Twenty years earlier, Pirandello had argued that the problem was twofold, and that both aspects were insurmountable. First of all, outwardly no actor can ever appear as the physical embodiment of a character simply because no two people can look the same, while inwardly no actor can eliminate his own personality and fill that vacuum with another. The stumbling-block is clear: it lies in Pirandello's perception of the dramatis personae as existing both before and after the play is performed, and not as simply being brought into existence by the performance itself. We have seen in Chapter 2, how in *Sei personaggi* the entire play is posited on the belief that the Characters' existence precedes the text, and that their transferral from a pre-textual to a post-textual existence and the travesties that occur during the transition are presented as being their problem, not the author's. It is reconfirmed at the close of the play in the 1925 version when the Director calls for light, so destroying the theatrical illusion. When the lights are again turned off the Mother, Father, and Son, but not the two little children who died during the performance, reappear like ghosts to occupy the stage, while the Stepdaughter runs down the steps and out of the auditorium, leaving behind the theatrical space altogether. The Director had wanted the lights to dispel the fiction, to show that it was all illusion; the directions are destined to confirm the reality of the Characters:

Come l'autore, per fare opera viva, deve immedesimarsi con la sua creatura, fino a sentirla com'essa sente se stessa, a volerla com'essa vuole se stessa; così e non altrimenti, se fosse possibile, dovrebbe fare l'attore.

Ma anche quando si trovi un grande attore che riesca a spogliarsi del tutto della propria individualità per entrare in quella del personaggio ch'egli deve rappresentare, l'incarnazione piena e perfetta è ostacolata spesso da ragioni di fatto irrimediabili: dalla figura stessa dell'attore per esempio.[34]

Just as the author has to merge wih his character in order to make it live, to the point of feeling as it feels, desiring as it desires itself, so also to no lesser degree, if that can be accomplished, must the actor.

But even when one can find a great actor who can strip himself completely of his own individuality and enter into that of the character

---

[34] Pirandello, *Spsv* 215 (tr. Bassnett and Lorch, 27).

that he is playing, a total, full incarnation is often hindered by unavoidable facts: for example, by the actor's own appearance.

The care Pirandello takes with the presentation of his characters' appearance can be judged from the descriptions that precede their entry on to the stage. Sometimes they take the form of a caricature, much as an artist (Pirandello was a skilled caricaturist and one of his sons, Fausto, was a painter) might do a sketch, exaggerating certain physical traits to the disadvantage of the subject. Such as is the case of Dr Hinkfuss in *Questa sera si recita a soggetto*, whose intellectual authority (and much of what he says in his disquisitions on theatre is complex and interesting) is persistently undermined by that one aspect of his persona over which he has no control, his appearance:

In frak, con un rotoletto di carta sotto il braccio, il Dottor Hinkfuss ha la terribilissima e ingiustissima condanna d'essere un omarino alto poco più d'un braccio. Ma se ne vendica portando un testone di capelli così. Si guarda prima le manine che forse incutano ribrezzo anche a lui, da quanto sono gracili e con certi ditini pallidi e pelosi come bruchi.[35]

Wearing a dinner-jacket with a large roll of paper under his arm, Dr Hinkfuss suffers the terrible, unfair burden of being such a miniscule man, hardly more than an arm's length. But he gets his own back by having a huge head of hair. He looks first at his tiny hands that perhaps revolt him as well, given that they are so slender with tiny, hairy little fingers like grubs.

In a stylistic move that is very typical of his writings Pirandello uses diminutives to reduce metaphorically as well as physically the stature of the man. He is an 'omarino' whose 'ditini' on his 'manine' provoke disgust; the contrasting size of his 'testone' does nothing to improve matters for him. At the same time, the playwright exploits the signifying potential of what is perhaps the single most important constituent of our public identity and the aspect of self over which we have the least control—our physical appearance. The body occupies a uniquely important position because while it contains the self and makes it separate and unique, it is also the threshold by which others come to know us, or think they know us. Traditionally employed in literature metonymically, as access to the character's soul or

---

[35] *Maschere nude, Opera omnia*, 202.

psychology, Pirandello's sketches, which are often a highly effective form of character assassination, are energized by their own cruelty.

There is no detectable difference in his approach to portraiture between the plays and the narratives. In both cases the reader (for the detail assumes of course a reading rather a viewing of the play) is presented with a thumbnail sketch which lingers over the grotesque appearance of the individual. In *Il fu Mattia Pascal*, for example, the description of the poor, duped tutor Pinzone 'd'una magrezza che incuteva ribrezzo' ('he was so thin it was repellent') is followed by a portrait of the corrupt estate-manager, Batta Malagna, who appropriates in a series of dishonest financial transactions the protagonist's family estate, but whose wife will succumb to the sexual advances of a very much more attractive and younger protagonist. And the following description alone would ensure that her choice of lover would have the reader's complete sympathy:

Scivolava tutto: gli scivolavano nel lungo faccione, di qua e di là, le sopracciglia e gli occhi; gli scivolava il naso su i baffi melensi e sul pizzo; gli scivolavano dall'attaccatura del collo le spalle; gli scivolava il pancione languido, enorme, quasi fino a terra, perchè data l'imminenza di esso su le gambette tozze, il sarto, per vestirgli quelle gambette, era costretto a tagliargli quanto mai agiati i calzoni; cosicchè da lontano, pareva che indossasse invece, bassa bassa, una veste, e che la pancia gli arrivasse fino a terra.[36]

Everything was crooked about him: his eyebrows and eyes were crooked in his long face; his nose was crooked above his silly moustache and collar; his shoulders were crooked on his neck; even his stomach hung crooked, an enormous, drooping belly reaching almost to the ground. This was because his stomach stuck out so much that his tailor was obliged to cut his trousers extremely generously in order to clothe his legs, with the result that, from a distance, he looked as though he were wearing a long jacket and his belly reached to the ground.

As well as taking a delight in portraiture and caricature, Pirandello also used appearance as a contributing factor in the plot. In *Enrico IV*, for example, the treatment excogitated with

[36] Pirandello, *Tutti i romanzi*, i. 336 (tr. *The Late Mattia Pascal*, 29). I have used the published translation here, although it does not render the meaning of 'scivolare'—to slip or slide. The inference is that the character is so grossly overweight that his flesh goes its own way and hangs in rolls pulled down by the force of gravity.

tragic consequences by the doctor to effect the Emperor's 'cure' is postulated on a trick, the visual interchangeability of mother and daughter. It entails replacing an oil portrait of the mother, Donna Matilda, commissioned when she was her daughter's age, with the living presence of her daughter dressed in the same clothes that her mother wore for the portrait. (His audience, watching with the naked eye, would have had to take on trust the point that the daughter is the spitting image of her mother at that age, although it is worth recalling that in Pirandello's day the theatre-going public had recourse to binoculars much more than today.)[37]

I referred to two problems that Pirandello claimed faced actors in 'Illustratori, attori e traduttori' and I now want to turn to the second, which raises the question of how far actors can enter into the character whose part they assume. Here his work as director led to a very marked change of attitude. Seventeen years after Pirandello wrote the essay, practices had changed sufficiently for him to feel a new confidence in his actors' ability to respond to his demands. His own theatre company was made up of a group of actors from whom he could select those he felt best suited to the part. This was in itself a novelty, because it assumed that actors would not be repeating the same role—or playing themselves playing a part—with localized adjustments. He also aimed to rehearse the actors so intensively that they came to identify with the characters whose parts they were to take, so that it would be inconceivable for them to speak anything other than the words assocated with that character. In an article for *La Tribuna* of 1924, Osvaldo Gibertini described Pirandello's innovations as follows:

A tal scopo, Pirandello farà moltissime prove non in teatro ma a casa, spiegando e rispiegando agli attori il valore di ciascuna parola e di ciascuna frase per se stesse e in rapporto alla costruzione di tutto un dramma finchè avrà ottenuto che via via, non già l'attore si sia impadronito della parte del personaggio, ma bensì il personaggio si sia impadronito dell'attore, lo abbia assorbito in sé, in modo da 'costringerlo' ad agire e parlare secondo la nuova vita da cui è ormai stato investito e invaso.[38]

---

[37] By using binoculars, theatre audiences are also able to create their own field of vision. See Ch. 8 for a discussion of appearance and gender in Pirandello.

[38] Osvaldo Gibertini, 'Luigi Pirandello e la Compagnia d'arte', *La Tribuna* (27 Nov. 1924). There is a clear parallel here with Pirandello's representations of the creative moment for the writer.

To this end Pirandello will hold lots of rehearsals away from the theatre, at home, explaining over and again to the actors the value of every word and every phrase both in itself and in relation to the construction of the entire play, until he reaches a point where gradually it is no longer the actor who has taken control of the character's role, but the character who has taken control of the actor, who has taken him into himself, in such a way that he is 'forced' to behave and speak according to the new life which has by now entered him and possessed him.

The Pirandellian twist at the end of the description which sees the character dominate the actor rather than, as might be expected, the other way round, is confirmed in an interview Pirandello himself gave in France the same year and which was subsequently published in Italy: Here he describes the methods he adopted with his actors:

fare cominciare materialmente le prove dopo un intenso lavoro personale, intimo, profondo, che fa di ogni attore il personaggio quale veramente dovrebbe essere se vivesse. Io aiuto [. . .] questo lavoro con colloqui durante i quali spiego all'interprete prima lo spirito generale del lavoro, poi lo spirito particolare che è nel personaggio affidatogli, e quando tutti gli artisti si sono assimilati questo duplice pensiero, quando sono riuscito a compiere uno per uno in tutti questo miracolo necessario di spirituale transubstatazione [sic], allora li riunisco tutti insieme e spiego loro come debbono muoversi, come debbono parlare, quale tono di voce, quali accenti debbono usare.[39]

to get the rehearsals physically under way after intense, exhaustive, and in-depth work in private, which will make of each actor the character as he really should be were he to live. I help [. . .] this work with talks where I explain to the actor who is to interpret the role first the overall spirit of the play, then the particular spirit that belongs to the character entrusted to him and when all the artists have assimilated this double thought, once I have managed to carry out step by step in everybody this necessary miracle of spiritual transubstantiation, then I bring them all together and I explain to them how they must move, speak, what tone of voice, what accents they must use.

So his confidence in the ability of his acting company is directly related to the preparatory work he did with them. According to his stage and set designer Virgilio Marchi, Pirandello's proce-

---

[39] Luigi Pirandello in interview with L. Lacour, '*La Mise en scène* de Pirandello', *Arte drammatica* (5 Sept. 1925).

dures were intended to empty the actor of identity, 'assentarsi dal proprio io' ('empty himself of his own self'), with a perhaps unintended side-effect in some cases: 'deve risultare anche logico come egli abbia presso certi attori la fama di maestro che uccide gli attori'[40] ('it must also be perfectly clear why he has the reputation among some actors of being a *maestro* who kills actors').

What is significant about Pirandello's work as director is that it gave him the means to retain control over every step in the play's journey from text to performance, allowing him to exercise what some might see, as Marchi suggests, as an autocratic power over his actors. The interdependency of character and author that was traced in Chapter 2 through the three short stories that opened the way to *Sei personaggi in cerca d'autore* is reaffirmed here. In view of this, it is clear why Pirandello was fundamentally hostile to a directors' theatre, where the task of the director is not so much one of mediating between actor and text as interpreting the text afresh. Throughout his career as playwright, Pirandello never moved towards a position where he reduced his own control over the text. He exercised control in the written text through the inclusion of unusually detailed stage directions, nor within those instructions did he propose areas where the director or the company might make choices about the staging of the work. The more the work appears to enjoy an autonomy, the tighter the playwright's hold. But I would argue that this kind of control is very far removed from what Derrida in his defence of Artaud termed 'theological theatre':

The stage is theological for as long as it is dominated by speech, by a will to speech, by the layout of a primary logos which does not belong to the theatrical site and governs it from a distance. The stage is theological for as long as its structure, following the entirety of tradition, comports the following elements: an author-creator who, absent and from afar, is armed with a text and keeps watch over, assembles, regulates the time or the meaning of the representation, letting this latter *represent* him as concerns what is called the content of his thoughts, his intentions, his ideas. He lets representation represent him through representatives, directors or actors, enslaved interpreters

[40] Virgilio Marchi, 'Ricordi sul "Teatro d'Arte"', *Teatro Archivio* (4 May 1981), 24 n. 27.

who represent characters who, primarily through what they say, more or less directly represent the thought of the 'creator'.[41]

Pirandello exhibits none of the confidence that Derrida sees in traditional theatre that his word will be obeyed, or indeed that his word carries authority with anybody. Instead he presents himself as beset on all sides by quarrelsome and uncollaborative people, be they chararacters, actors, directors, or, of course, audience. For the Italian playwright, the staging of a play is always the product of an adversarial and never a collaborative relationship.

The clearest evidence we have of the change in Pirandello's attitude towards actors comes in *Questa sera si recita a soggetto* which was written and first performed in Berlin in 1929. He had arrived in Berlin the previous year after his own theatre company had folded. The play is the last in the trilogy and certainly the most undervalued of his repertoire. It opens with the arrival of the audience in the auditorium who sit down waiting expectantly for the curtain to rise, but instead the director, Dr Hinkfuss, appears in front of the curtain and delivers a lengthy speech in which he explains what he intends to do. At the same time he introduces his actors who appear disenchanted, almost truculent. At last the curtain rises on a 'rappresentazione sintetica della Sicilia con una processioncina religiosa'[42] ('a synthetic representation of Sicily with a sort of religious procession'). In a play that is replete with echoes of other plays and performances, this scene revives memories of the spectacular opening procession in Pirandello's one-act play *Sagra del Signore della Nave* (*The Festival of Our Lord of the Ship*) which was chosen for the inaugural night of the Teatro d'Arte at the Odescalchi. But the procession in *Questa sera si recita a soggetto* is cut short by a sudden burst of jazz, while the set changes into a nightclub interior where three dancers and a singer are performing before an audience which includes Sampognetta, one of the protagonists in the story Dr Hinkfuss has selected as his source.[43]

---

[41] Jacques Derrida, *Writing and Difference* (London, Routledge and Kegan Paul, 1978), 235.

[42] *Maschere nude, Opera omnia*, i. 222.

[43] The story's title 'Leonora addio' comes from *Il Trovatore*, a story of pathological jealousy and appalling cruelty. The play has the same ingredients but the focus switches to performance.

Set in Sicily, it is a tale of jealousy which revolves around the La Croce family. Sampognetta himself is a somewhat vacant and ineffectual father and husband who dies early on in a brawl in the nightclub, leaving his Neapolitan wife Signora Ignazia and their four beautiful and talented daughters to fend for themselves. One of them becomes a highly successful singer, well able to support her family. But their independent and liberated lifestyle (with the connotations of 'looseness' often associated with women performers) so horrifies the bigoted air-force officer, Rico Verri (who descends from a long genealogy of the pathologically jealous in Pirandello's fictions), married to one of the daughters, Mommina, that to ensure that his wife's reputation remains unblemished, he keeps her incarcerated at home, together with their two young daughters. His jealousy is motivated purely by his fear of gossip. When Mommina's mother and sisters arrive in town for a performance of *Il Trovatore*, Verri refuses to allow them to enter the house to see his wife and explains his behaviour with the following comment: 'Se tu sapessi lo scandalo che seguitano a dare! Ne parlano tutti in paese, e figurati la mia faccia . . .'[44] ('If you only knew the scandal that they are giving rise to! Everybody is talking about them in town, and you can imagine how I come out of it . . .').

After Verri's departure, Mommina tries to explain to her children what theatre is. She begins by describing the sense of occasion, the glamour, the build-up of expectation, and then she moves on to the story, trying to create for them the experience of theatre by singing the gypsy's song from the opera. But it reminds her that it was the very song that she sang on the night her father was killed and, overcome by the pain and suffering that she has endured, she collapses and dies. At this moment of exceptional emotional intensity the play is operating at three levels of reality; there is the death of the gypsy in Verdi's *Il Trovatore*, Mommina's own death which is 'improvised' and not scripted in the story selected by Dr Hinkfuss, and the collapse of 'The First Actress' who, as she performs as Mommina singing an extract from Verdi's opera, is physically overwhelmed by the passion evoked by the role. For Marta Abba

[44] *Maschere nude, Opera omnia*, i. 285.

playing the part of Mommina, her collapse would have been a re-enactment of her own collapse at the end of the first night of *La nuova colonia* (*The New Colony*) which happened exactly, to the day, one year before Pirandello finished writing *Questa sera si recita a soggetto*.[45] Pirandello's play concludes with the gradual return to consciousness of 'The First Actress' and the agreement of the actors, who have rushed on to the stage in a shocked attempt to revive her, that they cannot work like this, scripts are needed to protect the actors from their roles. In the words of one actor:

Ecco le conseguenze! Ma noi non siamo qua per questo, sa! Noi siamo qua per recitare parti scritte, imparate a memoria. Non pretenderà mica che ogni sera uno di noi ci lasci la pelle![46]

And that's the result! But we are not here for that you know! We are here to perform written roles that we have learnt by heart. You can hardly expect that one of us each night loses our life!

Where *Sei personaggi in cerca d'autore* addressed issues related to the problematic relationship between the text and its performance as seen from the point of view of the author of the work, *Questa sera si recita a soggetto* turns the spotlight on the director and *his* actors (as Dr Hinkfuss insists on calling them) and neatly eliminates the play-script with the claim that it does not exist. So who authors the work, who is the power behind the performance? Dr Hinkfuss rashly claims at the beginning of the play, in a reference to the two earlier plays in the trilogy, that where the author won hands down on the two previous occasions by resorting to means more dishonest than fair, this time having eliminated the author at the outset, it is he, the director, who will be the victor. As could be expected, for the best-laid plans are always a recipe for disaster, his confidence is misplaced. His problem is that he has identified the wrong enemy and while he stands guard against the unexpected return of the

---

[45] *Questa sera si recita a soggetto* was finished on 24 Mar. 1929. The first night of *La nuova colonia* was in Rome on 24 Mar. 1928. For the first time in her association with Pirandello, Marta Abba received a very bad press for her performance as La Spera.

[46] *Maschere nude, Opera omnia*, i. 294. It is worth bearing in mind how much trickery and deception is behind this play. Just as its title *Questa sera si recita a soggetto* accompanies a play that is everything but improvised, so the special effects, the rich array of theatrical devices, emanate not from the director on stage but the play's author.

author, it is the actors who in all senses steal the show. What he did not take into account in his vision of a director-led theatre, which combines technique with technology, is what happens when actors are given parts but no script. From his knowledge of his rival's work, he should have seen the warning signs. In *Enrico IV* for example, the eponymous protagonist who has for many years managed to live his life within the safe confines of a story and a script created, on this occasion, not by a writer but by history, finds himself plunged into an unscripted existence where violent death is the outcome of the unpredictable.[47] In *Questa sera*, too, the actors have been asked to adopt roles in a story in which no more than an outline has been devised. In his prefatory comments on the play Pirandello compares the skills of improvisation displayed by the performers of the *commedia dell'arte* with those of the acting profession in his day, and finds his contemporaries wanting, claiming that it is difficult nowadays to find actors capable of improvisation. Yet, time and again, the play that follows disproves his contention. Even the *chanteuse* who sings every night her repertoire of songs of love and desertion cries tears which for some are pure performance, but for others are 'real', and once the disenchanted actors have entered their roles they unite to evict the director from stage. (Although it should be remembered that after he is banished Hinkfuss does control the lights and therefore creates the effects of the dramatic scene that unfolds.)

TUTTI GLI ALTRI [*Spingendo il Dottor Hinkfuss giù dal palcoscenico*]. Sì, Sì, se ne vada! se ne vada!

IL DOTTOR HINKFUSS. Mi cacciate via dal mio teatro?

L'ATTORE BRILLANTE. Non c'è più bisogno di lei!

TUTTI GLI ALTRI [*Spingendolo ora per il corridoio*]. Vada via! Vada via![48]

ALL THE OTHERS [*Pushing Dr Hinkfuss down from the stage*]. Yes, yes, off with you! Off you go!

DR HINKFUSS. Are you throwing me out of my theatre?

COMIC ACTOR. We no longer need you!

[47] Where Pirandello's theatre draws attention to the risks an unscripted performance bring, Meyerhold, Stanislavsky's closest collaborator, argued that in the new theatre actors would not only interpret but also create their roles and so finally the theatre of improvisation would be born. See *La rivoluzione teatrale* (Rome, Riuniti, 1962), 46.

[48] *Maschere nude, Opera omnia*, i. 274.

8

Performing Women

Woman is different from man, forever incomprehensible
and mysterious, strange and therefore apparently hostile.

(Sigmund Freud, 'The Taboo of Virginity')

Off-stage, in his essays and occasional journalism, Pirandello
held steadfastly to the view that the performance of a play would
always come a poor second to the text. But, as we saw in the
previous chapter, working in and for the theatre as writer and
director led him to adopt a more responsive, pragmatic approach to the problems of performance. Whatever the frustrations—and there were many, as his correspondence and indeed
his plays make clear—he thrived on the hurly-burly of theatre
life. Working with his own theatre company gave him more
control over every aspect of the play's production than he could
ever have imagined possible, while the arrival of Marta Abba in
1925 gave him the experience of working with an actress who,
although a young and dedicated disciple, also brought her own
distinctive acting style. Their collaboration was at its most intense between 1925 and 1928, the years of the Teatro d'Arte,
but it continued long after the theatre company closed, only
ending with Pirandello's death in 1936. In Marta Abba, the
playwright had not only found an actress with whom he could
work, but also an actress for whom he wrote parts, so that in
some of the plays we shall look at, the actress preceded the
character. Abba entered Pirandello's life at a time when the
domination of women protagonists on the European stage
which was such a feature of theatre from the late nineteenth
century onwards was itself undergoing an interesting evolution.

The late nineteenth century had seen the rise of the heroine
who represented universal aspirations towards emancipation,
dignity, and self-determination. The 'woman question' had
been posed in terms of her legal and civic rights and Ibsen,

Henry James, Bernard Shaw, Chekhov, and Tolstoy had created a succession of powerful women protagonists who combined a sense of their own worth with an awareness of the futility of their lives. The form taken by the struggle to escape the constraints of society, to bring authenticity into their existence, may well have been determined by considerations of gender, but the aspirations that informed their choices held true for men as well as women. All this spilled over onto the stage. In a fascinating study of one of the key figures of the period, Eleonora Duse, Cesare Molinari draws the reader's attention to how the transition from a Romantic-tragic theatre to a bourgeois realist canon was accompanied by a switch from male to female in the lead role:

A sua volta questa centralità dell'eroina nella produzione drammatica derivava da un'inedita attenzione prestata alla posizione della donna nella società; il problema riguarda, da un lato, ovviamente, la famiglia, considerata più che mai pilastro dell'intero edificio sociale—donde il gran numero di drammi incentrati sull'adulterio (ma è fenomeno antico—senza i cornuti non ci sarebbe teatro in occidente); ma riguarda altresì il ruolo ormai decisivo che le donne svolgono nella vita sociale e mondana propriamente dette.[1]

In its turn this centrality enjoyed by the heroine of dramatic productions derived from a new attention paid to the position of women in society; the problem concerns, on the one hand, obviously, the family which is seen, now more than ever, as pillar of the whole social edifice—hence the large number of plays which focus on adultery (although it is of course an ancient phenomenon—without cuckolds there would be no Western theatre); but it concerns in equal measure the by now decisive role that women play in social and worldly life as such.

By the 1920s the emphasis had changed to become a matter not so much of what woman wanted, but of what she was and what she appeared to be. We find, on stage at least, that while the practice of taking woman as protagonist continued, the issues that were addressed as a consequence were of a very different nature. As the site rather than the originator of a problem, woman became a spectacle to be viewed, a visual construct, a being who was all surface. What happened in these

---

[1] Cesare Molinari, *L'attrice divina: Eleanora Duse nel teatro italiano fra i due secoli* (Rome, Bulzoni, 1974), 144.

plays, some of which we shall be looking at in this chapter, was often neither intended by her nor willed by her and questions of guilt or innocence, right or wrong, were no longer foregrounded. As we shall see, Pirandello shared in the tendency of much modernist writing to explore woman in terms of spectacle—a tendency that was in part produced by an underlying unease about woman and in part facilitated by the increased presence of the visual image in culture, from photography to cinema.

This chapter will discuss two of Pirandello's plays taken from a decade of work between 1922 and 1932, much of it dedicated to the talents of Marta Abba, but I shall turn first to an earlier novel, *Quaderni di Serafino Gubbio operatore*, where two of the chapter's main concerns are articulated: the actress and the look. As the novel concerns itself with the world of silent cinema and one of the two plays is about theatre, I am drawing on two genres, narrative and the play, to represent three different media—theatre, novel, and cinema.

At the time of writing *Quaderni di Serafino Gubbio operatore* Pirandello had more personal experience of the film industry than of theatre. It was his friend Nino Martoglio who first drew him into film when he founded a production company which aimed to adapt for the screen the works of great writers. Scriptwriting was a lucrative occupation, so in 1904 Pirandello presented a script which was based on a short story of his called 'Nel segno' ('On Target') and although the film was never made, it led to a lifelong interest in the medium. When Pirandello came to write *Quaderni* he asked another friend who worked at Cinestudio in Rome, Arnaldo Frateili, if he would instruct him in the technical aspects of film production.[2] While

---

[2] By 1907 there were some 52 cinemas in Rome (120 in Paris and 340 in Berlin). It was said that after Cines started up in Rome, the city's history could be divided into three epochs—imperial, papal, and cinematographic. In the early 1920s Pirandello described with some strength of feeling the disastrous effect the burgeoning film industry was having on the Roman cityscape to the journalist Enrico Roma (Gian Pietro Brunetta, *Cent'anni di cinema italiana* (Rome and Bari, Laterza, 1981), 30): 'Il poeta, facendomi l'elogio del paesaggio mi additava con rammarico una vasta tettoia di vetro, spalancata proprio davanti alla finestra, che ne guastava l'incomparabile bellezza. Era il teatro di posa di uno dei cento stabilimenti cinematografici, i quali avevano rinchiusa la città imperiale in una cinta inespugnabile di celluloide, nei cui margini perforati erano riprodotte fatalmente rimpicciolite le arcate solenni dell'Acquedotto di Claudio.'

the novel benefits from his familiarity with the film studio, his more limited knowledge of the screen-actress can be seen in the presentation of the protagonist, Varia Nestoroff,[3] who reads today like a literary cliché. There is a cautionary note to be sounded, though, for alongside Delia of *Ciascuno a suo modo* (*Each in His Own Way*) or Donata of *Trovarsi* (*Finding Oneself*) Varia Nestoroff is disadvantaged by the fact that she does not have the verbal autonomy enjoyed by women on stage. In the novel Gubbio confers on himself the authority to speak for or on behalf of Nestoroff, whereas in the plays the women protagonists will speak for themselves. Even if the observation is exactly the same, its meaning will change according to who gives utterance to it, so that when Serafino says in relation to Nestoroff that 'Un angelo, per una donna, è sempre più irritante d'una bestia' ('An angel, for a woman, is always more irritating than a beast') the comment sounds faintly misogynistic and unpleasant, whereas in the play, because it is Delia herself who speaks the line, the innuendo is removed. Descended from an exotic but murky background, Russian-born, Berlin-, Paris-, and Vienna-bred—'Un'avventuriera russa, un'attrice, se non qualcosa di peggio!'[4] ('a Russian adventuress, an actress, if not something worse!')—she speaks perfect Italian, lapsing into French when distraught, which, given her excitable nature, happens frequently. The cameraman, Serafino Gubbio, whose profession makes him both literally and metaphorically the novel's focalizer, first knew her when she was part of an international bohemian set of artists, painters, and sculptors, living on the island of Capri. She modelled for and seduced a talented young artist, Giorgio Mirelli, who was then under Gubbio's tutelage, before going on to seduce his closest friend, the Baron Aldo

(As he praised the panorama to me, the poet regretfully pointed out a huge glass dome stetched out immediately before the window which broke the incomparable beauty. It was the film studio for one of the hundred cinematographic establishments which had enclosed the imperial city in an impregnable celluloid belt in whose perforated edges were reproduced in fatally shrunken form the solemn arches of Claudius' Acqueduct.') See also Elaine Mancini, *Struggles of the Italian Film Industry during Fascism, 1930–35* (Ann Arbor, UMI Research Press, 1985), for an account of the Italian film industry and Pirandello's involvement in it.

　[3] Varia Nestoroff reappears in *Ciasuno a suo modo* (1924) as Delia Morello (for a discussion of the play see Ch. 3, pp. 90–1 and 95–7). Although in the play she is by profession an actress, the play is not about acting.
　[4] Luigi Pirandello, *Tutti i romanzi*, ii. 563 (tr. Scott Moncrieff, 70).

Nuti, who was in his turn engaged to be married to Giorgio's sister. (This part of her life-story provides the backgound to Nestoroff's reappearance, with a different name, on- and off-stage in *Ciascuno a suo modo*.) With her red hair, green eyes, and feline elegance she has the seductive appearance of a *diva*. Many of her traits belong to the *femme fatale* of nineteenth-century decadent and symbolist writing, although her apparent indifference to her victims' misfortunes is symptomatic of a new female stereotype that will come to dominate in the cinema—the vamp:

> The fate of the Italian *femme fatale* is often as dreadful as that of her lovers, and this makes her even more appealing. She takes the form of a force against which one is powerless, since she herself is dominated by something stronger than herself. This may well be the reason for the name given to her in awe, which also defines her: *diva,* goddess. The man whom she touches and condemns becomes the victim of a kind of holocaust; he is sacrificed to a mysterious superior power. There is something almost religious in the audience's worship of the *dive*.[5]

The fascination of the figure lies in the peculiar nature of the power which she exercises over men, but over which she herself has no control.

While Varia Nestoroff may enjoy the attributes associated with an actress off-stage, she lacks the necessary skills. She cannot act—she is not even capable of keeping to 'i limiti entro i quali gli attori debbono muoversi per tenere in fuoco la scena'[6] ('the limits within which which the actors have to move to keep the picture in focus'), whose outer frame is delineated by chalk marks on the ground, so that during filming she often strays beyond the fixed camera's reach. (The camera did not follow the actors but remained fixed in position so the performance area was marked off like a stage.) Walter Benjamin's influential essay 'Art in the Age of Mechanical Reproduction', which draws on Pirandello's novel to illustrate the alienation inherent in the production and consumption of celluloid images, set the agenda for subsequent critical readings, but for the purposes of

---

[5] Pierre Leprohon, *The Italian Cinema*, tr. R. Greaves and O. Stallybrass (New York, Praeger, 1972), 34. Quoted in Mary Ann Doane, *Femmes Fatales. Feminism, Film Theory, Psychoanalysis* (New York and London, Routledge, 1991), 127.

[6] Pirandello, *Tutti i romanzi*, ii. 521 (tr. Scott Moncrieff, 7).

this chapter I shall begin by focusing on the presentation of Nestoroff herself, both the characteristics attributed to her and her role in the structural and thematic interplay in the novel between the story on the set and the lives of the protagonists. Varia Nestoroff may not be much of an actress within the area delineated on the set where the fiction is enacted, but beyond it, in the 'real' world, she is a woman whose life should be read as one sustained performance.

Two traits dominate in the presentation of her. First of all: the frequency with which she is linked to the animal kingdom. Her former lover Aldo Nuti in an impassioned speech declares that she is a viper whose poison has yet to be drawn—a familiar topos in the history of misogyny which is put almost verbatim into the mouth of another character in *Ciascuno a suo modo*. More substantial is the connection established between what the film's title identifies as its two protagonists *The Lady and the Tiger*, with, of the two, the lady described as being 'more tigerish than the tiger'. When the cameraman, Serafino Gubbio, sees her again after many years he is momentarily uncertain if it is her or not—it both is and is not. The style of dress and the strange tawny colour of her hair are not, but in the end they cannot conceal what is authentically her: 'l'incesso dell'esile elegantissima persona, con un che di felino nella mossa dei fianchi'[7] ('the motion of her slender, exquisite body, with a touch of the feline in the sway of her hips'). In his second notebook his comment on how she has been compared to the tiger purchased a few days previously by the film company gives rise to a convoluted comparison between animals and humans, contrasting the way a tiger kills, hungrily and instinctively, with human beings, who kill gratuitously and knowingly. After this lengthy parenthesis, he returns to the question of Nestoroff's own actions, drawing attention to his belief that she has killed, but not by her own hand. Her former lover, Giorgio Mirelli, killed himself after finding her *in flagrante delictu* with his best friend, Aldo Nuti.

The link between woman and tiger is resumed at the end of the novel in a climax which sees the merging of the film's 'fiction' with the novel's 'reality'. The tiger has been kept drugged in a cage in preparation for what is intended to be

---

[7] Pirandello, *Tutti i romanzi*, ii. 539 (tr. Scott Moncrieff, 33).

both its first and its final film performance. The plan is that it will be introduced into a much larger cage decorated with foliage and trees so that it has the appearance of her natural habitat and there it will be shot dead by the lead actor. At Nestoroff's instigation, Aldo Nuti, who has arrived unexpectedly at the film studio and seems set to stir up her current lover's smouldering jealousy, substitutes him for this crucial scene. The episode goes grotesquely but predictably wrong. The man who has temporarily become an actor for the woman he loves, turns the gun on her and shoots her dead, before he in turn is mauled to death by the tiger. While the tragedy unfolds before his eyes, the cameraman, Serafino, captures the entire episode on celluloid. The film, we learn from him later, is in such demand that both he and the company have grown rich on the royalties.

It is a powerful *mise-en-scène*: a double death in an episode which sees the 'fiction' of the film and the 'reality' of the narrative merge—spatially as well as thematically, for Nestoroff is positioned just beyond, on the outside of the concealed bars marking out the acting area of the story. The tiger is both woman and beast—in the time it takes to shoot the woman dead, the animal is able to pounce. This criss-crossing of two levels of narrative, the one purporting to be real and the other claiming to be fiction prefigures the disturbing, meta-theatrical finale of (among others) *Sei personaggi in cerca d'autore, Enrico IV*, and *Questa sera si recita a soggetto*. It informs the whole of *Ciascuno a suo modo* where the distinction between reality and fiction, which is conventionally mapped out in the theatre by separating the stage from the auditorium, is erased; in the words of one actor whose role is to play the part of a member of the audience: 'E ci sono dunque in teatro gli attori del dramma vero, della vita?'[8] ('And so are there actors from the real drama, from life, in the theatre?'). But the 'reality' that Gubbio films is also real in the sense that it is physically present, embodied, as he films it. By capturing it on celluloid he turns it into pure image. The episode sums up the difference between theatre and cinema; as Christian Metz expressed it in the opening to his psychoanalytic study of the cinema, reality in theatre 'is physically present, in

---

[8] Pirandello, *Maschere nude, Opera omnia*, i. (Milan, Mondadori, 1984), 158.

the same space as the spectator. The cinema only gives it in effigy, inaccessible from the outset, in a primordial *elsewhere*.'[9] Earlier in the novel there is an impassioned indictment of cinema; it is seen as a medium which attracts actors away fom the stage because it pays well and requires little effort. It films by breaking up episodes into fragments, taking them out of sequence, so that an actor may go through the motions not knowing whether he is playing the part of the husband or the lover. Actors share a hatred of the camera bordering on the superstitious because they have no live contact with an audience. He describes the alienation of acting for the screen as follows:

Qua si sentono come in esilio. In esilio, non soltanto dal palcoscenico, ma quasi anche da se stessi. Perchè la loro azione, l'azione *viva* del loro corpo *vivo,* là su la tela dei cinematografi, non c'è piu: c'è *la loro immagine* soltanto, colta in un momento, in un gesto, in una impressione, che guizza e scompare.[10]

Here they feel as though they are in exile. In exile, not only from the stage, but also in a sense from themselves. Because their action, the *live* action of their *live* bodies, there, on the screen of the cinematograph, no longer exists: it is *their image* alone, caught in a moment, in a gesture, an expression, that flickers and disappears.

Metz goes on to comment on how they confusedly feel that their bodies have been suppressed, deprived of reality. The first night never comes for them—they never see a public. At least in the theatre there is a reciprocity between actor and audience, both are present, but there is no equivalent in the cinema because the two exist in different temporal dimensions:

During the screening of the film, the audience is present, and aware of the actor, but the actor is absent, and unaware of the audience, and during the shooting, when the actor was present, it was the audience which was absent . . . The exchange of seeing and being-seen will be fractured in its centre, and its two disjointed halves allocated to different moments in time, another split. I never see my partner, but only his photograph.[11]

[9] Christian Metz, *The Imaginary Signifier: Psychoanalysis and the Cinema*, tr. Celia Britton *et al.* (Bloomington, Ind., Indiana UP, 1982), 61.
[10] Pirandello, *Tutti i romanzi*, ii. 585 (tr. Scott Moncrieff, 106).
[11] Metz, *Imaginary Signifier*, 95.

Performing for a camera does mean that the actress can at a later stage watch herself in performance, but this produces for Nestoroff an uncanny effect as she looks upon an image that she experiences as being both her and not her at one and the same time. When she reappears in *Ciascuno a suo modo* it is as actress turned spectator, who has come to watch another actress perform as her on stage. So there are two actresses both performing a part in which they pretend to be the same woman. One does not need to take questions of performance, identity, and observation as far as this play does to realize that theatre draws attention to the act of spectatorship in a way that cinema does not. By foregrounding processes of looking, these plays draw attention to the fact that the audience is part of the theatrical event.

It had been Pirandello's intention to call the novel by the simple and less self-conscious title *The Tiger*. The shocking finale is prefigured early in Serafino Gubbio's narrative when he invites the reader to imagine himself out shooting; lying low waiting for the prey to fly overhead, the reader opens the newspaper he has taken along with him to find an item announcing the death of a friend who, while crossing an African plain, is 'assaltato, sbranato e divorato da una belva'[12] ('attacked, torn in pieces and devoured by a wild beast'). The savagery of the beast, and, with it, the attraction it holds for Gubbio and Nestoroff who are repeatedly drawn to its cage, is one strand running through the book, but equally important is the connection made between woman and beast. A common enough motif in cultural and scientific circles, animality in a woman is often linked to either a criminal disposition or sexual appetite. Both are hinted at in Nestoroff's case. It is suggested that she is sexually frigid and promiscuous, while her conduct seems to indicate a woman devoid of a sense of moral or social responsibility. But Varia Nestoroff has an additional complication in that she has both to contend with a presentation of her which draws on a familiar topos in the history of misogyny— woman as closer to the animal kingdom than man, partaking more of nature than culture—and the quintessentially Pirandellian dilemma that is not the prerogative of one sex but

---

[12] Pirandello, *Tutti i romanzi*, ii. 553 (tr. Scott Moncrieff, 54).

is the consequence of being human, namely the horror that follows self-awareness.

Serafino Gubbio, the all-seeing I/eye who watches her dispassionately and intently both with and without a camera, is, he likes to believe, immune to her appeal as *femme fatale* combined with *femme sauvage*, but at the same time he does not deny that he feels an affinity with her which he attributes to their common experience of being on the margins of society. Both are positioned outside the body social, the Lacanian symbolic so hated by Pirandello's *raisonneurs*. There is, though, a clear distinction to be made between a man who is an outsider by choice, and in full consciousness of where he speaks from and the penalties it carries, and a woman who, in the absence of self-knowledge, finds herself there for reasons beyond her control:

Studio, dunque, senza passione, ma intentamente questa donna, che se pur mostra di capire quello che fa e il perchè lo fa, non ha però in sè affatto quella 'sistemazione' tranquilla di concetti, d'affetti, di diritti e di doveri, d'opinioni e d'abitudini, ch'io odio negli altri. [. . .] Ha in sé qualche cosa, questa donna, che gli altri non riescono a comprendere, perchè bene non lo comprende neppure lei stessa. Si indovina però dalle violente espressioni che assume, senza volerlo, senza saperlo, nelle parti che le sono assegnate. [. . .] E non c'è verso di tenerla in freno, di farle attenuare la violenza di quelle espressioni. Manda a monte ella sola più pellicole, che non tutti gli altri attori delle quattro compagnie prese insieme. Già esce dal *campo* ogni volta; quando per caso non ne esce, è così scomposta la sua azione, così stranamente alterata e contraffatta la sua figura, che nella sala di prova quasi tutte le scene a cui ella ha preso parte, risultano inaccettabili e da rifare.[13]

I study this woman, then, without passion but intently, who, albeit she may seem to understand what she is doing and why she does it, yet has not in herself any of that quiet 'systemization' of concepts, affections, rights and duties, opinions and habits, which I abominate in other people. [. . .] She has something in her, this woman, which the others do not succeed in understanding, because even she herself does not clearly understand it. One guesses it, however, from the violent expressions which she assumes, involuntarily, unconsciously, in the parts that are assigned to her. [. . .] And there is no way of keeping her in check, of making her moderate the violence of these expressions. She alone ruins more films that all the other actors in the four companies put

---

[13] Pirandello, *Tutti i romanzi*, ii. 555–6 (tr. Scott Moncrieff, 58–9).

together. For one thing she always moves out of the *picture*, when by any chance she does not move out, her action is so disordered, her face so strongly altered and disguised, that in the rehearsal theatre almost all the scenes in which she has taken part turn out useless and have to be done again.

Varia Nestoroff is an actress who cannot act on demand because her body is already in performance; transformed into the theatre of her unconscious, it acts out the repressed.[14] Her body has its own script which is hidden from her consciousness. The 'something in her', which becomes elsewhere 'questa ossessa che è in lei e che le sfugge'[15] ('the demon which exists in her and always escapes her'), gives rise to the convulsive movements, the disordered actions, and violent expressions whereby the body becomes the medium for the unconscious and uncontrollable expression of the repressed trauma. How can she act on demand when 'her body has already been transformed into a theatre for forgotten scenes'?[16] Her condition exhibits the characteristics of 'conversion hysteria' according to the definition provided by Laplanche and Pontalis: 'the psychical conflict is expressed symbolically in somatic symptoms often very varied—they may be paroxystic (e.g. emotional crises accompanied by theatricality) or more long-lasting (anaesthesias, hysterical paralyses, 'lumps in the throat', etc.)'.[17] Nestoroff's condition provides an early example of a gender divide that becomes pervasive in Pirandello's writings. Male protagonists have to endure the consequences of a capacity for recollection and lucidity (even the eponymous hero of *Enrico IV* is shown fully recovered from his amnesia) that by its very excessiveness bars the way to a full participation in contemporary life, and conversely female characters suffer exclusion as a consequence of the repression of their past, which inhibits their understanding of themselves and the present.

[14] I am aware that medicalizing the condition of literary heroines carries its own risks. *The Times*, for example, reviewing *Hedda Gabler* on 21 Apr. 1891, summed up the protagonist as follows: 'Hedda Gabler is manifestly a lunatic of the epileptic class'.

[15] Pirandello, *Tutti i romanzi*, ii. 557 (tr. Scott Moncrieff, 61).

[16] Hélène Cixous and Catherine Clément, *The Newly Born Woman* (Manchester, Manchester UP, 1986), 5.

[17] J. Laplanche and J.-B. Pontalis, *The Language of Psychoanalysis* (London, The Hogarth Press, 1985), 194.

The other trait associated with Nestoroff, hysteria, has a history going back to Hippocrates, but it occupies a singularly important position in the late nineteenth century when, first with the work of Charcot and later that of Breuer and Freud, it made a significant contribution to the origins of psychoanalysis. While according to Freudian psychoanalytic practice the doctor has to learn to listen to the patient, to hear the words that are spoken, for his predecessor, Charcot, the doctor had to learn to look, to watch his patient. As a malady expressed through representation, where the body itself becomes the means for the uncontrolled expression of the unconscious conflict that rages within her, the woman hysteric provided Charcot and his male colleagues with a rich spectacle. From the famous photographs of hysterics that he commissioned at La Salpêtrière in the 1880s—he founded a photographic studio within the asylum—the viewer can see how he succeeded in theatricalizing what was construed as madness by staging spectacular demonstrations in which he hypnotized his patients. He produced a series of stills, but what we see is very similar to the visual impression left by the description in *Quaderni di Serafino Gubbio operatore* of the one occasion when Varia Nestoroff can and does perform as requested. What she performs is a dance, the 'dance of death'. Dance here is linked to hysteria and animality, as through her body she seeks to abreact the past that possesses her:

Tra i penosi contorcimenti di quella sua strana danza macabra, tra il luccichio sinistro dei due pugnali, ella non staccò un minuto gli occhi da' miei, che la seguivano, affascinati. Le vidi sul seno anelante il sudore rigar di solchi la manteca giallastra, di cui era tutto impiastricciato. Senza darsi alcun pensiero della sua nudità, ella si dimenava come frenetica, ansava, e pian piano, con voce affannosa, sempre con gli occhi fissi ne' miei, domandava ogni tanto:
—*Bien comme ça? Bien comme ça?*
Come se volesse saperlo da me; e gli occhi erano quelli d'una pazza.[18]

Through the painful contortions of that strange morbid dance, behind the sinister gleam of the daggers, she did not take her eyes for a moment from mine, which followed her movements, fascinated. I saw the sweat on her heaving bosom make furrows in the ochreous paint with which she was daubed all over. Without giving a thought to her nudity, she dashed about the ground as in a frenzy, panted for breath,

---

[18] Pirandello, *Tutti i romanzi*, ii. 598–9 (tr. Scott Moncrieff, 127–8).

and softly, in a gasping whisper, still with her eyes fixed on mine, asked
now and again:

    '*Bien comme ça? Bien comme ça?*'

As though she wished to be told by me; and certainly her eyes were the
eyes of a madwoman.

Just as the Salpetrière hysterics performed before Charcot,
and by so doing, for him, so Nestoroff performs for Gubbio 'the
painful contortions of that strange, morbid dance', her eyes
those of a 'madwoman' as she is recorded by the camera and
watched, impassively, by him. In their essay on hysteria, Cixous
and Clément refer to the practice by women in Southern Italy
who if they think they have been bitten by a tarantula, arrange
to expel the effects of its bite by dancing the tarantella. As the
spider is not to be found in that part of the world, the authors
conclude that the symptoms experienced by its victims are psychical phenomena and that through the convulsive movements
of the dance (performed in the presence of others) the venom,
what Pirandello refers to as 'a demon which exists in her', is
expelled. By the time Pirandello wrote his novel, the figure of
the hysteric had long since escaped confinement in the mental
asylum and the home to become both a symbol of the malaise of
the new woman and, in the hands of Surrealists such as André
Breton and Louis Aragon, the fountain head of artistic inspiration. We shall see shortly how the convulsive, uncontrolled
movements of her body, those very attributes that make conscious acting impossible for Nestoroff, will later become intrinsic to Pirandello's inscriptions of femininity in plays dominated
by women's roles, so that, instead of being a limitation, they
become a hallmark of the performance. Soon bodily movements previously associated with the hysteric take on broader
connotations, implying a woman in the throes of profound
distress. In *Ciascuno a suo modo*, when Varia Nestoroff's counterpart, Amalia Moreno, attends the first night of the play, she
assures her entourage that she can manage the situation, but
the signs that she is out of control can be read from her body:
she is 'pallida, convulsa' ('pale, convulsive') with a 'viso
stravolto' ('distraught face') and a body that is 'tutt'un fremito'
('trembling through and through'). Time and again these
women are betrayed by the language of their bodies. Before
turning to inscriptions of femininity in his theatre, however, I

shall comment briefly on Pirandello's view of women's social and political rights.

Although the character traits associated with Nestoroff in *Quaderni di Serafino Gubbio operatore* are the same as those used by Pirandello in his plays to create other female protagonists, they are no longer presented as being a hindrance to acting and instead become an intrinsic part of the character in performance. What occasions this change in his perception? There is certainly no clear signal that his political stance on the woman question changed over the years. In the fifteen years after his move to Rome in 1891, the city had seen feminism become an important issue, encouraged by a number of prominent women engaged in literary and social activities: amongst them he personally knew Grazia Deledda (who was to be the model for his protagonist in *Suo marito*), Sibilla Aleramo, Matilde Serao, and Ada Negri. The presence of these four women writers in Italian literary life did not stop him many years later from expressing the view that women and culture do not mix.[19]

Meanwhile the campaigning work of these women among others had resulted in the First National Women's Congress, which was held in Rome in 1917. Pirandello himself contributed to the debate as early as 1909 with a short, dismissive article called simply 'Feminismo' (where feminism is referred to as 'una vescica piena di vento' ('a bladder full of wind'), just one, according to him, among the many empty beliefs that fill history) which appeared in the political-military journal *La Preparazione*, a publication obviously intended for a male readership.[20] His views on the matter were unambiguously reactionary, although three at least of his works take as protagonists women who show themselves to be outstanding in their chosen professions—writing (*Suo marito*), teaching (*L'esclusa*), and acting (*Trovarsi*).

What did develop were Pirandello's views of the theatre and acting in particular; his closer involvement with the stage came at a time when Italian theatre was rapidly catching up with practices prevalent elsewhere in Europe, and also at a time

[19] G. Villoroel, 'Colloqui con Pirandello', *Giornale d'Italia* (Rome, 8 May 1924). (See Ch. 3, p. 98).

[20] A translation and analysis of 'Feminism' appears as an appendix to Maggie Günsberg, *Patriarchal Representations: Gender and Discourse in Pirandello's Theatre* (Oxford and Providence, RI, Berg, 1994), 195–207 (tr. or pp. 204–7).

when the European stage had switched from male-centred to female-centred plays. Varia Nestoroff was the product of Pirandello's limited understanding of the actress in 1916; yet his own theatre production in the decade between 1922 and 1932 was dominated by plays with female leads. Pirandello's understanding of acting was largely informed by the changing techniques that were making themselves felt more widely on the European stage and which in turn were largely due to women. In the late nineteenth century three women dominated the European and North American stage: Sarah Bernhardt, Ellen Terry, and Eleonora Duse. It was Duse who held Pirandello in thrall. Like so many professional actors, she was born into an acting family—indeed she was born while her parents were on tour, in a hotel-room in Vigevano in 1858, and she died while she herself was on tour in another hotel-room, this time in Pittsburgh on 21 April 1924. A profound change occurred in Italian theatre with the appearance on stage of Eleonora Duse. As the following quotation illustrates, taken from an article by Pirandello published in America in *The Columbian Monthly*, Duse embodied all his ideas of what great acting should be. In it he drew attention to the difference between a conventional acting style which was entirely 'external' and Duse's own technique based on fluidity; a physical expression of internal processes which Pirandello described in terms of an act of creation on the part of the actor rather than an act of imitation:

From the very beginning of her long career Eleonora Duse had one controlling thought—the ambition to disappear, to merge herself, as a real person, in the character she brought to life on stage.

Only by a hasty judgement could such an attitude be mistaken for an abdication of personality on an artist's part. As understood by Duse, it is her greatest title to glory, since this attitude implies obedience to the first duty of the actor—that supreme renunciation of the self, that carries as its reward the realisation not of one life only, but of as many lives as the actor succeeds in creating. And we shall see, too, that this attitude implies not, as some people conclude, an almost mechanical passiveness on the part of the actor, who must think of himself simply as an instrument for communcating an author's thoughts, but a spiritual creativity of the rarest kind.[21]

---

[21] Luigi Pirandello, 'The Art of Duse', *The Columbian Monthly*, 1/7 (July 1928). The essay can also be found in Eric Bentley (ed.), *The Theory of the Modern Stage: An Introduction to Modern Theatre and Drama* (Harmondsworth, Penguin, 1992), 158–69.

What he describes bears the mark of one of Pirandello's strongest convictions, that the act of creation, and he makes no distinction between the writer and the actor, can only take place on condition that the artist's conscious self gives way to alternative selves seeking self-expression, but other commentors who saw Duse in performance were similarly struck by these attributes. They all return to the same point, that Duse does not play a part but reincarnates a state of being. Acting becomes a means of giving expression, primarily visual, to inner processes of the psyche. Gerhardt Hauptman wrote that her greatness lay in her ability not to act so much as to 'reincarnate . . . to live these *states of mind* from which the characters must be developed'; James Agate, after seeing her in Pittsburgh in Ibsen's *The Lady from the Sea*, wrote that, unlike most actors who build and develop a role, she 'focused her mental energy on the *creation* of a role'; while in Moscow the Russian critic Alexei Suvorin wrote, 'she creates characters, *lives* them with a simplicity never before seen on stage'.[22]

What also emerges from contemporary accounts is the switch in attention away from the delivery of the spoken word to the semiotics of bodily movements. (She did not perform corseted, nor did she wear stage make-up.) She often turned to stage-props to make the telling gesture—a caress of a single flower or the arrangement of a vase of flowers—which has every appearance of being natural but was, according to George Bernard Shaw, the final stage in a complicated dance of her arms. A contemporary of hers noted that nobody seemed to ask if these gestures were strictly necessary. The implication that they were not, is, of course, in a strict sense true, but Duse developed them to help establish the basis for a different kind of relationship between herself and her audience—one in which the spectators concentrate as hard on looking at her as they do on listening to her. What it added up to was a performance technique in which her relationship with her audience was paramount—Charlie Chaplin was struck by her investment in the relationship.

[22] From, in order: G. Pontiero, *Eleanora Duse: In Life and Art* (Frankfurt-am-Main, 1982), 120–1; J. Stokes, M. R. Booth, and S. Bassnett, *Bernhardt, Terry, Duse: The Actress in her Time* (Cambridge, CUP, 1988), 168; W. Weaver, *Duse: A Biography* (London, Thames and Hindson, 1984), 236.

A nervous, slightly morbid style of acting had been introduced into Italy by Sarah Bernhardt during her famous Italian
tour of 1882 and it has been suggested that Duse, whose first
great success was to come two years later, had acquired from her
a repertory of movements which, from the descriptions offered
by contemporary critics—'scatti nervosi' ('nervous starts'),
'smarrimento dei sensi' ('a confusion of the senses'), 'languore
delle membra' ('a languor in the limbs'), and 'fremito di tutta
la persona' ('shudder throughout the body')—borrow heavily
from contemporary accounts of what was construed as being
the neurasthenic woman. What is clear is the singularly effective
symbiosis between acting style and the new roles being created
by Ibsen and Strindberg, among others. In Cesare Molinari's
robust words, Duse's heroines suffer 'un generico stato di
disagio squisitamente femminile. Un disagio che nasce
dall'esclusione delle donne dalla vita pratica'[23] ('a generic state
of awkwardness which is exquisitely feminine. An awkwardness
produced by women's exclusion from practical life'). Eleonora
Duse was strongly identified with Ibsen's theatre which she had
brought to Italy in 1891 with *A Doll's House* and presented in
Milan, and over the next decade she won universal recognition
for her interpretations of Ibsen's heroines (in 1908 she performed an entire season of Ibsen plays in Berlin). In Milan on
5 May 1921, the night which saw the disastrous première of *Sei
personaggi in cerca d'autore* in Rome, Duse returned to the stage
after an absence of some twelve years, with Ibsen's *The Lady from
the Sea*. Although there were other plays in Duse's repertoire,
including Alexandre Dumas's *The Lady of of the Camelias* and,
less successfully, the theatre of her lover Gabriele D'Annunzio,
her name was indissolubly associated with Ibsen's heroines and
what was known as the *fin de siècle* woman. In the words of Barba
and Savarese: 'Duse has created her own style, she has created
for herself a sort of convention that is quite hers, through which
she effectively became the woman of modern times, with all her
complaints of hysteria, anaemia and nerve trouble and with all
the consequences of these complaints; she is, in short, the *fin de
siècle* woman.'[24]

---

[23] Molinari, *L'attrice divina*, 112.
[24] E. Barba and N. Savarese, *The Secret Art of the Performer: A Dictionary of Theatre
Anthropology* (London and New York, Routledge, 1991), 156.

Marta Abba's own style of acting had strong affinities with that practised by Eleonora Duse. According to Mirella Schino, Abba 'riprenderà una gestualità inarrestabile, una intensità fisica e vocale inquietante, fuori moda tra i comici ma di grande effetto per il pubblico'[25] ('was to adopt a relentless gestuality, a disquieting vocal and physical intensity, out of fashion among other actors but very effective with the public'). It was the experience of working intensively with her that led Pirandello to revise his views of acting so that he came to see it as a process in which the actress discovers traits within her which may well have been hidden from her, but which give her the means to identify with the character she is to embody on stage.[26] Of the plays written for Marta Abba, *Trovarsi* represents a natural conclusion because here the relationship between the actress who performs in the theatre and the role she embodies (of an actress who performs on stage) are one and the same. As author as well as director of many of the plays associated with Abba, Pirandello contributed to the symbiosis between actor and character by creating roles that fitted her. For example, in one of the earliest plays written for her, called *L'amica delle mogli* (*The Wives' Friend*, 1927), taken from a short story bearing the same title of 1894, all the substantial changes that are made to the original story relate to the persona to be played by Abba. Gone is the placid girl of the story and in her place is, in the words of one theatre critic, 'una creatura drammatica ed inquieta, nella quale le compresse energie della giovinezza esplodono con violenza' ('a restless, dramatic creature in whom the compressed energies of youth explode with violence'). Her appearance naturally enough changes to fit Abba's, but even her name is changed to Marta, recalling Abba's own habit of hanging on her dressing-room door the name of the character she was playing instead of her own.

Marta Abba was to stay with Pirandello's company for its full two and a half years of existence until August 1928. Her impact on his theatre was immeasurable, including the six plays in which he created roles for her which brought to his theatre a

---

[25] Mirella Schino, *Il teatro di Eleanora Duse* (Bologna, Il Mulino, 1992), 141.

[26] See Claudio Vicentini, 'Modelli di recitazione nel teatro di Pirandello', in *Alle origini della drammaturgia moderna: Ibsen, Strindberg, Pirandello* (Genoa, Costa e Nolan, 1987), 42.

new protagonist, the single woman. It is one of those curious ironies that just as he was identifying himself publicly with the Fascist regime, in artistic terms he moved away from the Fascist ideal of femininity as maternity and women defined purely in familial terms as mothers, wives, and daughters, to single and above all childless women, struggling to find an identity for themselves outside the parameters of the family. A cluster of disparate factors, personal, cultural, and technological, contributed to this highly productive and innovative period in Pirandello's career as dramatist which, if one takes as starting-point the pre-Abba play *Vestire gli ignudi* (*To Clothe the Naked*) of 1922 (which became part of her repertoire after she joined the 'Teatro d'Arte), dominates a decade of Pirandello's theatre and includes *Diana e la Tuda* (1925–6), *Come tu mi vuoi* (1930), and *Trovarsi* (1932). Also included in her repertoire was Ellida in Ibsen's *The Lady from the Sea*, a part made famous by Eleonora Duse. With the last of the plays Pirandello wrote for Abba, *Trovarsi* (1931–2), he created as central protagonist the figure of an actress and although we cannot know how far he had Eleonora Duse in mind, the play certainly contains echoes of Duse's performance in *The Lady from the Sea*.

Trovarsi is a play whose concerns are with theatre and theatricality, without the cinematic dimension that we shall find in other plays considered in this chapter. It is both a meta-play and, most unusually for Pirandello, a love-story. The famous actress Donata Genzi has travelled to the Riviera to enjoy a well-earned rest. There she meets Elj Nielson, an eligible but wild young man who shuns society and spends most of his time at sea. As his name suggests, he is modelled on the sailor in Ibsen's play, but he is a tamed version, lacking the threatening sexual presence so disturbing to domesticity that Ibsen's character, a true outsider, embodies. Initially attracted to him because he has not the slightest idea of who she is, she begins a passionate affair with him, which comes to an abrupt halt when he watches her on stage for the very first time. After he flees the theatre, horrified at the sight of her making exactly the same gestures with her stage-lovers as she does in privacy with him, she chooses to stay with her profession, rather than follow him. It is an abrupt, but entirely fitting conclusion to an affair in which it was clear from the start that there was a heavy price to be paid in terms of her loss of self-determination.[27] The signals that the relationship was destined to end are present in an extraordinary episode at the beginning of Act II. Donata is seen on stage examining the bite-marks that her lover Elj had left imprinted in her flesh when he rescued her from the high seas after their boat had capsized. His claim, supported by the doctor, is that they are a testimony to his struggle to save her life, but she knows better. Her interpretation is different:

DONATA. Mi pare che alle bestie, per non perderle, si usa fare un marchio sull'anca.
ELJ. Ma che paragoni!
DONATA. Tu me l'hai fatto alla nuca.
DOTTORE. E fortuna che l'istinto lo portò a farglielo.[28]

DONATA. It seems to me that with cattle, so as not to lose them, it's customary to brand them on the flank.
ELJ. But what a comparison!
DONATA. You've branded me on the neck.
DOCTOR. It's fortunate that instinct led him to do it!

The scar left where Elj sank his teeth into her is a branding mark, a sign to herself and to others that she has passed into his ownership. In one of Pirandello's deft underminings of established cliché, the transaction is sealed not with a ring or a kiss, but 'con un morso, di cui mi resterà il segno finchè campo' ('with a bite whose mark will remain with me for as long as I live'). When she appears in this scene she is dressed a little oddly in a 'vestaglia, e con un accappatoio soprammesso' ('nightdress with a bathrobe flung over it'). The stage directions explain that it is because she is about to be examined by the doctor, but her unusual dress is also a reference to Duse's appearance on stage in *The Lady from the Sea* where she appears in Act I 'chiusa in un grande accappatoio'[29] ('enveloped in a large bathrobe').

[27] A similar example of the continuity between performance on- and off-stage is provided by a journalist who visited a young actress while she was ill. At one point in the interview, she gave her pillow 'un colpo di gomito' ('a prod with her elbow') with a gesture which he instantly recognized as identical to one made by Duse on stage. *L'Arte drammatica* (4 Jan. 1896), quoted in Schino, *Il teatro di Eleonora Duse*, 142.

[28] Luigi Pirandello, *Maschere nude, Opera omnia*, iv (Milan, Mondadori, 1949), 198.

[29] Claudio Vicentini, 'Il repertorio di Pirandello capocomico e l'ultima stagione

Trovarsi is also and more importantly a play about acting. Before Donata first appears on stage, friends and admirers are seen discussing animatedly the attributes needed to be a good actress. The well-worn cliché that women are natural performers because they have an innate gift for dissimulation is discarded. Far from suggesting that women simply imitate or reflect the creations of a male mind, a real actress *lives* a part so completely that she is the character she is playing (in Pirandello's eulogy to Duse, acting is not 'an instrument for communicating an author's thoughts, but a spiritual activity of the rarest kind'). What Pirandello establishes in the opening scene is that acting has nothing to do with mimicry or pretence. Instead of playing a role given us by nature (such as motherhood), or chance (such as being a twelfth-century German Emperor), actors are the creators of their own roles, and by living in full consciousness of what they are doing they give themselves a plenitude most of us could never aspire to. Although Pirandello's views on acting are not gender-specific, it is a woman who seems to have inspired him and it is through another woman that his ideas were realized on stage.

Just as acting is often associated with insincerity and mimicry, so falling in love is often seen as a moment of total authenticity described in the expression 'letting go' or, in *Trovarsi*, 'shutting one's eyes'. By bringing the two together in the play, Pirandello manages to expose their respective mythologies. When Donata appears in Act I, she describes the moment when she returns to herself at the end of a performance as a loss of self, and it is this very search for selfhood that leads her to Elj, for his philosophy of life seems to hold out the promise of a truly authentic, instinctive experience. She is therefore disturbed when she realizes that she is making the same gestures with him as with her stage-lovers. It comes to her that as she tries to forge a role and a life for herself beyond the stage, it is her lover who is doing it for her. He knows her, he would argue, and her needs. What he reads as love, she experiences as possession. When he makes love to her, she experiences a syndrome that is common to many of Pirandello's heroines: she feels detached from her

della sua drammaturgia, pp. 86–7, sees in *Trovarsi* an attempt to construct Marta Abba as Eleanora Duse's spiritual heir.

own body. While the eponymous hero of *Enrico IV* can refer to the moment a man and a woman are naked in bed together as the occasion when all pretence, all sham, is dropped, for Donata it merely registers the alienation of self from a body no longer hers, now that it has become object of another's desire. She explains the sensation in a long discussion about female and male sexuality with a friend, Elisa. It is a courageous or possibly audacious illustration, on the male author's part, of a comment made by the play's ever perpicacious *raisonneur*, Salò, to Volpes: 'Tu sei quello dell'esperienza [. . .] Che, per sapere, bisogna prima provare. Io so invece che ho provato sempre soltanto ciò che m'ero prima immaginato'[30] ('You are the exponent of experience [. . .] That, in order to know one has to first experience it. I know instead that I have always experienced only that which I had first imagined').

Trovarsi ends a cycle of plays written for Marta Abba where Pirandello depicts women who are, for all their neuroses, strong-willed and uncompromising, much more so than their weak and vacillating male counterparts. But, as we shall see, he does not hold out much hope for his heroines as they struggle to attain a life they can call their own. Only in the conclusion to *Trovarsi* does he show that, by living a part in full consciousness of what one is doing, is one freed, like Donata, of the imprisoning gaze of the other. The audience is physically present but she refuses to engage with it. Acting becomes a strategy for resistance. Salò says to Donata:

Ebbene, voi avete al contrario questo dono: di poter vivere sulla scena, sapendovi guardata da tutti, cioè con tanti specchi davanti, quanti sono gli occhi degli spettatori.[31]

Well, you on the other hand have this gift; of being able to live on the stage, knowing yourself watched by everyone, that is to say, with as many mirrors before you as the audience has eyes.

She replies quite simply: 'Ma io non vedo gli spettatori' ('But I don't see the audience'). There is a terrible pathos, however, about this selfhood that has no self beyond the stage.

Alienated, suffering a permanent condition of self-alienation, or so it would appear judging from the position from which

---

[30] Pirandello, *Maschere nude, Opera omnia*, iv. 179.
[31] Ibid. 183.

Pirandello's women protagonists speak; it is as if the voice were outside the body that it refers to so obsessively. It is striking how, throughout Pirandello's writing where the problem of women's bodies is not 'resolved' by child-bearing, real tensions emerge. The non-maternal female body is trapped as object of desire; as Susan Sontag noted in the programme notes to her 1980/1 production of *Come tu mi vuoi*:

Essersi creati dal desiderio degli altri è una caratteristica della siuazione umana, ma è particolarmente tipica della situazione delle donne. L'edificio culturale dell'oppressione delle donne può essere riassunto dai modi in cui è sottinteso che le donne, a differenza degli uomini, sono create dal fatto che sono desiderate.[32]

To be created by other people's desires is a characteristic of the human situation, but it is particularly typical of the situation women find themselves in. The cultural edifice of women's oppression can be summarized by the ways that it is understood that women, unlike men, are created out of the fact that they are desired.

In *Il giuoco delle parti* (*The Rules of the Game*, 1918) Silia compares her condition to that of a prisoner. In her case surveillance is maintained by the male gaze, which works like Foucault's Benthamite mechanism of 'panopticism', with the consequence that she never forgets, even momentarily, that she is caught in a woman's body.[33] The very disjointedness of the language communicates her self-alienation as she tries to explain to her lover why it is that she feels as though she is living a life in prison: 'questo mio corpo, quando mi dimentico che è di donna, e nossignori, non me ne debbo mai dimenticare, dal modo che tutti mi guardano . . .'[34] ('even my own body, when I can forget that it is a woman's, and how can I ever forget, the way you all look at me . . .'). Julia Kristeva, writing about Céline, has commented on how in his case linguistic disjointedness, created by the frequent use of three dots followed by an exclamation mark, has the effect of dividing sentences into their constitutive parts, so making them independent of the central

[32] See Jennifer Stone, 'Beyond Desire: A Critique of Susan Sontag's Production of Pirandello's *Come tu mi vuoi*', *The Yearbook of the British Pirandello Society*, 1 (1981), 147–61.
[33] The panopticon was an architectural form for a prison designed in such a way as to allow the guards to keep the inmates in their cells under constant surveillance.
[34] Pirandello, *Maschere nude*, ii (1993), 138.

verb.[35] What then emerges are sentences whose meaning is incomplete. The same point can be made of the descriptions that have been left us of Duse's speaking style which was then adopted by Abba, with its absence of fluency and broken syntax so that grammatical and logical links are weakened. Donata in *Trovarsi* also struggles to resist the identification between her and her body:

vedendomi talvolta richiamata da certi sguardi al mio corpo, trovarmi donna [. . .] Non vedo più la ragione che io debba riconoscere il mio corpo come la cosa più mia, in cui io debbo realmente consistere per gli altri.[36]

Seeing myself sometimes recalled by certain glances at my body and I find myself a woman. [. . .] I no longer see the reason why I should consider my body as that which is most me, in which I must really exist for others.

Fulvia in *Come prima, meglio di prima* (*As Before, Better than Before* 1921) is described in the stage directions as having an:

evidente sdegno e un vero intimo odio per la sua bella persona, come se da un pezzo non le appartenesse più, e non sapesse più neppure com'esso è, non avendo mai, se non con feroce ribrezzo, condiviso la gioia che gli altri ne han preso.[37]

an evident scorn and a real intimate hatred of her beautiful body, as if for some time now it no longer belonged to her, and she no longer even knew what it was like, never having shared, except with fierce disgust, in the pleasure others had taken in it.

The disgust that these women feel for their bodies is their response to men's perception of their sexuality. To be defined by your body is to be given a gendered identity. Whatever ruptures the male psyche, no man in Pirandello's writing can be heard addressing the body/self split in similar terms. Where the male at least enjoys the illusion of a unitary self located within the body, adult women who are not defined by the maternal role experience a self that is split off from the body. The male body is universalized and therefore in a sense non-sexed, the

[35] See Julia Kristeva, 'From one Identity to Another', in *Desire in Language*, tr. Thomas Gora, Alice Jardine and Leon Roudiez (New York, Columbia University Press, 1982), 141.

[36] Pirandello, *Maschere nude, Opera omnia*, iv. 145.

[37] Pirandello, *Maschere nude*, ii (1993), 527.

woman is seen uniquely in terms of her sex. In response to
Ersilia's cry of 'Chi sono?' ('Who am I?') the reply comes back:
'Prima di tutto una bella ragazza' ('Above all else a pretty girl').
The question that these protagonists put to themselves over and
over again is how they might escape such a limiting condition.
The actress Delia Morello of *Ciascuno a suo modo* is, like her
precursor in *Quaderni di Serafino Gubbio operatore*, a *femme fatale*;
men have killed themselves—and each other—for her, leading
to mayhem among the town's eligible bachelors. But she is as
much a victim as they are, for when she looks at herself she
suffers an alienation verging on disgust:

DELIA. [. . .] Mi stringo e non mi sento. Le mani—me le guardo—non
mi sembrano mie. [. . .] Apro la borsetta, ne cavo lo specchio; e
nell'orrore di questa vana freddezza che mi prende, non potete
immaginarvi che impressione mi facciano, nel tondo dello specchio,
la mia bocca dipinta, i miei occhi dipinti, questa faccia che mi sono
guastata per farmene una maschera.

DORO (*appassionato*). Perchè non ve la guardate con gli occhi degli
altri?[38]

DELIA. [. . .] I clutch hold of myself and I can't feel anything. I look at
my hands and it's as if they were somebody else's. [. . .] I get the
mirror out of my handbag and then what happens? Can you imagine, in this horrible, blank, frozen state, what it does to me to look
in that little disc of mirror and see my painted mouth, my painted
eyes? I don't have a face any more! I've traded it in for a mask!

DORO (*with feeling*). That's only because you can't see it as other
people see it!

Until now Doro has been the one man she felt understood
her, so she responds to his unfeeling comment as though it
were an act of betrayal on his part: 'Anche voi?' ('You too?').
But precisely because his immunity to her confers on his comments a privileged status, we should pursue its implications a
little further. Of all Pirandello's problematic women, the only
one who seems to derive any pleasure from her body is 'una
vergine matura', Anna Rosa of *Uno, nessuno e centomila*. She is
admittedly protected by her virginity (and in other ways too),
but she is also a fully realized narcissist, able to make herself
both the subject and the object of the gaze.

---

[38] Pirandello, *Maschere nude, Opera omnia*, i. 84 (tr. *Each in His Own Way*, 87).

Solo del suo corpo pareva si compiacesse sempre, per quanto a volte non se ne mostrasse per nulla contenta, anzi dicesse di odiarselo. Ma se lo stava a mirare continuamente allo specchio, in ogni parte o tratto; a provarne tutti gli atteggiamenti, tutte le espressioni di cui i suoi occhi così intensi, lucidi e vivaci, le sue narici frementi, la sua bocca rossa e sdegnosa, la mandibola mobilissima, potevano essere capaci. Così, come per un gusto d'attrice; non perchè pensasse che per sè nella vita, potessero servirle se non per giuoco: per un giuoco momentaneo di civetteria o provocazione.[39]

Her body alone, it appeared, gave her a never-failing pleasure, although at times she exhibited anything but satisfaction with it, and even asserted that she hated it. Nevertheless, she was constantly surveying it in the mirror, in its every part and feature, trying out every conceivable pose, every expression of which her intently gleaming and vivacious eyes, her trembling nostrils, her red, disdainful mouth and her exceedingly mobile lower jaw were capable. This was due, rather, to the actress in her; it was not because she fancied that in life they could be of any use to her except as a game, a momentary game of coquetry and flirtatiousness.

Her narcissism makes of her an actress in a performance in which she is her own audience. It is not so different from Doro's recommendation to Delia that, if she cannot bear to gaze upon herself, she should try to adopt the position of the other; the effect is the same for it makes a woman resistant to specular appropriation by male desire.

The image of the woman trapped in the gaze of the other is developed in Pirandello's essay on humour of 1906, where it is deployed to illustrate the difference, fundamental to his theory of humour, between 'perception' (*avvertimento*) and 'feeling' (*sentimento*). He explains his thesis by drawing on a hypothetical case that, it could be argued, is as revealing about his assumptions as it is about his aesthetics:

Vedo una vecchia signora, coi capelli ritinti, tutti unti non si sa di quale orribile manteca, e poi tutta goffamente imbellettata e parata d'abiti giovanili. Mi metto a ridere. *Avverto* che quella vecchia signora è il *contrario* di ciò che una vecchia rispettabile signora dovrebbe essere. Posso così, a prima giunta e superficialmente, arrestarmi a questa impressione comica. Il comico è appunto un *avvertimento del contrario*. Ma se ora interviene in me la riflessione, e mi suggerisce che quella

---

[39] Pirandello, *Tutti i romanzi*, ii. 888 (tr. Putnam 245).

vecchia signora non prova nessun piacere a pararsi così come un papagallo, ma che forse ne soffre e lo fa soltanto perchè pietosamente s'inganna che, parata così, nascondendo così le rughe e la canizie, riesca a trattenere a sè l'amore del marito molto più giovane di lui, ecco che io non posso più riderne come prima, perchè appunto la riflessione, lavorando in me, mi ha fatto andar oltre a quel primo avvertimento, o piuttosto, più addentro: da quel primo *avvertimento del contrario* mi ha fatto passare a questo *sentimento del contrario*. Ed è tutta qui la differenza tra il comico e l'umoristico.[40]

I see an old lady whose hair is dyed and completely smeared with some kind of horrible ointment; she is all made-up in a clumsy and awkward fashion and is all dolled-up like a young girl. I begin to laugh. I *perceive* that she is *the opposite* of what a respectable old lady should be. Now I could stop here at this initial and superficial comic reaction: the comic consists precisely of this *perception of the opposite*. But if, at this point, reflection interferes in me to suggest that perhaps this old lady finds no pleasure in dressing up like an exotic parrot, and that perhaps she is distressed by it and does it only because she pitifully deceives herself into believing that, by making herself up like that and by concealing her wrinkles and gray hair, she may be able to hold the love of her much younger husband—if reflection comes to suggest all this, then I can no longer laugh at her as I did at first, exactly because the inner working of reflection has made me go beyond, or rather enter deeper into, the initial stage of awareness: from the beginning *perception of the opposite*, reflection has made me shift to a *feeling of the opposite*. And herein lies the precise difference between the comic and humor.

The words printed in italics in the text identify the two stages in the process from the comic to the humorous, so that what starts out as a gut response to a perceived discrepancy between appearance and reality translates, on reflection, into a deeper understanding of the underlying reasons behind it. It is a transition, Pirandello claims, that takes the perceptive observer away from the attitude of cruelty that is inherent in the comic to the compassionate stance that he identifies as the essence of humour. This process occurs purely in the mind of the man (in this case Pirandello) who looks: there is no change in the appearance of the woman who is the object of the gaze. What takes place is the product of the superior understanding of the (male) subject. The first of several examples offered by

---

[40] Pirandello, *Spsv* 127 (tr. *On Humor*, by Antonio Illiano and Daniel P. Testa (Chapel Hill, NC, The University of North Carolina Press, 1960), 113).

Pirandello (the others all come from literary texts), it provides a succinct and highly visual illustration of his theory.

If we put to one side the theory and look instead at the illustration he provides, what do we find? The object of the humorist's, of Pirandello's attention, is an old woman dressed to appear much younger—mutton dressed as lamb—but she has not been very successful in her attempts to disguise her age. Pirandello conjures up before the reader's eyes an object of derision and disgust: her dyed hair is 'unto' ('smeared' but closer to 'greasy') with 'orribile manteca' ('horrible ointment') and she is 'goffamente' ('clumsily') made-up. He begins to laugh because she is the opposite of what a *respectable* (my italics this time) old lady should be. With the sentence *'Avverto* che quella vecchia signora è il *contrario* di ciò che una vecchia rispettabile signora dovrebbe essere' ('I *perceive* that she is *the opposite* of what a respectable old lady should be'), Pirandello introduces the notion of respectability into the text for the first time and also, in a neat move, he changes the terms of the discussion by concluding not, as one might expect, that she does not look like a respectable old lady, but that she is not what a respectable old lady should be. In other words, to make his point, he chooses to conflate appearance and reality; by authorial sleight of hand you are what you look like. Then a process of reflection sets in and what he began by seeing as grotesque becomes on further consideration a sign of her suffering and pain. Compassion succeeds cruelty. The reason given for her attempts at disguise is that she is trying to hold on to the love of a much younger husband. There is no hint of the fact that her dilemma, as he hypothesizes it, is the product of a set of highly coded, and very tenuous, social assumptions about older women and younger men; Debenedetti wrote of this passage that Pirandello 'fa violenza alle sagome più consuete della vita reale, in cui—di solito—le mogli sono più giovani dei mariti'[41] ('does violence to the most common features of real life, in which—usually—wives are younger than their husbands'), but there is no critique, implicit or explicit, of a commonly held *doxa* which says men should marry younger women. Although her anxieties are traced back to her feeling that her hold on her

---

[41] Giacomo Debenedetti, 'L'umorismo di Luigi Pirandello', *Nuovi argomenti*, (Apr.–June 1968), 180.

husband is insecure, which is, as Pirandello's 'perhaps' acknowledges, pure conjecture, from the opening words one wonders if her problem does not lie simply in her failure to apply make-up skilfully. Just as the premiss for his example of *umorismo* is embedded in questionable but unquestioned assumptions, so too is its frame. She is spectacle, he the seeing I/eye who can ascertain the truth through the power of the gaze—the passage opens with 'Vedo' ('I see'). To see is to know, but where Pirandello differs from realist writers is in his argument that seeing means seeing beyond or beneath appearance, that there is a deeper truth that lies beneath the surface. Appearance can deceive, but one can learn to look through as well as at.

So far we have seen instances of men who believe that looking will give them an understanding of the women they observe. We now move on to cases where the enigma posed by woman seems to be bound up with questions of truth and knowledge. It is no longer a question of trying to understand an individual woman in all her singularity, but of trying to comprehend woman, the sex which by metaphorical displacement is all that is mysterious, unfathomable, oracular. In the group of plays that we shall turn to, the supposition that one can penetrate beyond the surface to an inner truth is rejected—here the protagonists are all surface. These women resist interpretation. Massimo Bontempelli's *Nostra Dea* (*Our Goddess*) is a play that appeared, quite literally, to 'lift the veil off the enigma of femininity'.[42] After listening to Bontempelli describe his plans for a new play, Pirandello urged him to write it for the Teatro d'Arte. After months of procrastination, it was finally written hurriedly in the space of a fortnight, and handed over to Pirandello for nearly a month of rehearsals before its first night on the 22 April 1925. It was to be the most frequently performed play in the company's repertoire, bringing such critical acclaim to Marta Abba herself, in her second play as a professional actress, that from then on she often used the name Dea on her dressing-room door. In the wake of its success, Pirandello urged its author to come up with another play for the Teatro d'Arte, proposing that he should take the plot from one of his short stories, as Pirandello himself had done many times with his own theatre.

---

[42] Sarah Kofman, *The Enigma of Woman: Woman in Freud's Writings* (Ithaca, NY, Cornell University Press, 1985), 113.

Clearly feeling the need to push Bontempelli that bit further, Pirandello returned to him a few days later with a story taken from a recently published collection called *La donna dei miei sogni* (*The Woman of my Dreams*). Bontempelli finally completed the play, which he called *Minnie la candida* (*Minnie the Ingenuous*), in the spring of 1927, but after just one day of rehearsals it was abandoned because Marta Abba disliked it.

Nostra Dea embodies the pornographer's perfect fantasy by taking as its protagonist a woman who is all surface. Dea's identities are created by her dressmaker and effected by her maid. Every change of dress is accompanied by a change of personality and identity. To read Dea one must read her wardrobe. The nodal points in the plot accompany changes of dress, so obviating the need for a verbal explanation; what disappears from the dialogue returns in the costume. The play is a visual materialization at the level of wardrobe of the modernist preoccupation with the dissolution or fragmentation of character.[43] She has no past, no future, she can only live in the present: resting between clothes 'in combinazione', she is a living breathing mannequin, inert and inexpressive:

Sta ritta in mezzo alla scena con la faccia al pubblico, le braccia pendenti lungo i fianchi, inerte, lo sguardo assolutamente inespressivo; ha qualche cosa di abbandonato e insieme rigido, come i manichini.[44]

She stands upright in the middle of the stage facing the public, her arms hanging down her sides, inert, her gaze absolutely devoid of expression; she has something about her that is both inert and rigid, like puppets have.

The description of Dea from the stage directions at the opening and the close of the play echoes a partisan description of Eleonora Duse's own acting style offered by a rival of hers, the older prima donna, Adelaide Ristori, in the following extract from an interview given by her: 'She has a rather curious manner

---

[43] Although critics received the play very warmly on the whole, their interpretations vary widely. Vincenzo Cardarelli, for example, who argues interestingly that the play is in a sense an exacerbation of bourgeois comedy, also claims that with Dea Bontempelli has gone to extreme lengths simply to represent the typical female traits of inconsistency and volubility. See Vincenzo Cardarelli, *Il Tevere* (24–5 Sept. 1925).

[44] Massimo Bontempelli, *Nostra Dea e altre commedie* (Turin, Einaudi, 1989), 94.

of gesture that has an automated quality, a certain stiff letting
go of her arms down her sides with her body tired and drooping, a certain angular way of lifting her arm, holding it in a
rather mechanical stiffness.'[45] Dea herself is not capable of
combining the two sounds needed to articulate the word 'io'—
Italian for 'I'—and she therefore never acquires subjectivity.
The plot is determined by the clothes selected for Dea to wear,
until the denouement when the malicious intention to use her
as an instrument to inflict the maximum misery on others by
dressing her as a serpent—venomous, vicious, and extremely
seductive—is averted when the clothes are torn off her back by
a man who thereby neutralizes the evil created by women.
Reduced to rags, her clothes in shreds, Dea circulates the ball-
room begging alms before finally being returned to the state of
mannequin. Bontempelli has fun with some well-established
literary clichés. The exploited, prostituted, and victimized dressmaker of nineteenth-century fiction becomes a fanatical, and
almost demonic figure, a 'grande fabbricatrice di divinità' ('a
great maker of gods'), while the mistress–maid relationship is
inverted, as Anna the maid ominously comments: 'la signora
Dea, la faccio io, due o tre volte al giorno' ('it is I who make
madame Dea, two or three times a day'). Where the heroine's
identity is demoted to a function of costume, her physical reality
is similarly displaced, as is shown by her doctor who practises
what he calls a 'semeiotica ambientale', which entails visiting his
patient's home only in her absence, and making his diagnosis
on the basis of 'clues' left in her apartment.

Not only did Pirandello produce the play and introduce
changes to the script (the end of Act I was cut), but he was in
the habit of giving a brief presentation of the play to the public
before each performance. Although he was generous in his
praise for the work, it was noted that his introductory remarks
were at odds with the work itself. According to a letter sent to
Bontempelli, the gap between Pirandello's comments which
'avevano il tòno di presentare una commedia per lo meno
ponderosa—nel senso romantico della parola', ('had the tone
of one presenting a play that was to say the least weighty—in the
Romantic sense of the word') and the play, the 'irridiscente e

---

[45] Adelaide Ristoro in an interview with Leone Fortis in 1897.

maliziosa trama di *Nostra Dea*—leggera come un *chiffon*' ('*Nostra Dea*'s irridescent and mischievous plot—as light as chiffon'), produced a sense of disquiet among the audience.[46] Successive critics have noted the close link between the ideas informing Bontempelli's play and Pirandello's own theatre and in particular *Come tu mi vuoi*. Luigi Baldacci goes further, to note that if it had not been for Pirandello's adoption of the play, it could easily have been read as a light-hearted satire on his work:

È un *Come tu mi vuoi* (che però verrà dopo) immaginato e realizzato da una sarta. Il che significa che c'è anche un margine di divertimento nei confronti dello stesso Pirandello. Se Pirandello, dimostrando la liberalità della sua intelligenza, non avesse tenuto a battesimo questa commedia, si sarebbe potuto pensare a una satira antipirandelliana.[47]

It is a *Come tu mi vuoi* (which, however, comes afterwards) imagined and realized by a dressmaker. Which means that there is a degree of amusement at Pirandello's expense. If Pirandello had not acted as godfather to this play, thereby demonstrating the generosity of his own intelligence, one might have taken it for an anti-Pirandellian satire.

Pirandello's *Come tu mi vuoi* (*As you desire me*) was published and first performed in 1930. Unlike so much of his theatre, it has no source in any of his stories or novels. The play opens in Berlin in the late 1920s where the protagonist, L'Ignota (the Unknown Woman), pursues a career as a dancer in a nightclub. She lives with her lover Salter, but she is desired also by his sexually indeterminate daughter Mop. Like Dea, L'Ignota's identity revolves around appearance and when a photographer 'verifies' that she is Cia, the long-lost wife of a friend of his in the Veneto, she abandons her dissolute life and accompanies him to Italy. There, dressed in the clothes that Cia wore some ten years before when she posed for her portrait, L'Ignota causes some disquiet by looking more like the portrait than Cia ever did. (It recalls an episode with the artist Max Liebermann who

---

[46] Giovanni Artieri, letter to Massimo Bontempelli, 22 Oct. 1927. Quoted in *Nostra Dea e altre commedie*, 266.

[47] Ibid. 267. This is not the only example of a mutual creative debt. Another is to be found in Bontempelli's *Il figlio di due madri* (1929) which owes a debt to Pirandello's *La ragione degli altri* (1915). Where in Pirandello's play Livia manages to become mother to a child that is not hers through the symbolic authority of the father, in Bontempelli's narrative physical maternity is challenged by a male protagonist who is both the biological son of Arianna and the reincarnation of Luciana's dead son.

responded to a client dissatisfied with his portrait with the comment; 'this painting, my dear Sir, resembles you more than you do yourself'.[48]) When Salter arrives with a deranged woman from a Viennese asylum—a woman without speech and without features—who, he claims according to his documentation, is Cia, L'Ignota decides to return with her lover to Berlin.

Both Pirandello and Bontempelli owe a considerable artistic debt to Frank Wedekind's *Die Erdgeist (Earth-Spirit)* and *Die Büchse der Pandora (Pandora's Box)*, plays that Wedekind worked on intermittently between 1892 and 1913.[49] For censorship reasons, however, they were not permitted a public performance until 1918. The plays reached a much wider audience when in 1929 G. W. Pabst turned them into a film, *Die Büchse der Pandora (Pandora's Box)*, with the American actress Louise Brooks playing the part of Lulu. The concentration of female identity on surface and by extension costume is the idea informing all four plays, so that what is striking is the extent to which they rely upon the visual representation of the woman protagonist for their effect. Appearance replaces psychology as the motivating impulse behind their narratives. As what occurs is often neither of the protagonist's volition nor under her control, the plays communicate a sense of hopelessness and aimlessness. Like Bontempelli's Dea, Lulu is a succession of clothes. When *Erdgeist* opens we meet Lulu's Pierrot costume before we meet her but, as one of her admirers, the artist Schwarz, observes, it is as though her body has been born in the costume.[50] Her skin is indistinguishable from her dress, both are of silk. Her 'naturalness' rests in the fact that she is pure artifice (indeed in an earlier draft of the play Lulu is suspected of dyeing and artificially curling the hair in her armpits). In the course of the two plays the enigmatic Lulu is implicated in the deaths of three husbands, several admirers, and the wife of the man who

---

[48] See E. H. Gombrich, 'The Mask and the Face', in *The Image and the Eye* (Oxford, Phaidon, 1982), 136.

[49] In an interview with *L'Impero* (11 Apr. 1925), Pirandello said that the company intended to perform works by Wedekind, Strindberg, Shaw, and Claudel during the next season.

[50] 'Der ganzer Körper im Einklang mit dem unmöglichen Kostüm, als wäre er darin zur Welt gekommen' ('Her whole body was as much in harmony with this impossible costume as if she had been born in it'), Frank Wedekind, *Erdgeist: Die Büchse der Pandora* (Munich, Wilhelm Goldmann, 1980), 16–17.

became her third husband. Furthermore there is a strong intimation that she enjoys an incestuous relationship with her father; she has an affair with her husband's son, and among her admirers are a schoolboy whose main preoccupation is that he may be expelled, and a lesbian, the Countess Geschwitz, who later, in Pabst's film, was to be the first 'screen lesbian'. Lulu herself embraces death when it comes to her in the figure of Jack the Ripper—the first man in relation to whom she is more desiring than desired and the only man who does not look directly at her. Whenever something unpleasant happens Lulu changes dress and her exhibitionist fascination with dress is crucial to her presence as spectacle. Lulu aspires to be what Dea unwittingly is, she simply wishes to be that which others see her as being: 'Ich habe *nie* etwas anders sein wollen also wofür man mich genommen hat' ('I have *never* wanted to be anything other than what people take me for').

Pirandello must have known the work of both Pabst and Wedekind. Although it can only be conjectured that he knew Pabst's film adaptation of the plays from when he was living in Berlin between 1929 and 1930, he was sufficiently impressed by Pabst as a film director to recommend him as second choice after Eisenstein whom he met in Berlin, to make a film version of his story 'Acciaio' ('Steel'). In the event neither director was available. But more compelling evidence of Pirandello's familiarity with the Lulu plays comes from within *Come tu mi vuoi* where the first act, which is clearly intended primarily as an indictment of the social mores of 1920s Berlin, is a reworking of *Erdgeist*. Still more interesting are the similarities between L'Ignota, Lulu, and Dea. All three young women are presented to us without any reliable information about their background. Even the first index of identity—forename and surname—is missing. These are anonymous, unidentified women who circulated like currency with the potential to pass into any man's possession. Naming, a father's prerogative, which he later confers on the husband, is a statement of ownership. As they circulate among men, so their names change, L'Ignota changes name three times, Lulu four times, but the speed and insignificance of the changes means that no one name sticks long enough to provide an identity. So depersonalized are their names (only the name Dea, Goddess, remains constant no matter how many roles she adopts) that they come to represent Woman as sex, rather than as individual members of their sex. In the absence of a statement as to who they are, the protagonists construct themselves, or are constructed, visually through the dress they wear: it is their 'look' that authenticates their identity.

In three of the plays with parts written specifically for Marta Abba—Tuda in *Diana e la Tuda*, L'Ignota in *Come tu mi vuoi*, and Donata in *Trovarsi*—the woman protagonist is accompanied by a male artist who is trying to 'capture' her image through his medium: oils, photography, or clay. Because these elusive, enigmatic women are of uncertain provenance and background, and because they themselves cannot or will not provide a coherent account of themselves, their identity is construed almost entirely from their appearance. So their selfhood is bound up in the gaze of others. Icons, such as photographs and portraits, usually thought of simply as *aides-mémoire,* are here granted more extensive powers as a means to establish who somebody is. In *Come tu mi vuoi* L'Ignota's legal identity suddenly becomes a matter of some urgency when a man who insists that she is his lost wife stands to lose his inheritance if the claim cannot be verified. Photographs and portraits acquire a new and alarming significance. Even more strikingly, in *Trovarsi*, Giviero's reputation for having such an intimate knowledge of Donata does not come from a personal friendship (in fact they have never met) but from his collection of portraits of her: 'Tanti—appunto— tanti—non uno solo—e tutti diversi l'uno dall'altro' ('So many—it's exactly that—so many—not just one—and all of them different from one another'). So a woman's identity can be authenticated, her personality known, through more or less accurate visual representations of her. The etymology of *theatre*, from the Greek *theatron*, 'place of viewing', and *theasthai*, 'to look upon, to contemplate', related of course to *theoria*, meaning speculation, contemplation, reminds us of the privileged position that sight has in our access to knowledge. In 'Science and Reflection', Martin Heidegger traces the etymology of both *theatre* and *theory* back to the same root:

The word 'theory' stems from the Greek verb *theorein*. The noun belonging to it is *theoria*. Peculiar to these words is a lofty and mysterious meaning. The verb *theorein* grew out of the coalescing of two root words, *thea* and *horao*. *Thea* (cf. theatre) is the outward look, the aspect, in which something shows itself, the outward appearance in which it offers itself. Plato names this aspect in which what presences shows what it is, *eidos*. To have seen this aspect, *eidenai* is to know. The second root word in *theorein*, *horao* means: to look at something attentively, to look it over, to view it closely. Thus it follows that *theorein* is *thean horan*, to look attentively on the outward appearance, wherein what presences becomes visible and, through such sight—seeing—to linger with it.[51]

In Pirandello's writings, sight is frequently a central metaphor in the search for truth; Pirandello's own male characters often resort to seeing-aids—telescopes, lenses, spectacles, and cameras—as against the poor, benighted feminist of 'Feminismo' whose wrong-thinking is embodied in her myopia. He himself describes the confusion induced by living through four decades, each of which is associated with a different kind of lighting.

Pirandello had, from the outset, recognized the importance realism gave to the role of sight in the cognitive process, but he did not just accept it as a philosophical and cultural given. Instead, he used his writings to set about investigating its function and its effects. Sight informs his novels both at the level of the writing—a number of characters in his early narratives are presented visually as caricatures, physically grotesque and deeply repulsive, as though the transparency, and therefore invisibility, of the realist mirror had been replaced by the distorting mirrors of the fairground—and plot, where sight and seeing are catalysts causing things to happen. Paradoxically, nowhere is this more apparent than in *Quaderni di Serafino Gubbio operatore*, where Serafino's alienation stems precisely from the dissociation his function as cameraman brings between seeing and doing. The seeing I/eye, like the camera's lens, is passive, it sees purely to record, never to act—or, as the violent finale serves to remind us—to react.

But what emerges in *Quaderni di Serafino Gubbio operatore*, is a concern for the problematic nature of sight and seeing which the novel presents as both more complex and more compromis-

[51] Martin Heidegger, 'Science and Reflection', in *The Question Concerning Technology and Other Essays*, tr. William Lovitt (New York, Harper and Row, 1977), 163.

ing than previously suggested. The notebooks of the title are written by a man who, in the wake of the traumatic episode with the tiger in the film-studio, has stopped speaking. He has also stopped working. As cameraman, he used to set up the equipment, 'prestare i miei occhi alla macchinetta' to check 'fin dove arriva a *prendere*'[52] ('apply my eyes to the machine so that I can indicate how far it will manage to *take*'), measure out the number of metres of film required, and then, when the time came, turn the handle, varying the speed according to the tempo of the scene. Where a cameraman today would watch through the camera lens, Gubbio films by turning a handle but without looking through the camera's aperture. The end of his professional career does not mean the end of his watching of others. Quite the contrary: as we have seen, the novel's opening reveals that he now does little else: 'Studio la gente nelle sue più ordinarie occupazioni'[53] ('I study people in their most ordinary occupations'); in his search for knowledge, 'study' and 'watch' have been conflated, and with them epistemology and voyeurism. There are three stages to his voyeurism; first he watches people as they go about their daily business ('studio')—at this stage they do not notice; then he looks them in the eye ('guardo')—at this stage they notice and their eyes 's'aombrano' ('veil over'); and finally in those cases where he goes on to scrutinize them ('scrutarli'), they are so disturbed and confused that it would not take much for them to attack him. Serafino Gubbio is one of Pirandello's *raisonneurs*, the outsider who dedicates himself to watching others and records what he sees on paper. The problem, he learns, is that looking is not enough and the novel acts as an early warning of the failure of the gaze to reveal.

Theatre was not the only cultural medium of the period to suggest that woman was all surface. A striking aspect of modernism's preoccupation with the indeterminacy of woman's identity was the growing fascination with clothes; dress that can dissemble, conceal, and construct the bearer's self. The most startling representation of this preoccupation can be found in Surrealist art; Man Ray, Salvador Dali, and Oscar Dominguez offer their versions of the creation-myth. In Ray's 'The Enigma

---

[52] Pirandello, *Tutti i romanzi*, ii. 521 (tr. Scott Moncrieff, 7).
[53] Ibid. 519 (tr. Scott Moncrieff, 3).

of Isadore Ducasse' (1920), Dali's 'Night and Day Clothes of the Body' (1936), and Dominguez's 'Electrosexual Sewing Machine' (1934), it is the sewing-machine that makes woman. In Surrealist images of feminine beauty, clothing and the female body appear to be indissolubly sewn together and, frequently, as in the work of Max Ernst and Giorgio De Chirico, the inanimate form of the mannequin replaced woman. Why displace identity on to a woman's wardrobe? Beyond the arts, a new visual semiotics of dress had also come into being, moving perception of it away from the idea that dress was a means of covering the body (but bearing signs of its owner's social status and wealth) towards a concept of dress as an expression or revelation of individual identity. It was not after all so long since women's dress had been a question of bustles, whale-bone stays, and tight-lacings which caused such concern at the turn of the century that the Reform Dress Movement was launched in England to fight the manipulation and distortion of the female body induced by women's clothes. Changes brought about by the technology of the sewing-machine and developments in textiles and fabrics contributed to the changing significance of clothes. Photography made possible the proliferation of fashion plates so that the 'image' or 'look' could be reproduced and made accessible to a wide audience. Gradually the barriers between pure and applied arts began to give—a process both illustrated and advanced by the surge of creativity in Russia in the years immediately following the Revolution. Soon leading artists such as Delaunay, Goncharova, and Léger were engaged in costume-design both for the stage and for the screen.

One area where we can particularly see the assumption that clothes are a manifestation of a core identity is in the cultural representations of androgyny or cross-dressing. The three plays by Bontempelli, Pirandello, and Wedekind all use clothes to raise questions about sexual identity. In Act I of *Come tu mi vuoi* Pirandello communicates his vision of Berlin in the 1920s as a degenerate and reprehensible society by giving Mop, Slater's daughter who competes with her father for L'Ignota's attention, a pair of pyjamas and a masculine haircut. The opening stage directions describe her face as 'segnata d'un che d'ambiguo che fa ribrezzo' ('marked by something ambiguous that puts one off'). In *Nostra Dea*, when the protagonist is dressed in masculine clothes, her stride lengthens, her physical appetites increase, she knows her own mind; the shy, acquiescent, inviting young woman of the day before has vanished, to her suitor's comical dismay and confusion. Wedekind's representation of Lulu's most constant and loyal suitor, the Countess Geschwitz, with her mannish lesbianism, is an embodiment of the pioneering sexologist Havelock Ellis's concept of the third sex. In all three examples sexual indeterminacy is attached to a woman's appearance. The anxiety these plays testify to is an expression of a widespread unease. Traditionally held views of masculinity and femininity as complementary were being undermined on a number of fronts, from women fighting for emancipation to women replacing men in civic society during the 1914–18 war.[54] The appalling experience of trench warfare itself delivered a serious blow to received notions of masculinity. Emergent theories of the psyche, with their emphasis on the role of the unconscious in determining behaviour, also undermined presuppositions about sexual difference. In all this, of course, men had much more to lose than women. The disquiet so evident in works written by men does not extend to those written by women. When, for example, Virginia Woolf addressed the subject, she produced a witty celebration of androgyny in her novel *Orlando* (1928), where her eponymous hero/ine discovers that her sex and personality change along with her clothes. Far from this being a source of anxiety, it is accompanied by nothing other than pleasure.

The displacement of identity on to clothes and the continuum between body and dress are developed still further on stage in avant-garde spectacle such as Dadaist performance, where the body becomes a screen constantly imprinting redefinitions and transformations. As early as 1909 the young Kokoschka had caused uproar in Vienna with the staging of his play *Mörder Hoffnung der Frauen* (*Murder Hope of Womankind*), a battle between the sexes enacted through progressive mutual mutilation and culminating in Man's killing of Woman and his departure from a stage red with blood and flames, by covering the actors' bodies in a web of painted lines which traced or

---

[54] See Ch. 7, 'Male Hysteria: W. H. R. Rivers and the Lessons of Shell Shock', in Elaine Showalter, *The Female Malady: Women, Madness and English Culture, 1830–1980* (London, Virago, 1988), 167–94.

represented the network of nerves. Where Dea's dress in Bontempelli's play projects inwards to manufacture an identity, so erasing the gap between dress and 'self', Kokoschka's characters' interiority is displaced on to the surface, so they are just nerves, flesh, and blood. Clothes and body, textiles and skin, become indistinguishable. As a result the concept of theatricality itself extended to include all aspects of self-presentation offstage as well as on. It became a part of life.[55]

As character is displaced on to dress, so the body assumes the function of self-expression or self-revelation. Dance had been largely absent from the theatre in the nineteenth century, but in the period under discussion it returns to the stage, not to tell a story in the manner of a masque, but to display the heroine. L'Ignota is the only professional dancer in our three plays, and we first see her wearing the costume for the serpentine dance she invents for performance in the nightclub. But Lulu and Dea also dance. Indeed Lulu is only truly alive when dancing; it is her body's only means of self-expression. Nietzsche saw dance as an expression of human liberation, but in the world of our protagonists it is a morally ambiguous *métier* associated with display, sexual voyeurism, and seduction. It is always performed before a male gaze that pays for the privilege. In *Come tu mi vuoi* Pirandello brings together dance, drink, and debauchery; in *Erdgeist* the connection between dance, dress, and voyeurism is made when a young avant-garde director is told by his father (who will himself later put Lulu back into circulation by making her dance in public) that nobody is going to pay money to see her dance in a raincoat. Lulu is told by Schön that she will dance before anyone who pays to watch her and later he adds, 'Solang du noch einen Funken Achtung vor dir selbst hast, bist du keine perfekte Tänzerin'[56] ('As long as you keep a spark of self-respect you can't be a perfect dancer'). The nature of the dance is not specified in these plays, although we are clearly not talking about classical dance; it is, however, described variously as 'serpentine', 'convulsive', and 'extravagant', adjectives that,

[55] See Erika Fischer-Lichte, 'From Theatre to Theatricality: How to Construct Reality', *Theatre Research International*, 202 (Summer 1995), 106–13.

[56] In both *Come tu mi vuoi* and *Erdgeist* the presentation of woman as image is also represented visually through the presence of framed reproductions of Lulu and L'Ignota; portraits or copies that the audience are invited to compare with the 'original' model.

as we have seen, are associated with the 'uncontrollable' writhings of Charcot's hysterics at La Salpetrière. Again we find the idea of the body over which the mind has no control, a reflection on woman as the sex closest to animal. In Wedekind's play Lulu is first seen being carried immobile into a circus-ring where the animal-tamer instructs her as his whip caresses her. What is interesting is that dance is not simply referred to, but that our protagonists are watched by a paying public in the auditorium as they dance by themselves on stage. These are moments which carry no narrative, the only reason for their inclusion is that they focus the spectator's gaze on the dancer.

The dances enacted on stage reflect the influence Isadora Duncan, Loïe Fuller, Maud Allen, and others had exercised over traditional classical dance by creating unballetic bodily movements of their own, producing a writing of the female body which was markedly different from the concepts of grace and harmony inherent in classical inscriptions. Dance and dress, passivity and presence; what is so marked about these three protagonists is that the emphasis falls not on doing but on performing—appearance is everything. In classic realism dress is used as a key to the personality of its wearers, but at the same time, for the device to be effective, the reader or viewer must remain unaware of the extent to which the understanding of the protagonist is determined by outer trappings: in these plays dress is foregrounded either to deny any continuity between outer and inner, or to question a concept of interiority. To step into a costume is to step into a role; many of the costumes of Lulu, Dea, and L'Ignota are designed to be looked at by the public before whom they perform. They are all surface, they do not yield to interpretation.

The primacy of the image in creating an identity is emphasized in both *Erdgeist* and *Come tu mi vuoi* in scenes where the audience is invited to compare the protagonists to their respective portraits in oils. In both cases the portrait was commissioned for private consumption, but where in Wedekind's play its presence simply arouses a voyeuristic pleasure among the male spectators on stage, in Pirandello's play it is used, together with photographs and documents, to authenticate a woman's legal identity and is the subject of discussion among the actors on stage. So important is the heroine's 'look' that it outweighs speech as signifier. It is true that these plays were written at the end of a period which had seen the nineteenth-century dominance of language increasingly challenged, but I would argue that this shift in the presentation of the heroine on stage owes much to the arrival of cinema. The years of silent cinema saw a productive exchange between theatre and cinema; while silent cinema had from its inception borrowed its plots from nineteenth-century literary melodrama, theatre explored the potential available to it for communication without words.

Pirandello's involvement with cinema as spectator and writer led also to several essays on the subject. In 1929, after the advent of sound, Pirandello wrote two newspaper articles,[57] 'Contro il film parlato' ('Against the Speaking Cinema') and 'Se il film parlante abolirà il teatro' ('Will the Talkies Kill the Theatre?') where he discusses the issues raised by the new technology. Insistent that the discovery of sound must not be used to produce filmed theatre, he argued that the new emphasis on words was mistaken as it detracted from the power of the image, cinema's most fundamental and compelling asset. Narration, he wrote, with some disingenuousness, should be left to the novel, and drama to the theatre, while cinema should hold fast to its own visual language and capitalize on it: 'il cinema dovrebbe trasformarsi in pura visione' ('cinema should transform itself into pure vision'). It is, perhaps unexpectedly, the advent of sound that leads Pirandello to argue that the threat cinema posed to theatre had been averted. In the days of silent film, he argued, the cinema, defined as 'muta espressione di immagini e linguaggio di apparenze'[58] ('mute expression of images and language of appearances') had accustomed its huge public to a new language of sight. Theatre, worried by its formidable rival, hastened to turn itself into a theatre of spectacle by closely studying cinematic technique, but now it was the turn of cinema to seek to emulate, quite misguidedly, the stage, and theatre had nothing further to fear.

[57] 'Contro il film parlante', *Corriere della sera* (19 Apr. 1920). 'Se il film parlante abolirà il teatro', *Anglo-American Newspaper Service* (London and New York, June 1919). Both essays can be found in Francesco Càllari, *Pirandello e il cinema* (Venice, Marsilio, 1991), 118–20 and 120–6 (tr. Bassnett and Lorch, *Pirandello in the Theatre*, 152–7).

[58] Pirandello, 'Se il film parlante abolirà il teatro', 122.

If Pirandello is correct to argue that the rivalry between cinema and theatre was at its most intense during the years of silent cinema, when theatre had most to lose from an audience accustomed to following narratives through what they saw rather than what they heard, that rivalry may well be expected to have had repercussions on the way in which character was represented. In the introduction to her collection of essays on feminism, semiotics, and cinema, Teresa de Lauretis notes that narrative cinema, spoken as well as silent, is the genre in which 'the representation of woman as spectacle—body to be looked at, place of sexuality and object of desire—so pervasive in our culture, finds its most complex expression and widest circulation'.[59] This is not to suggest that the two media, cinema and theatre, were interchangeable. Where, for example, silent cinema had the possibility of close-up, allowing facial expressions to be a vehicle for self-expression, theatre had the voice whose signifying capacity included tone as well as content. Nor could the signifying techniques developed by the one medium simply be transferred to the other. In the absence of the voice in silent cinema, bodily movements required an exaggerated expressivity to be understood, facilitated by a closeness of range unobtainable in conventional theatre. Nor did the body need to be a constant unity as it did on stage (despite experiments by the Futurists); it could fragment, or parts of the body could be emphasized over others. What screen and stage did share however was that both sought to remedy their respective lack, voice in the case of cinema, close-up in the case of theatre, by maximizing the potential afforded by dress and bodily movement.

But even if the move towards the representation of woman as image was at least in part an effect of the impact of the cinema on theatre-going audiences, it is reasonable to assume that the consequences of the shift in attention away from the spoken word to the visual image were not purely technical in character and that, in the shadow of the authority which our culture invests in the word, the redefinition of woman as dramatic spectacle carried an ideological price for woman. For Pirandello the figure of the actress on stage and on screen

---

[59] Teresa de Lauretis, *Alice Doesn't: Feminism, Semiotics, Cinema* (London, Macmillan, 1984), 4.

Bibliography

AA VV, *Atti del congresso internazionale di studi pirandelliani* (Florence, Le Monnier, 1967).

—— *Lectures pirandelliennes* (Abbeville, F. Paillart, 1978).

—— *Pirandello e il teatro* (Milan, Mursia, 1994).

—— *Testo e messinscena in Pirandello* (Urbino, La Nuova Italia Scientifica, 1986).

Abba Marta, *Caro Maestro . . . Lettere a Luigi Pirandello (1926–1936)*, ed. Pietro Frassica (Milan, Mursia, 1994).

Adorno, T. W., 'The Essay as Form', *New German Critique*, 32 (1984), 151–71.

Alberti, Alberto Cesare, *Il teatro nel fascismo, Pirandello e Bragaglia* (Rome, Bulzoni, 1974).

Alfonzetti, Beatrice, *Il trionfo dello specchio* (Catania, Collana di studi di filologia moderna, 1984).

Alford, C. Fred, *The Self in Social Theory: A Psychoanalytic Account of its Construction in Plato, Hobbes, Locke, Rawls and Rousseau* (New Haven, Yale University Press, 1991).

Alonge, Roberto, *Pirandello tra realismo e mistificazione* (Naples, Guida, 1972).

—— 'Madri, puttane, schiave sessuali e uomini soli', in R. Alonge *et al.*, *Studi pirandelliani: Dal testo al sottotesto* (Bologna, Pitagora, 1986).

Altieri Biagi, Maria Luisa, 'La lingua in scena: Dalle novelle agli atti unici', in AA VV, *Tutto Pirandello* (Agrigento, Edizione del centro nazionale di studi pirandelliani, 1986), 209–67.

Andersson, G., *Arte e teoria: Studi sulla poetica del giovane Luigi Pirandello* (Stockholm, Almquist and Wiksell, 1966).

Angelini, Franca, *LIST: Il Novecento*, i (Bari, Laterza, 1976), 418–20.

—— *Serafino e la tigre* (Venice, Marsilio, 1990).

Archi, Paolo, *Il tempo delle parole: Saggio sulla prosa di Pirandello* (Palermo, Palumbo, 1992).

Ashley, Kathleen M. (ed.), *Victor Turner and the Construction of Cultural Criticism. Between Literature and Anthropology* (Bloomington, Ind., and Indianapolis, Indiana University Press, 1990).

Baldacci, Luigi, *Massimo Bontempelli* (Turin, Borla, 1967).

Bàrberi Squarotti, G., *La forma e la vita: Il romanzo del Novecento* (Milan, Mursia, 1987), 54–74.

—— *Le sorti del 'tragico'. Il Novecento italiano: Romanzo e teatro* (Ravenna, Longo, 1978), 137–99.

Barilli, Renato, 'Pirandello e Bontempelli: Dalla seconda alla terza età', in *Pirandello e la drammaturgia tra le due guerre* (Agrigento, Centro nazionale di Studi Pirandelliani, 1985), 261–75.

Barilli, Renato, *Pirandello: Una rivoluzione culturale* (Milan, Mursia, 1986).

Bassnett, Susan, and Lorch, Jennifer (eds.), *Luigi Pirandello in the Theatre: A Documentary Record* (Reading, Harwood Academic Publishers, 1993).

Bassnett McGuire, Susan, 'Art and Life in Luigi Pirandello's *Questa sera si recita a soggetto*', in *Themes in Drama* 2, 1980 ('Drama and Mimesis', ed. J. Redmond), 81–102.

——*Luigi Pirandello* (London, Macmillan, 1983).

Bauman, Richard, *Story, Performance, and Event: Contextual Studies of Oral Narrative* (Cambridge, Cambridge University Press, 1986).

Benjamin, Walter, 'The Storyteller', in *Illuminations* (London, Fontana, 1992), 83–109.

Bentley, Eric, *The Pirandello Commentaries* (Evanston, Ill., Northwestern University Press, 1986).

——(ed.), *The Theory of the Modern Stage: An Introduction to Modern Theatre and Drama* (Harmondsworth, Penguin, 1992).

Besant, Annie, *A Study in Consciousness* (London, Theosophical Publishing Society, 1904).

——and Leadbeater, C. W., *Thought-Forms* (London, Theosophical Publishing Society, 1905).

Biasin, Gian Paolo, and Perella, Nicholas J. (eds.), *Pirandello 1986* (Rome, Bulzoni, 1987).

Bigazzi, Roberto, 'I *Sei personaggi* e l'autore', *Modern Language Notes*, 97/1 (Jan. 1982), 41–55.

Binet, Alfred, *Les Altérations de la personnalité* (Paris, Félix Alcan, 1892).

Borsellino, Nino, *Ritratto di Pirandello* (Bari, Laterza, 1983).

Boswell, John, *The Kindness of Strangers: The Abandonment of Children in Western Europe from Late Antiquity to the Renaissance* (Harmondsworth, Allen Lane, 1988).

Brunetta, Gian Pietro, *Cent'anni di cinema italiana* (Rome and Bari, Laterza, 1981).

Brustein, Robert, *Beyond Objectivism amd Relativism* (Oxford, Blackwell, 1983).

Büdel, Oscar, *Pirandello* (London, Bowes and Bowes, 1966).

Burns, Elizabeth, *Theatricality: A Study of Convention in the Theatre and in Social Life* (London, Longman, 1972).

Cambon, Glauco (ed.), *Pirandello: A Collection of Critical Essays* (Englewood Cliffs, NJ, Prentice Hall, 1967).

Cantoro, Ugo, *Luigi Pirandello e il problema della personalità* (Bologna, Gallo, 1954).

Cappello, Giovanni, *Quando Pirandello cambia titolo: Occasionalità o strategia?* (Milan, Mursia, 1986).

Carlson, Marvin, 'The Structure of the Drama', *Semiotica*, 76/3–4 (1989), 267–73.

Cascetta, Annamaria, *Teatri d'Arte tra le due guerre a Milano* (Milan, Vita e pensiero, 1979).

Castri, Massimo, *Pirandello Ottanta*, ed. Ettore Capriolo (Milan, Ubulibri, 1981).

Cauldwell, Lesley, *Italian Family Matters: Women, Politics and Legal Reform* (London, Macmillan, 1991).

Cerina, Giovanni, *Pirandello o la scienza della fantasia* (Pisa, ETS, 1983).

Cometa, Michele, *Il teatro di Pirandello in Germania* (Palermo, Edizioni Novecento, 1986).

Croce, Benedetto, *La letteratura della nuova Italia*, vi, Ch. 54 (Bari, Laterza, 1974).

——*La letteratura italiana per saggi storicamente disposti*, ed. M. Sansone (Bari, Laterza, 1968), iv, 326–49.

Cudini, Piero, 'Mattia Pascal tra evocazione ed epifania', *Rivista di studi pirandelliani*, 1 (Sept.–Dec. 1978), 7–16.

D'Amico, Alessandro, and Tinterri, Alessandro, A. *Pirandello capocomico: La Compagnia del Teatro d'Arte di Roma 1925–28* (Palermo, Sellerio, 1987).

D'Amico, Maria Luisa Aguirre, *Album Pirandello* (Milan, Mondadori, 1992).

D'Amico, Silvio, *Storia del teatro italiano* (Milan, Bompiani, 1936).

Dashwood, Julie (ed.), *Luigi Pirandello: The Theatre of Paradox* (Lampeter, Edward Mellen Press, 1996).

De Castris, Arcangelo Leone, *Il decadentismo italiano* (Bari, De Donato, 1974).

——*Storia di Pirandello* (Bari, Laterza, 1962).

Debenedetti, Giacomo, *Il romanzo del Novecento* (Milan, Garzanti, 1971), 304–414.

De Grazia, Victoria, *How Fascism Ruled Women: Italy 1922–1945* (Berkeley, University of California Press, 1992).

Della Terza, Dante, 'Luigi Pirandello e la ricerca della distanza umoristica', in AA VV, *Studi in memoria di Luigi Russo* (Pisa, Nistri-Lischi, 1974), 404–22.

De Meijer, Pieter, 'La prosa narrativa moderna', in *Letteratura italiana*, iii. *Le forme del testo, 2. La prosa* (Turin, Einaudi, 1992), 759–847.

Derrida, Jacques, 'The Theatre of Cruelty and the Closure of Representation', in *Writing and Difference* (London, Routledge and Kegan Paul, 1978), 232–50.

Doane, Mary Ann, *Femmes Fatales, Feminism, Film Theory, Psychoanalysis* (New York and London, Routledge, 1991).

Donati, Corrado, *Saggi pirandelliani* (Urbino, Università degli studi, 1984).

——*La solitudine allo specchio* (Rome, Lucarini, 1980).

Ellenberger, Henri, F., *The Discovery of the Unconscious: The History and Evolution of Dynamic Psychiatry* (London, Allen Lane, 1970).

Emerson, Caryl, 'The Outer Word and Inner Speech: Bakhtin, Vygotsky and the Internalization of Language', *Critical Inquiry*, 10/2 (1984), 245–64.

Ferrario, Edoardo, *L'occhio di Mattia Pascal: Politica e estetica in Pirandello* (Rome, Bulzoni, 1978).

Firth, Felicity, 'Fixed for Death: Pirandello on Birth, Babies and Children', *The Yearbook of the Society for Pirandello Studies*, 14 (1994), 54–60.

Fischer-Lichte, Erika, 'From Theatre to Theatricality: How to Construct Reality', *Theatre Research International*, 20/2 (Summer 1995), 106–13.

Forrester, John, *The Seductions of Psychoanalysis: Freud, Lacan and Derrida* (Cambridge, Cambridge University Press, 1991).

Freud, Sigmund, *Case Histories*, i. *'Dora' and 'Little Hans'* (The Pelican Freud Library, 8; Harmondsworth, Pelican, 1977).

Geerts, W., Musarra, F., and Vanvolsem, S. (eds.), *Luigi Pirandello: Poetica e presenza* (Rome, Bulzoni, 1987).

Gioanola, Elio, *Pirandello e la follia* (Genoa, Il Melangolo, 1987).

Giddens, Anthony, *Modernity and Self-Identity: Self and Society in the Late Modern Age* (Oxford, Polity, 1991).

Giudice, Gaspare, *Luigi Pirandello* (Turin, UTET, 1963).

Gledhill, Christine (ed.), *Stardom: Industry of Desire* (Routledge, London and New York, 1991).

Goody, Jack (ed.), *Literacy in Traditional Societies* (Cambridge, Cambridge University Press, 1968).

Greco, F. C. (ed.), *Pulcinella: Una maschera tra gli specchi* (Naples, Edizioni scientifiche italiane, 1990).

Guglielmi, Guido, *Ironia e negazione* (Turin, Einaudi, 1974).

——*La prosa italiana del Novecento* (Turin, Einaudi, 1986), 57–155.

——'La tradizione del nuovo', in *Da De Sanctis a Gramsci: Il linguaggio della critica* (Bologna, Il Mulino, 1976), 160 ff.

Guglielminetti, Marziano, *Il romanzo del Novecento italiano: Strutture e sintassi* (Rome, Riuniti, 1986), 55–98 and 161–84.

Günsberg, Maggie, *Patriarchal Representations: Gender and Discourse in Pirandello's Theatre* (Oxford and Providence, RI, Berg, 1994).

Halbwachs, Maurice, *On Collective Memory* (Chicago and London, University of Chicago Press, 1992).

Harrison, Thomas, *Essayism: Conrad, Musil and Pirandello* (Baltimore and London, The Johns Hopkins Press, 1992).

Holquist, Michael, *Dialogism: Bakhtin and his World* (London, Routledge, 1990).

Illiano, Antonio, *Metapsichica e letteratura in Pirandello* (Florence, Vallecchi, 1982).

Jacques, Francis, *Difference and Subjectivity: Dialogue and Personal Identity* (New Haven, Yale University Press, 1991).

James, William, *The Principles of Psychology* (Chicago, The University of Chicago, 1990).

Janner, A., *Luigi Pirandello* (Florence, La Nuova Italia, 1948).

Kerby, Anthony Paul, *Narrative and the Self* (Bloomington, Ind., Indiana University Press, 1991).

Kroha, Lucienne, 'Behind the Veil: A Freudian Reading of Pirandello's *Così è (se vi pare)*', *The Yearbook of the British Pirandello Society*, 12 (1992), 1–23.

Lacan, Jacques, *The Seminar*, ii. *The Ego in Freud's Theory and in the Technique of Psychoanalysis, 1953-II*, tr. Silvana Tomaselli (Cambridge, Cambridge University Press, 1988).

Laplanche, J., and Pontalis, J.-B., *The Language of Psychoanalysis* (London, The Hogarth Press, 1985).

Lauretis, Teresa de, *Alice Doesn't: Feminism, Semiotics, Cinema* (London, Macmillan, 1984).

Lauretta, Enzo, *Luigi Pirandello, storia di un personaggio 'fuori di chiave'* (Milan, Mursia, 1980).

—— (ed.), *Pirandello e il teatro* (Milan, Mursia, 1993).

—— (ed.), *Lo strappo nel cielo di carta: Introduzione alla lettura del 'Fu Mattia Pascal'* (Rome, La Nuova Italia Scientifica, 1988).

—— (ed.), *Il teatro nel teatro di Pirandello: La trilogia di Pirandello* (Agrigento, Centro nazionale di Studi Pirandelliani, 1977).

Lepschy, Anna Laura, *Narrativa e teatro fra due secoli: Verga, Invernizio, Svevo, Pirandello* (Florence, Olschki, 1984).

Lepschy, Giulio, 'Teoria del discorso e soggettività', in *Tra linguistica storica e linguistica generale* (Pisa, Pacini, 1985), 193–207.

Licastro, Emanuele, *Luigi Pirandello dalle novelle allle commedie* (Verona, Fiorini, 1974).

Livio, Gigio, *Teatro grottesco del Novecento: Antologia* (Milan, Mursia, 1965).

Lorch, Jennifer, 'The 1925 Text of *Sei personaggi in cerca d'autore* and Pitoëff's Production of 1923', *The Yearbook of the British Pirandello Society*, 2 (1982), 32–47.

Lucente, Gregory, ' "*Non conclude*", Narrative Self-Consciousness and the Voice of Creation in Pirandello's *Il fu Mattia Pascal* and *Uno, nessuno e centomila*', in *Beautiful Fables: Self-Consciousness in Italian Narrative from Manzoni to Calvino* (Baltimore, The Johns Hopkins Press, 1986).

Lugnani, Lucio, *L'infanzia felice e altri saggi su Pirandello* (Naples. Liguori, 1986).

——*Pirandello: letteratura e teatro* (Florence, La Nuova Italia, 1970).

Luperini, Romano, *Luigi Pirandello: Il fu Mattia Pascal* (Turin, Loescher, 1990).

Macchia, Giovanni, *Pirandello e la stanza della tortura* (Milan, Mondadori, 1981).

MacClintock, Lander, *The Age of Pirandello* (Bloomington, Ind., Indiana University Press, 1951).

MacIntyre, Alistair, *After Virtue: A study in Moral Theory* (London, Duckworth, 1990).

Maclean, Marie, *Narrative as Performance: The Baudelairean Experiment* (London, Routledge, 1988).

Malvani, Francesca, 'Être et paraître chez Proust et Pirandello', *Francofonia*, 11 (Autumn 1986), 65–85.

Mancini, Elaine, *Struggles of the Italian Film Industry during Fascism, 1930–35* (Ann Arbor, UMI Research Press, 1985).

Marchesini, Giovanni, *Le finzioni dell'anima: Saggio di etica psicologica* (Bari, Laterza, 1905).

Mazzacurati, Giancarlo, *Pirandello nel romanzo europeo* (Bologna, Il Mulino, 1987).

Meynaud-Jeuland, Maryse, 'A propos des didascalies des *Sei personaggi in cerca d'autore*', *Revue des études italiennes*, 14/1 (Jan.–March. 1968), 72–87.

Milioto, Stefano (ed.), *La donna in Pirandello* (Agrigento, Centro nazionale di studi pirandelliani, 1988).

Molinari, Cesare, *L'attrice divina: Eleanora Duse nel teatro italiano fra i due secoli* (Rome, Bulzoni, 1974).

Morabito, Roberto, *Parola e scrittura* (Rome, Bulzoni, 1984), 89–116.

Moses, Gabriel, ' "Gubbio in Gabbia": Pirandello's Cameraman and the Entrapments of Film Vision', *Modern Language Notes*, 94/1 (Jan. 1979), 36–60.

Mumford, Lewis, *The City in History: Its Origins, its Transformations and its Prospects* (Harmondsworth, Pelican, 1973).

Negri, Gaetano, *Segni dei tempi* (Milan, Hoepli, 1893).

Ong, Walter J., *Orality and Literacy: The Technologizing of the Word* (London, Methuen, 1982).

Pennica, Gilda (ed.), *Pirandello e la Germania* (Palermo, Palumbo, 1984).

Pfister, Manfred, *The Theory and Analysis of Drama* (Cambridge, Cambridge University Press, 1991).

Pirandello, Luigi, *Lettere a Marta Abba* (Milan, Mondadori, 1995).

Piroué, Georges, *Luigi Pirandello: Sicilien planétaire* (Denoël, Paris, 1988).

Pontiero, Giovanni, *Eleonora Duse: In Life and Art* (Frankfurt-am-Main, Peter Lang, 1986).

Pullini, Giorgio, *Tra esistenza e coscienza: Narrativa e teatro del '900* (Milan, Mursia, 1986), 138–56.

Puppa, Paolo, *Dalle parti di Pirandello* (Rome, Bulzoni, 1987).

Raffaelli, Sergio, *La lingua filmata: Didascalie e dialoghi nel cinema italiano* (Florence, Casa Editrice Le Lettere, 1992).

Ragusa, Olga, *Pirandello: An Approach to his Theatre* (Edinburgh, Edinburgh University Press, 1980).

Ricoeur, Paul, *Oneself as Another*, tr. Kathleen Blamey (Chicago and London, University of Chicago Press, 1992).

Schino, Mirella, *Il teatro di Eleonora Duse* (Bologna, Il Mulino, 1992).

Sciascia, Leonardo, *La corda pazza*, in *Opere 1956–71*, ed. Claude Ambroise (Milan, Bompiani, 1987).

—— (ed.), *Omaggio a Pirandello: Almanacco Bompiani 1987* (includes the *Almanacco letterario Bompiani 1938*) (Milan, Bompiani, 1986).

—— *La Sicilia come metafora* (Milan, Mondadori, 1979).

Scrivano, Enzo (ed.), *Pirandello e la drammaturgia tra le due guerre* (Agrigento, Centro nazionale di studi pirandelliani, 1985).

Serri, M., 'L'immagine dell'attrice in Pirandello', *Rivista di studi pirandelliani*, 4/2 (Oct. 1984), 7–33.

Sipala, Paolo Mario, *Capuana e Pirandello: Storia e testi di una relazione letteraria* (Catania, Bonanni, 1974).

Sogliuzzo, Richard, *Luigi Pirandello: The Playwright in the Theatre* (New York and London, Metuchen and The Scarecrow Press, Inc., 1982).

Spacks, Patricia Meyer, *Gossip* (Chicago, University of Chicago Press, 1985).

Spera, Francesco, '*Così è* (la parodia pirandelliana)', in G. Bàrberi Squarotti (ed.), *Lo specchio che deforma: Le immagini della parodia* (Turin, Tirrenia, 1988), 267–80.

—— 'La finzione del popolare: Il teatro rusticano di Pirandello', in G. Bàrberi Squarotti (ed.), *Letteratura in scena: Il teatro del Novecento* (Turin, Tirrenia, 1985), 105–20.

Squarzina, Luigi, *'Ciascuno a suo modo' di Pirandello e il teatro totale delle avanguardie* (Rome, Bulzoni, 1987).

Steiner, Wendy, *Pictures of Romance: Form against Content in Painting and Literature* (Chicago, University of Chicago Press, 1988).

Stocchi-Perucchio, D., *Pirandello and the Vagaries of Knowledge* (Stanford, Calif., ANMA Libri, 1991).

Stone, Jennifer, *Pirandello's Naked Prompt: The Structure of Repetition in Modernism* (Ravenna, Longo, 1989).

Szondi, Peter, *Theory of Modern Drama* (Oxford, Blackwell, 1987).

Tilgher, A., 'Luigi Pirandello', in *Voci del tempo* (Rome, Libreria di Scienze e Lettere, 1921), 78 ff.

—— 'Il teatro di Pirandello', in *Studi sul teatro contemporaneo* (Rome, Libreria di Scienze e Lettere, 1923).

Tissoni Benvenuti, Antonia, *L'"Orfeo' del Poliziano con il testo critico dell'originale e delle successive forme teatrali* (Padua, Editrice Antenore, 1986).

Turner, Victor, *Dramas, Fields and Metaphors: Symbolic Action in Human Society* (Ithaca, NY, and London, Cornell University Press, 1990).

—— *The Ritual Process, Structure and Anti-Structure* (New York, Aldine, 1969).

—— and Bruner, Edward M. (eds.), *The Anthropology of Experience* (Urbana, Ill., and Chicago, University of Illinois Press, 1986).

Venè, Gian Franco, *Pirandello fascista: La coscienza borghese tra ribellione e rivoluzione* (Venice, Marsilio, 1981).

Vicentini, Claudio, 'Modelli di recitazione nel teatro di Pirandello', in *Alle origini della drammaturgia moderna: Ibsen, Strindberg, Pirandello* (Genoa, Costa e Nolan, 1987).

—— *Pirandello: Il disagio del teatro* (Venice, Marsilio, 1993).

Weaver, William, *Duse: A Biography* (London, Thames and Hudson, 1984).

Whitaker, Thomas R., *Fields of Play in Modern Drama* (Princeton, Princeton University Press, 1977).

Witt, Mary Ann, 'Modes of Narration in *Sei personaggi*', in W. Geerts, F. Musara, and S. Vanvoselm (eds.), *Luigi Pirandello: Poetica e presenza* (Rome, Bulzoni, 1987), 607–16.

Index